Fundamentals of Railway Line

铁路线路基础

Ma guozhong Chen Tao
马国忠 陈 韬 编

西南交通大学出版社
· 成都 ·

图书在版编目（CIP）数据

铁路线路基础 = Fundamentals of Railway Line：英文 / 马国忠，陈韬编．—成都：西南交通大学出版社，2018.8

ISBN 978-7-5643-6250-8

Ⅰ．①铁… Ⅱ．①马… ②陈… Ⅲ．①铁路线路－英文 Ⅳ．①U21

中国版本图书馆 CIP 数据核字（2018）第 133149 号

Fundamentals of Railway Line

铁路线路基础

马国忠　陈　韬　编

责任编辑	张文越
封面设计	何东琳设计工作室
出版发行	西南交通大学出版社 （四川省成都市二环路北一段 111 号 西南交通大学创新大厦 21 楼）
发行部电话	028-87600564　028-87600533
邮政编码	610031
网　　址	http://www.xnjdcbs.com
印　　刷	四川煤田地质制图印刷厂
成品尺寸	170 mm × 230 mm
印　　张	19.75
字　　数	446 千
版　　次	2018 年 8 月第 1 版
印　　次	2018 年 8 月第 1 次
书　　号	ISBN 978-7-5643-6250-8
定　　价	68.00 元

课件咨询电话：028-87600533
图书如有印装质量问题　本社负责退换

前　言

《铁路线路基础》长期以来是交通运输专业重要的专业基础课程之一，其相关内容和知识的学习为后续专业课程的学习奠定铁路线路方面的基础知识。学生通过对本课程的学习，了解有关铁路线路基本结构、功能和作用，掌握铁路线路工程的基本计算方法。

本教材是为培养我国铁路技术相关国际合作所需的既能熟练掌握铁路线路专业知识，又能熟练运用专业英语进行对外交流的复合型人才而专门编写的教材，旨在培养学生专业技能的同时强化学生相关的专业英语水平，拓展学生的专业视野，提高学生利用英语直接从事和研究铁路技术相关的实际与理论工作。本教材也可作为交通运输专业双语教学用书，也可作为铁路运输部门从事实际工作的生产人员、技术人员和管理人员的专业英语参考用书。

本教材共8章，系统地介绍了铁路线路中轨道、路基、桥梁、隧道等内容，主要包括轨道的分类、结构、组成、标准，道岔的组成、功能、标准，无缝铁路的设置、特点及意义，轨道维护、维修的内容和标准，路基、桥梁、隧道建筑物的组成、分类和建设等。每个单元包括三部分，第一部分是文中涉及的重要知识点、技术点。第二部分是用专业英语介绍的铁路线路知识。第三部分是专业英语词汇，紧扣课文内容，提供与课文内容相关的常用单词。

本教材力求通俗易懂，在编写过程中参考了大量已出版的相关国内外铁路线路教材内容以及专业文献，且得到了各铁路相关专业老师的协助。在此，致以衷心的谢意。由于编写的时间有限，书中难免会出现不足和疏漏之处，为此，恳请使用本书的广大读者批评、指正。

编　者

2018年6月

CONTENTS

CHARPTER 1 INTRODUCTION ······ 1

1.1 The origin and development of railway ······ 1

1.2 History and development of china railway ······ 4

1.3 Status and development of high speed railway ······ 7

1.4 Role and advantage of railway ······ 11

1.5 Composition of railway line ······ 12

CHARPTER 2 TRACK ELEMENTS ······ 14

2.1 Introduction ······ 14

2.1.1 Traditional track structure ······ 15

2.1.2 Features of track ······ 19

2.2 Rail ······ 23

2.2.1 History ······ 23

2.2.2 The function of rails ······ 26

2.2.3 The length and weight of rails ······ 27

2.2.4 Rail profile ······ 29

2.2.5 Chemical composition and manufacture ······ 33

2.2.6 Rail life and maintenance ······ 35

2.3 Sleeper ······ 39

2.3.1 Functions of sleeper ······ 40

2.3.2 Timber sleepers ······ 40

2.3.3 Reinforced concrete sleepers ······ 45

2.3.4 Sleeper spacing ······ 50

2.3.5 Other types of railway sleeper ······ 53
2.4 Rail joints and rail fastenings ······ 56
2.4.1 Rail joints ······ 56
2.4.2 Rail fastening ······ 64
2.5 Track ballast ······ 75
2.5.1 Purposes of ballast ······ 76
2.5.2 Ballast materials ······ 77
2.5.3 Ballast section ······ 80
2.5.4 Phenomena occurred over the ballast ······ 83
2.6 Rail creep ······ 86
2.6.1 Causes of creep ······ 87
2.6.2 Measurement of creep ······ 89
2.6.3 Adjustment of creep ······ 90
2.6.4 Anti-creep devices ······ 91
2.6.5 Gauge rods and rail brace ······ 92
2.7 Railroad level crossing ······ 93
2.7.1 Overview ······ 93
2.7.2 Protection arrangements of level crossings ······ 94
2.7.3 Construction of level crossings ······ 95
2.7.4 Choice of Crossing Panel Type ······ 96
2.8 Ballastless track ······ 98
2.8.1 Introduction ······ 98
2.8.2 Different ballastless track system ······ 99
2.8.3 Ballastless track of Chinese high-speed railway ······ 103

CHARPTER 3 TRACK GEOMETRY ······ 109
3.1 Introduction ······ 109
3.2 Basic track geometry elements ······ 110
3.2.1 Track gauge ······ 110
3.2.2 Track alignment(or profile) ······ 112
3.2.3 Cross level ······ 114
3.2.4 Track twist(or warp) ······ 115

3.2.5 Rail cant …… 116
3.2.6 Gradients …… 118
3.2.7 Surface (or longitudinal level) …… 121
3.2.8 Irregularity …… 122
3.3 Track super-elevation …… 123
3.3.1 Track plane acceleration …… 124
3.3.2 Equilibrium super-elevation and balanced speed …… 125
3.3.3 Super-elevation deficiency and super-elevation excess 126
3.3.4 Permissible speed with respect to radius, super-elevation and super-elevation deficiency …… 128
3.3.5 Rate of super-elevation and rate of super-elevation deficiency …… 129
3.3.6 Tilt technology …… 129
3.4 Track transition curves …… 130
3.4.1 Curves …… 130
3.4.2 The function of transition curves …… 133
3.4.3 The geometric features of transition curves …… 134
3.4.4 Shapes of transition curves …… 136
3.4.5 Length of transition curves …… 138
3.5 Gauge Widening of Curves …… 141
3.5.1 Geometrical requirements for rolling stocks negotiating (traversing) curved tracks …… 142
3.5.2 Gauge widening for vehicle …… 143
3.5.3 Gauge widening for locomotives …… 144
3.5.4 Maximum gauge widening on curves tracks …… 146
CHARPTER 4 TURNOUTS …… 149
4.1 Introduction …… 149
4.1.1 Concept …… 149
4.1.2 Type of turnouts …… 150
4.2 Structure of normal simple turnout …… 156
4.2.1 Components of normal simple turnout …… 156

4.2.2 Switches ··· 159
4.2.3 Crossings ··· 166
4.2.4 Lead rail ··· 174
4.3 Turnouts Sleepers ··· 176
4.4 Installation and maintenance of turnouts ··· 178
CHARPTER 5 CONTINUOUS WELDED RAIL (CWR) ··· 181
5.1 Overview ··· 181
5.2 Fundamentals theory of CWR ··· 184
5.2.1 Rail temperature force and temperature stress ··· 184
5.2.2 Rail temperature ··· 185
5.2.3 Longitudinal resistance and diagram of rail temperature ··· 190
5.3 Welding methods of CWR ··· 193
5.3.1 Chemical or thermit welding ··· 193
5.3.2 Flash butt welding ··· 195
5.3.3 Gas butt welding ··· 197
5.3.4 Electric arc welding ··· 197
5.3.5 Welding failure ··· 197
5.4 Regional CWR and Seamless Turnout ··· 198
5.4.1 Regional CWR ··· 198
5.4.2 Seamless turnout ··· 201
CHARPTER 6 TRACK MAINTENANCE ··· 203
6.1 Introduction ··· 203
6.1.1 Outline ··· 203
6.1.2 Good maintenance features ··· 204
6.2 Type of maintenance ··· 206
6.2.1 Period of maintenance ··· 206
6.2.2 Level of maintenance ··· 206
6.3 Contents of maintenance ··· 207
6.3.1 Maintenance of track geometry ··· 208
6.3.2 Maintenance of track components ··· 208
6.3.3 Maintenance of turnouts ··· 211

6.3.4 Maintenance of level crossings ········· 212
6.3.5 Maintenance of drainage ········· 212
6.4 Track maintenance activities ········· 213
6.4.1 Tamping ········· 214
6.4.2 Dynamic track stabilization ········· 216
6.4.3 Ballast cleaning ········· 216
6.4.4 Rail grinding ········· 217
6.4.5 Rail lubrication ········· 218
6.4.6 Replacement ········· 219
6.5 Maintenance management of Chinese railway ········· 220
6.6 High-speed rail line maintenance ········· 221
CHARPTER 7 RAILROAD SUBGRADE ········· 224
7.1 Subgrade design and construction ········· 225
7.1.1 Typical cross sections ········· 225
7.1.2 Geometric design ········· 229
7.2 Stability of subgrade ········· 235
7.2.1 Instability performance of subgrade ········· 236
7.2.2 Stabilization methods ········· 241
7.3 Subgrade drainage ········· 247
7.3.1 Introduction ········· 247
7.3.2 Drainage system ········· 248
7.3.3 Drainage problems ········· 251
CHARPTER 8 TUNNELS AND BRIDGES ········· 253
8.1 Tunnels ········· 253
8.1.1 Overview ········· 253
8.1.2 Tunnel cross-section ········· 254
8.1.3 Tunnel structure ········· 256
8.1.4 Tunnel construction ········· 266
8.1.5 Tunnel maintenance ········· 277
8.2 Bridges ········· 279
8.2.1 Bridge components ········· 279

8.2.2 Bridge type······282
8.2.3 Bridge construction······293
8.2.4 Bridge maintenance······295
8.3 Choice of tunnels vs. bridges······296
TEST SHEET······299
REFERENCE······303

CHARPTER 1 INTRODUCTION

【Primary Contents】

(1) Origin and development of railway

(2) History and development of China Railway

(3) Features and development of high-speed railway

(4) Features and basic structure of railway line

1.1 The origin and development of railway[1][2]

In medieval times, people mostly traveled by foot or horseback and any form of transportation for moving goods. Before the beginning of the eighteenth century wheeled transport was generally hauled by horse and ran on surfaces which at the best was reinforced by a broken stone foundation and at the worst was simply a mud track. It was found at a very early stage of the development of land transport, that most road surfaces and foundations were very quickly damaged by heavy wagons on rigid wheels. The first railway tracks were laid down in the eighteenth century for horse drawn trains of wagons, initially having a surface of stone slabs or timber baulks. Actually the man who hit upon the idea of pulling the loads by a wheeled vehicle put on the timber baulks and drawn by horses is unknown now. But it was the beginning of the development of the principle of track system today.

The timber track proved unsatisfactory as loads grew heavier. As the Industrial Revolution progressed, to prolong the life of timber rails, the idea was developed further by adding wrought iron plates to reduce wear on the timber baulks. This evolved further first to cast iron plates and later to edge rails, enabling for the first time the use of flanged iron wheels. The first known railway, the line "Surrey Iron Railway", was inaugurated in 1803 in London. It was basically a railway drawn by horses, used for the transport of mining.

By the time locomotives came on the scene in the early nineteenth century, wrought iron rails had developed further and became strong enough to support these heavy engines without assistance from longitudinal timbers.

One of the biggest boons of science to the modern civilization is the invention of steam engine in 18th century. Nicholas Joseph Cugnot, a French mechanic was the first man to invent and construct a steam locomotive for roads in the year 1769. In 1804, Trevithick designed and constructed the first steam locomotive for railways. Later on George Stephenson perfected the steam locomotive in 1814 and finally led to the development of present day railway system as shoun in Fig. 1-1.

Fig. 1-1 Stephenson and his rocket locomotive

The first modern railway in the world was opened for traffic on 27 th September 1825 in England. This railway line was run between Stockton and Darlington and its width was 1,435 mm and the speed was 24 km/h. The planning and design of the railway line was carried out by Stephenson himself. George Stephenson was neither the inventor of steam locomotive nor the father of railways, but he indeed played a great role in perfecting the already available locomotives and constructing the present day railways, Fig. 1-1 shows Stephenson and his locomotive. This was followed by a spate of development of the railway system throughout the world.

In France, first railway was opened in 1828 with horse as a tractive power.

Though passenger traffic had started in 1832, but steam locomotives were used in 1842 as tractive power. The first railway line in America was laid in 1833 between Mohawk and Hudson. The first railway line in Germany was opened in 1835. The first railway in Italy and Netherlands were opened in 1839. The first railway line in China was in 1876.

The year of 1st opening of railways in different countries of the world is given in the following Tab. 1-1.

Tab. 1-1 Railroad opening year of major countries in the world

Country	Opening year	Country	Opening year	Country	Opening year	Country	Opening year
Britain	1825	Canada	1836	Switzerland	1844	Egypt	1855
American	1830	Russia	1837	Spain	1848	Japan	1872
France	1832	Austria	1838	Brazil	1851	China	1876
Belgium	1835	Holland	1839	India	1853		
Germany	1835	Italian	1839	Australia	1854		

As experience was gained and new technology evolved, rails steadily increased in size, both in length and cross section, and were made in steel rather than iron. Electric locomotive and diesel locomotive were appeared to replace steam locomotive.

In 1879, an electrical train model was built by Werner von Siemens presented in Berlin, with a third rail for the electrical supply. The overhead power cable was introduced in 1888 for the electrical tramways that replaced the animal-force and steam models. For the construction of the subway lines, with underground circulation, it became necessary to use this kind of power supply, provided that the smoke emission of the steam-locomotives made unfeasible that kind of mechanical-driving. The electrification of standard railways was focused preliminarily to the mountainous regions, as the hydroelectric power was widely available and the electrical locomotives had better features in all senses, both technical and economical.

In 1912, it was firstly tested a diesel locomotive. In 1924, an electric-transmission diesel locomotive were made and operated in the Soviet Union. In the same year, the steam engine were converted into an air transmission diesel locomotive in German. In 1925, the first diesel locomotive was put into operation in United States. As the efficiency, cleanliness and economy of the diesel engine are much more than steam locomotives, after the 2nd World War, the combustion engines were already very powerful, and in few decades diesel locomotives replaced almost entirely the steam-locomotives in those lines were electrification was not profitable.

The progressive drop of the manufacturing costs of engines led to the massive scale-production of trucks and buses, which, added to the great spread of highway networks occurred after the 2nd World War, made the railway become less popular. The airplane transportation replaced soon the railway in long-distance route and the buses and truck the short- and medium- distance ones. From 1950 until the Oil Crisis of 1973, lots of railway lines were dismantled all over the world.

Then, the increasing costs of energy, the introduction of shipment-containers, the more demanding pollution-control and the inrush of the high-speed rail technology helped the railway became again attractive and profitable.

1.2 History and development of china railway

The history of rail transport in China began in the late nineteenth century during the Qing Dynasty. Since then, it has become one of the largest rail networks in the world.

The first railways in China were built during the Qing Dynasty in the late 19th Century, meannhile, extensive railway networks were already in place in Europe, North America, India and Japan. The late arrival of railways in China was due both to the lack of industrialization and skeptical attitude of the Qing government. Although diverse and prominent personages such as Lin Zexu called for the building of railways in China in the mid-19th century, the conservative Qing court considered steam engines to be “clever but useless” contraptions, and resisted the railways.

However, a small railway network was constructed during the Qing Dynasty.

In the imperial capital, Beijing was designed as the center of the Chinese railway network. Several lines radiated out from Beijing. Four main lines are Beijing-Hankou Railway, Beijing-Fengtian Railway, Beijing-Zhangjiakou Railway and Tianjin-Pukou Railway. Beijing-Hankou Railway was from Beijing to Hankou,built from1897 to 1906. The Guangneiwai railway was extended west to Beijing and east to Fengtian by 1912 and renamed as Beijing-Fengtian Railway. The Tianjin-Pukou Railway, built from 1908 to 1912. It ran from Tianjin, which was connected by the Beijing-Fengtian Railway, to Pukou across the Yangtze River from Nanjing. The Beijing-Zhangjiakou Railway, built from 1905 to 1909, ran from Fengtan to Zhangjiakou.

After the 1911 Revolution, from 1911 to 1949, the construction of railway technology has been developed. Inside the Great Wall, about 3,600 km of railway was built. Among the completed lines were the Longhai Railway (Lingbao-Tongguan and Xi'an-Baoji sections), Zhejiang-Jiangxi Railway (Hangzhou-Pingxiang section) and the Guangdong-Hankou Railway (Zhuzhou-Shaoguan section). The Shanxi warlord Yan Xishan built the narrow gauge Datong-Puzhou Railway across Shanxi Province. The Japanese occupiers, using forced labor, built 5,700 km of railway in in the north of China and 900 km in the other parts of China. In 1941, construction began of the Yunnan Burma Railway, an attempt to link British occupied Burma with Kunming in Yunnan province. Ultimately, however, the project was aborted. By 1948, the number of usable kilometers of rail was estimated at only 8,000 km due to the war. When the People's Republic of China was established in 1949, China had constructed 27,380 km of railway, but only 24,090 km was kept, including 10,309 km in the northeastern part of China, and 919 km in Taiwan.

The end to decades of warfare in China allowed railway construction to proceed on a large-scale. In the 1950s, the government initiated numerous railway building projects to fill in missing links in the country's rail network. The government undertook a vigorous railway building campaign. In 1951, after extensive investment in reconstruction, China had restored the usable network to about 22,000 km. Most of the early reconstruction (about 11,000 km) was in East-North of China, From 1952, Chengdu-Chongqing Railway line—the first railway of the People's Republic, entered into operation. By end of the First Five Year Plan in 1957, 6,100 km of railroads were built, accounting for 18% of the national total. The lines completed during this period include the final sections of the Longhai and Xianggui railwayline, the Litang-Zhanjiang, Yingtan-Xiamen, Lancun-Yantai and Xiaoshan-Ningbo railway lines. These lines, along with the Baoji-Chengdu railway line (completed in 1958) and the 1,900 km Lanzhou-Xinjiang railway-line to Urumqi (completed in 1962), extended the national rail network to the Northwest and Southwest, and added connections between the coast and interior.

After China initiated market-oriented economic reforms in 1978, railway building slowed as state funds were directed toward higher return investments. It was not until the 1990s, after more than a decade of economic growth, that the state could commit the funds to renew large-scale railway building.

In 1990, the Lanxin railway line was extended with the railway line from Northern Xinjiang railway line to the Kazakh border. In 1999, the Southern Xinjiang railway line brought railway service to Kashgar in the far west.

The railway to Tibet however, was more difficult to build due to the high altitude and terrain. Rail lines were first extended to Xining in Qinghai, and by 1984 another section between Xining and Golmud was completed. It was not until 2006 that the whole of the Qingzang railway line was finished, linking Lhasa with rest of China. Since then, every province-level entity in China has a railway network.

Before the 1980s, due to the, ease of manufacture, and cheap coal price, steam locomotives dominated the Chinese railways. During the 1980s and 1990s, diesel and electric locomotives gradually replaced steam engines on the main lines. On some provincial rails, however, steam locomotives were not retired until the 21st century. In December 2005, last regular revenue mainline steam train finished its journey on the Jitong railway line, marking the end of the steam era. Nevertheless, there are still some steam locomotives used on the industrial railways in China.

In order to improve the efficiency and capacity of railway, from April 1, 1997 to April 2007, 18, the speed of China Railway has been increased six times and China Railway entered the era of fast transport and started to explore the technology of high-speed railway in China.

China in 2008 opened its first high-speed railway-Jingjin railway line with fully independent intellectual property rights and reaching 350 km/h speed.

Nowadays, China is developing an extensive high-speed rail system to relieve the pressure of both passenger and freight demand on its overcrowded existing rail system, improve transportation connections between its different regions, and promote the economy of less developed regions. China has upgraded parts of its existing rail network to achieve speeds of 190-250 km/h, and is building new high-speed rail network to enable speeds of 200 km/h or more. The government has announced plans to have approximately 30,000 km of high-speed lines in operation by 2020.

1.3 Status and development of high speed railway

Define high-speed railway has the following criteria:

(1) In 1970 the Japanese government decree No. 71 defined high-speed railwany as: the train in the main zone can be 200km / h above the speed to run mainline railway.

(2) 1985 the European Commission defined high-speed rail as: Passenger 300km / h, mixed passenger and freight transport line 250km / h.

(3) UIC(French: Union Internationale des Chemins de Fer) proposed high-speed rail as: the maximum speed should be at least 250km/ h, or the maximum speed of 200km / h the existing line.

High-speed railway has become an important trend in the world of railway development. Since the 1960s, nearly 10 countries' various types of high-speed railway put into operation. Most countries have achieved from high-speed railway a good social and economic benefits. In rail transport, especially rail passenger transport industry, which was sluggish, has injectdnew vitality.

High-speed railway has a great influence on socio- economic aspects of society, for example, they create economic development, expedite communication and reduce distance which makes the world a smaller place. In addition, there are some similar technical standards: they are designed along straight lines for rapid movement, and they adopt technology that minimizes maintenance.

According to incomplete statistics, by the end of 2015, worldwide operations of 250 km/h or more new high-speed railway line is about 30,000 km, of which

Japan 2,615 km, Geman 941.2 km, France 1985.9km, Spain 2066km, Italy 959km, Turkey 610km, Englan 97 km, China 20,719 km etc. With the development of economy,the world is building more and more high-speed rail (including new lines and transformation line).

High-speed railways in different countries have developed different highest speed. The Tokaido Shinkansen in Japan, which is a passenger line, allows maximum speed of 240 km/h, and the maximum speed trains actually run 210 km/h. The highest speed is designed for Cologne-Mainz / Rhine line of German and the north line of the French TGV and the TGV Mediterranean line, up to 330 km/h. In high-speed railway construction in Madrid, Spain-Barcelona high-speed rail line design speeds up, reaching 350 km/h. In addition, the French TGV east of the southern section of an extension, allows speed up to 350 km/h. Korea and China high speed rail allows speed reach 350 km/h, but their maximum operating speed of high-speed trains are only 300 km/h and350 km/h is the line reserved for speed, which is necessary. Rome, Italy-Florence high-speed rail in the original design standard is quite a little low, the maximum speed of only 250 km/h. High-speed railway is a systematic project, bringing together a variety of high technology, and especially high-speed train technology is the key. World except Japan, France, Germany, Italy and a few other countries is independently developed its own high-speed trains, most countries imported technology from them. This regard, the introduction of technology in China and Korea to be relatively successful. It takes a smaller price, in just a few years to master the world's most advanced high-speed train technology.

1. High-speed railway in Japan

Japan may be the ideal country, geographically, for high speed rail; its main island is relatively long and narrow, so that its relatively large population is concentrated in cities arrayed along a corridor. Japan opened its first high speed railway, between Tokyo and Osaka, in 1964. That railway was built to expand capacity in an overcrowded rail corridor. From its inception it earned enough revenue to cover its operating costs, and reportedly earned enough money within its first few years to pay back its construction costs.

The success of the Tokyo-Osaka line encouraged expansion, and the Japanese government has supported construction of other high-speed railway.

Currently, new lines are funded by public-private partnerships, part of the funding coming from the now-privatized regional rail companies, and the rest from the national and local governments. Since 1987, when the government began the privatization of Japan National Railways, all high-speed lines have been operated by private companies. In 2015, the high-speed rail network was 2615.7 kilometer in length.

2. High-speed railway in France

France opened its first high-speed rail railway in 1981, between Paris and Lyon. Its high-speed trains are referred to as TGVs (Trains à Grande Vitesse). In 2015, the system has approximately 1,985.9 km of high-speed railway.

Because of the relatively low population density of France and the central role of Paris (the nation's capital and largest population center), the French high-speed railway network has been developed as spokes radiating outward from Paris. Regional governments are responsible for a significant share of construction costs. The state-owned rail operating company, SNCF, reports that its TGVs have taken the dominant share of the air-rail travel market in several of the high-speed corridors, taking over 90% in the Paris-Lyon market (with a TGV travel time of less than two hours) and about 60% in corridors where the TGV travel time is around three hours.

3. High-speed railway in Germany

Germany opened its first high-speed railway in 1991. Its high-speed trains are called Intercity Express (ICE). Germany's network varies significantly from that of its neighbor, France. Due in part to the more geographically distributed political demands of a federal system of government and in part to a denser and more evenly distributed population, Germany's high-speed railway service has been developed to connect many hubs rather than centering on a single city. Germany's high-speed trains also have more stops than those of France, whose system emphasizes connecting distant city with few intermediate stops. These considerations have led Germany to put more emphasis on upgrading existing railway to accommodate higher speed service, and less emphasis on building entirely new high-speed railway. One result is that Germany's high-speed trains have longer average trip times than do those of France over comparable distances.

In 2015, the high-speed rail network was 941.2 kilometer in length.

4. High-speed railway in Spain

Spain opened its first high-speed rail line in 1992. Like France, its population density is relatively low by European standards, and, except for Madrid, the capital and largest city, which is located in the center of the country, the population is largely concentrated near the coasts. Spain's conventional rail network was built using a wider gauge (i.e., the distance between the two parallel rails) than the international standard. Its high-speed rail network is being built rauording to the international standard, producing two separate rail networks. Many trains have special equipment to allow them to operate on both networks.

Government spending on rail infrastructure (both high-speed and conventional) surpassed spending on roads in 2003. The Spanish government's Ministry of Public Works has a Strategic Plan for Infrastructure and Transport for the period 2005-2020. 44% of the total spending of the Plan is for railways, primarily for increasing the size of the high-speed rail network to about 10,000 km by the year 2020, and putting 90% of the population within 30 miles of a station. The high-speed rail network is seen as a way of improving mobility with less environmental impact than automobile or air travel, and as a way of promoting the development of Spain's regions, as well as creating transportation-related employment. In 2015, the high-speed rail network was 2,355.6 km in length, with more under construction.

5. High-speed railway in China

At present, China has become the country with the fastest pace of development and the largest scale of network. China has stepped into world's leading level in terms of high-speed railway technology. China proposes to develop high-speed railway and construct a rapid passenger traffic network with the eight south-north corridors and eight east-west corridors as the backbone. According to the middle-term and long-term railway network plan, the operational length of China high-speed railways will exceed 30,000 km by 2020, connecting all provincial capitals and cities with a population of at 500,000 people at least. Now, China high-speed railway has compatible operation of 200 km/h, 250 km/h, 300 km/h and 350 km/h trains, operational speed up to 350 km/h.

1.4 Role and advantage of railway[3]

It is obvious that railways are important to society. It is quite necessary to have railways to transport many of the economy's basic commodities. Railway can provide dependable, economical, and rapid movement for all types of commodities, especially those classed as bulk freight (lumber, coal, iron ore, wheat, building materials, and others), or for any other type moving in large volumes. Passenger traffic moves in comfort and with reasonably rapid speed. Railways share in the efficient handling of mass commutation traffic. Even for short haul and merchandise traffic the railways can provide a service that is prompt, dependable, and economical.

Railway plays an important part in the development of major industrial nations in the world. One reason for their importance is the efficiency of rail operations. The metal wheel on the metal rail produces a minimum of friction and permits railway locomotives to pull their loads with less energy than other vehicles. Foreign research shows a locomotive uses about one-fourth as much energy as a highway truck in moving one ton of material one mile. Because of this, railways can move three times as much freight per gallon of fuel as big trucks and 125 times as much as aircraft. This is a huge fuel saving, which also reduces air pollution. For example, railways – on a ton-mile basis-give off less than half the amount of exhaust emission released by diesel trucks. A recent study indicates that railway-despite carrying the lion's share of the intercity ton-mileage-are responsible for only slightly more than one percent of all air-pollution emissions from transportation sources.

Because of their vital role in society, railways operate as common carriers. Unlike private and contract carriers (the types most commonly found in the motor truck field), railways cannot concentrate on serving one class of shipper or commodity. Railways must provide sufficient equipment, facilities, and schedules to handle without discrimination to persons, places, or commodities all traffic offered. Providing sufficient capacity (which must sometimes remain unused for lengthy periods) to meet peak demands is one of the serious problems faced by railway management.

Except for the economic reason, railways also have brought political, social changes in the life of the society. Railways have the following advantages over other means of transportation.

(1) Railways have provided opportunity of meeting people from different parts of the country, which has resulted in the development of sense of national unity.

(2) Railways also have helped in the mass migration of the people in the holidays.

(3) Railways provide a safe and convenient mode of transport for the people.

(4) During famine, floods etc. railways play a vital role for transport goods from one region to the other.

(5) Railways have provided facilities for the transport of raw materials to the factories and the finished products to the people at reasonable cost, which has resulted in industrial development at a rapid rate.

(6) Due to speedy movement of the commodities through railways, price stability could be achieved.

1.5 Composition of railway line

Railway is a means of conveyance of passengers and goods on wheeled vehicles running on rails, and railway line is an important infrastructure of railway, and composed of the sub-base, superstructure and installations.

The sub-base known as subgrade is the bottom layer aimed at supporting, transmitting and distributing uniformly the loads to the natural terrain. It must work likewise as drainage layer, as well as to control the capillary rise of the water. Generally it is composed of granular aggregated material and special geotextile fabric to prevent the pollution of the superstructure with clays coming from the natural terrain. Bridge and tunnel building are important parts of sub-base, their structures are complex, difficult construction and high cost.

In the railway, the superstructure is known as the elements that compose the track. The track (the set of elements) guide the railway vehicle and allow a safe and comfortable running surface. In order to guide the railway vehicle safely, the track needs elements to absorb the huge loads that the vehicle transmits to the rails. The superstructure is composed by the rails, the sleepers, the fastenings, the ballast and the ancillary facilities (such as turnouts, crossings).The track must be an elastic ensemble in order to counteract the stiffness of the contact between wheel and rail, as well as be resistant to longitudinal, transversal and vertical loads.

The installations are composed by the electrical system, the signaling and the stations, etc.

There are two type of rail line, subject to the superstructure type: ballasted railroad and ballastless railroad. They distinguish because the function of providing stability to the ensemble of rails and sleepers is carried out, on one type, by the ballast, and on the other, by the ballastless (concrete slab).With the development of high-speed railway and urban rail transit, the trend of developing the ballastless railway line is more and more obvious, but the conventional ballasted railway line is still in largest occupation.

Professional Words and Expressions

locomotive 机车
high-speed railway(HSR) 高速铁路
infrastructure 基础设施
minimum speed limit 最小限制速度
operating conditions 运营条件
rolling stock 车辆
railway line 铁路线路
conveyance 位移
sub-base 下部基础
subgrade 路基
superstructure 上部建筑
steam locomotive 蒸汽机车
diesel locomotive 内燃机车
electric locomotive 电力机车
commom carriers 公共承运人
rail 钢轨
sleeper 轨枕
fastening 联结零件
ballast 道床
ancillary facilities 附属设备
turnout 道岔
elastic 弹性
installation 设施
electrical system 电气系统
signaling 信号
station 车站
conventional railway 既有线铁路
backbone 干线
ballasted railroad 有碴铁路
ballastless railroad 无碴铁路

CHARPTER 2 TRACK ELEMENTS

【Primary Contents】

(1) Structure and features of traditional track

(2) Function, features and structure of rail, sleeper, joint, fastener and ballast

(3) Reason, measurement and adjustment of rail creep

(4) Construction and safety protection of the level crossing

(5) Classification and structure of ballastless track

2.1 Introduction

Track supports the loads of cars and locomotives and guides their movements. The excellence of the track determines the permissible wheel loads, speeds, safety, and dependability of railroad operation. No modern railroad can hope to survive in a competitive economy if its track is a hindrance to safe, dependable, on-time service.

Track is an apparently simple structure. It appears to have changed little since over 200 years ago, when early track consisted of rough timbers laid parallel, with angle irons placed on the edges to form flange-ways guiding the wheels of colliery wagons on the timbers. Components have varied somewhat over the years and techniques for their use have improved. Flanges have been moved from the rail to the wheel, timbers with iron corner straps have been replaced, first with wrought iron rail, then with steel rail, and with sleepers closely spaced to insure lateral rigidity.

Track development came mostly through trial and error. Improved track brought heavier wheel loads, calling, in turn, for still better track, again leading to heavier wheel loads. In the early days, early construction and maintenance materials were those found along the right of way. Little attention was given to drainage or to soil characteristics. If the track settled, more ballast was tamped under the sleepers. Rational design principles came later, more as a means of explaining the structure already in use than as a basis for design.

2.1.1 Traditional track structure [4]

The track on a railway or railroad, also known as the permanent way, is the structure consisting of the rails, fastenings, sleepers (in British English, or cross sleepers in the United States) and ballast, plus ancillary facilities (such as turnouts, crossings). Fig. 2-1 shows the structure of traditional track. For clarity it is often referred to as railway track (British English and UIC terminology) or railroad track (predominantly in the United States).

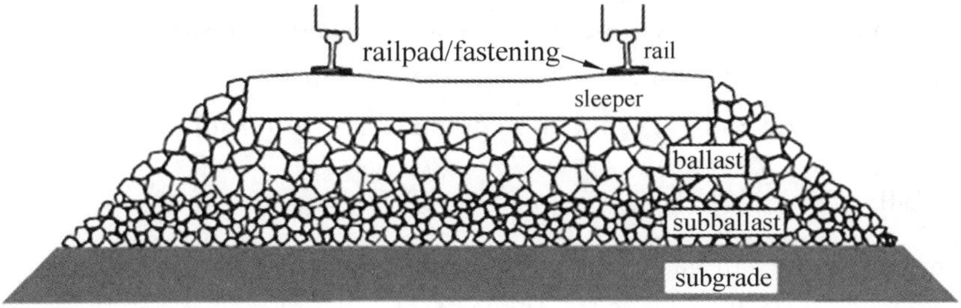

Fig. 2-1 The track structure

Rail are fixed to the sleepers by fastenings. Conventional construction with wood sleepers utilizes steel spikes driven into the sleepers through holes in the sleeper plate. In some cases, screw type fastenings are used to provide more resistance to vertical forces. Elastic, clip-type fastenings are used on concrete and, at times, on wooden sleepers to provide a uniform, resilient attachment and longitudinal restraint in lieu of anchors.

Track gauge or rail gauge is the distance between the inner sides of the heads of the two load bearing rails that make up a single railway line. Sixty percent of the world's railways use a standard gauge of 1,435 mm. Wider gauges are called broad gauge; smaller gauges, narrow gauge. Gauge is often intentionally widened slightly on curved track.

Rails are produced in fixed lengths and need to be joined end-to-end to make a continuous surface on which trains may run. The traditional method of joining the rails is to bolt them together using metal fishplates, producing jointed track. For more modern usage, particularly where higher speeds are required, the lengths of rail may be welded together to form continuous welded rail (CWR).

Track needs regular maintenance to remain in good order, especially when high-speed trains are involved. Inadequate maintenance may lead to a "slow order".

Track maintenance was at one time hard manual labor, requiring teams of laborers. Currently, maintenance is facilitated by a variety of specialized machines. Common maintenance jobs include changing sleepers (cross ties), lubricating and adjusting switches, tightening loose track components, and surfacing and lining track to keep straight sections straight and curves within maintenance limits.

The subgrade serves as the interface between the ballast and the native soil. Subgrade material is typically compacted or stabilized soil. Instability of the subgrade due to groundwater permeation is a concern in some areas. In some difficult locations, a semi-permeable geotextile fabric is used to separate the ballast and subgrade and prevent subgrade material from fouling the ballast.

1. Rail

A modern steel rail has a flat bottom and its cross section is derived from an I-profile.The upper flanges of the I-profile have been converted to form the railhead.

The rails should provide smooth running surfaces for the train wheels and they should guide the wheel sets in the direction of the track. The rails also carry the vertical load of the train and distribute the load over the sleepers. Lateral forces from the wheel sets, and longitudinal forces due to traction and braking of the train should also be transmitted to the sleepers and further down into the track bed. The rails also act as electrical conductors for the signaling systems.

2. Sleeper (cross ties in British English)

The sleepers provide support of the rails and preserve gauge, level, and alignment of the track. The sleepers transmit vertical, lateral, and longitudinal forces from the rail down to the ballast bed. They should also provide electrical insulation between the two rails. Nowadays, ballasted railway tracks are usually constructed with mono-bloc concrete sleepers. Timber sleepers have been used almost since the beginning of railway construction. In countries where the timber price is acceptable, timber sleepers are still frequently used. Sometimes, it is suitable to use steel sleepers.

3. Fastening

It is a means of fixing rails to sleepers. The terms rail anchors, railpads (sleeper plates in British English), chairs and track fastenings are used to refer to parts or all of a rail fastening system. Various types of fastening have been used over the years.

4. Track ballast

The track ballast comprises of the ballast and any sub-ballast layers and supports the track, drains water from the bottom of the sleepers and distributes the imposed track load to such a degree that the subgrade can resist the imposed bearing pressure adequately.

5. Railroad turnout

A railroad turnout or switch (in US) enables a train switched from one track to another. When a train traverses the railroad switch, the wheels change from rolling on one rail to rolling on another at the crossing. Under perfect conditions, the wheels traverse smoothly over the rail discontinuity and the magnitude of the wheel/rail contact force does not increase very much.

6. Subgrade[2]

Subgrade is the term used for the natural soil stratum, or embankment soil, after trimming off organic topsoil and made ground, upon which a road, pavement or railway track is constructed. It is also called formation level.

There are two type tracks: Ballasted track (Fig. 2-2 (a)) and Ballastless track (Fig. 2-2 (b)). Ballasted track is the most traditional track structure.

1) Ballasted track

A ballasted track is a structure in which the track skeleton is supported by ballast. From the bottom its structure is ballast, sleepers, rail fastening system, and rails .The ballast distributes the load from the sleepers and transmits it to the roadbed. And when the track has been deformed, the deformation can be repaired by tamping the ballast. But this structure is susceptible to track deformation caused by deformation of the ballast, so it requires regular maintenance work.

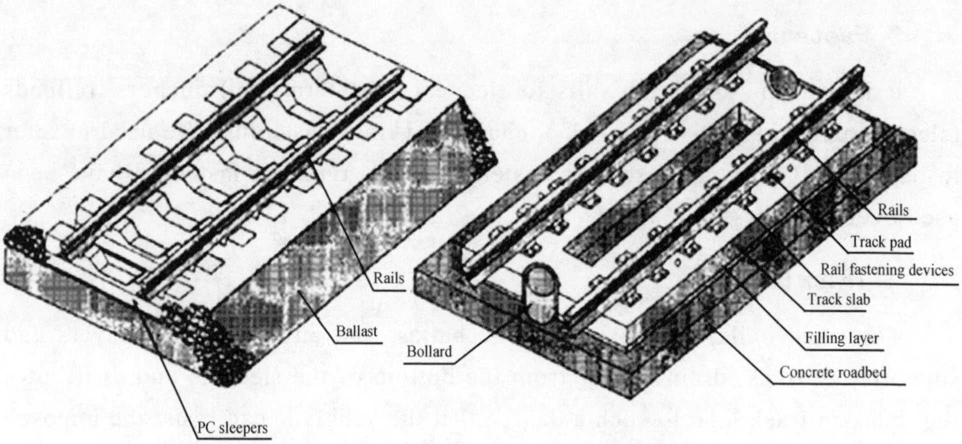

(a) Ballasted track (b)Ballastless Track

Fig. 2-2 Two types of railway track

2) Ballastless track

A ballastless track is a structure with the track structure directly supported by the roadbed. It does not include ballast, so regular maintenance to deal with deformation of ballast is unnecessary. But when the track is deformed, it is more difficult to repair than a track with ballast, because to repair this deformation the track's height is adjusted with track fastening system. This means that in order to lower the amount of maintenance work, the goal of using ballastless track, the amount of earth structure deformation of must be minimized. To do so, a highly stiff concrete roadbed or asphalt roadbed are used.

Advantages of ballasted track:

- Easy assembly and maintenance with heavy-machinery.
- not necessarily let the railroad out of service for installation or maintenance.
- Well-known service life and maintenance programs.
- Good absorption of efforts, noises and vibrations.
- Chance to reuse the ballast.

Drawbacks of ballasted track:

- More maintenance required.

• Degeneration of ballast, with damaging repercussion on drainage capabilities and elasticity.

• Increasing of the top level with each mechanized maintenance, since in each one a new ballast amount is added.

• The co-existence of circulations at different speeds cause undesired settlements.

• Dangerous flight of ballast in high-speed railroads.

Advantages of ballastless track:

• Ensures railroad stability.

• The maximum heights of the subgrade can be fitted to the minimum, since no alteration in the tracing will occur.

• Longer service life of materials.

• Almost no maintenance required.

• Allows the co-existence of circulations at different speeds.

Drawbacks of ballastless track:

• Higher construction costs.

• Requires a minimum time for concrete setting before allowing the railway traffic.

• More difficult repair, since the concrete must be demolished in order to re-build any section.

• More noisy than ballasted railway line

• Worse absorption of noise and vibrations

• Requires an accurate topographic-survey prior to the assembly, since there is no chance to use alignment and leveling machines as for the ballasted track.

2.1.2 Features of track

Track has been termed the permanent way, it is, unfortunately, far from permanent. There is no definite structural coordination. The rails, fastenings, sleepers, ballast, and subgrade experience differential movement between all components, with consequent wear and deterioration. Lateral stability and resistance to uplift depend on the embedment of sleeper in ballast and on the weight of rail and axle loads. Rail support varies in stiffness and local deformations in the roadbed cause (and are caused by) impact from dynamically applied loads of widely varying intensities. Drainage and deep-seated roadway instabilities require occasional correction; local reforming of surface, alignment, and gauge must be a continuing process. The effects of all adverse features are cumulative, and track materials-rail, sleepers, fastenings, and ballast-require routine attention and renewal at intervals that are all too frequent. In practice, track exists in various degrees of excellence and adherence to geometric design.

1. Load transmission on a ballasted railroad[2]

Track acts as an elastic, load-distributing structure. Load distribution is a function of stiffness and flexibility. In effecting this distribution, the rail absorbs and distributes wheel loads to the sleepers (through sleeper plate and sleeper pad) with diminished unit pressure, the sleepers distribute the loads to the ballast, ballast distributes loads to the subgrade, and the subgrade distributes the subgrade load to the natural ground.

Fig. 2-3 shows a principle sketch with the main dimensions. Load transfer works on the principle of stress reduction, which means layer by layer. The distribution function can be indicated roughly by assuming a 100 kN wheel load resting on the rail. The area of contract will be no more than 1 cm^2.The greatest stress occurs between wheel and rail thus 100 kN/cm^2. Subgrades, if reasonably firm, may have a supporting capacity of 5 N/cm^2. The track structure must reduce or distribute the 100 kN/cm^2 to 5 N/cm^2 or less, otherwise the subgrade will not support the track and train.

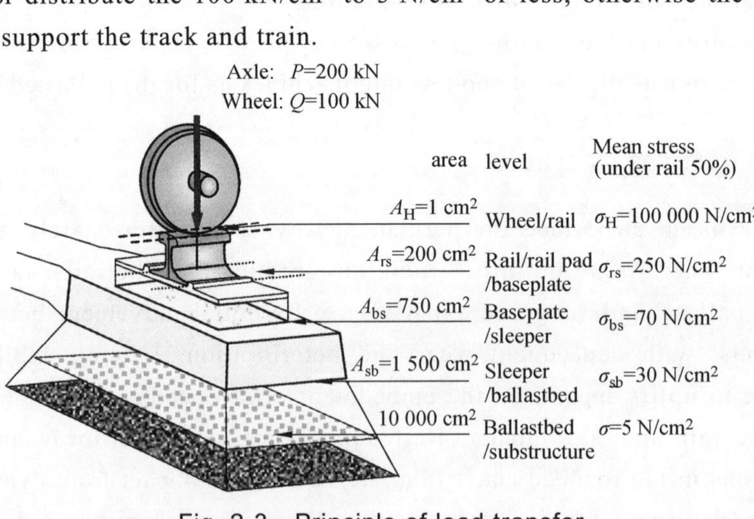

Fig. 2-3 Principle of load transfer

As shown in the figure 2.3, the 26% of the load from an axle is applied over the sleeper where the axle is placed. Likewise, the remaining load is distributed over the adjacent sleepers, placed 0.6 m apart, (21%, 11%, 5%). Considering the load of a conventional axle, the sub-ballast just reaches a pressure of around 0.4-0.6 kg/cm^2.

The Bearing Capacity of a soil is defined as the maximum load that a soil can bear without suffering significant deformations. Below are some results[5]:

Vegetable ground wet: 1 kg/cm^2.

Vegetable ground very wet: 0.5 kg/cm^2.

Vegetable ground mix with sand: 1.5 kg/cm^2.

Vegetable ground mix with dry clay: 4 kg/cm^2.

Mix debris, vegetable ground and dry clay: 2 kg/cm^2.

Dry clay: 6 kg/cm^2.

Ground little compact: 1.5 kg/cm^2.

Ground compact: 2.5 kg/cm^2.

Fine Sand non compacted: 3 kg/cm^2.

Fine Sand compacted: 5 kg/cm^2.

Median Sand compacted: 7 kg/cm^2.

Rock and Sand compacted: 5.5 kg/cm^2.

Rock and Sand very hard: 9 kg/cm^2.

In Europe it is established that the railroad subgrade must have a minimum bearing capacity of 1.0 kg/cm^2, despite it varies depending on[2]:

- Load per axle.
- Railroad type.
- Circulation speed.
- Thickness of the ballast layer.
- Climate of the zone.
- Groundwater level (water table).

2. Track stresses

Track Stress is load (force) divided by the area over which it is applied, that is,

$$\text{Stress}=\text{load}/\text{area}=P/A \tag{2-1}$$

Stress may be expressed in pascals (or in kilograms per square centimeter).

vertical Bending stress: The vertical component of wheel loads causing deflection.

lateral Bending stress: From lateral components of wheel loads, from hunting and nosing action, and from thermal forces and brake applications.

Shearing stress: From the vertical and lateral components of wheel loads damaging the metallic structure of the rail.

Longitudinal stress: Due to wave action under the passage of car wheels; also due to thermal forces.

Torsional or twisting stress: Due to the eccentricity of applied loads and to lateral flexibility; also due to the tendency of a rail to rotate about its points of lateral and longitudinal restraint.

Contact stress: A concentration of local shearing and bending stresses on the rail surface and immediately below the point of load application. Some of these stresses are well understood and can be expressed quantitatively; others are still somewhat of a mystery. The purpose of track is to transfer train loads to the formation.

3. Requirements of track

Certain requirements must be met for the track to perform its load-distributing function satisfactorily.

a. Stiffness

Stiffness or resistance to deflection is a function of bending strength and is measured by the amount of deflection and by the modulus of track elasticity. Vertical deflection is the single best indicator of track strength, life, and quality. Excessive deflection causes differential movement and wear between all track components. Deflection leads to deterioration of ballast through abrasion and powdering of the particles, to the formation of water and ballast pockets, to muddy and pumping track, to permanent deformation, and to increased train resistance. Pressures transmitted to the subgrade must be within the supporting capability of that subgrade. There should also be enough stiffness so that the pressure pulses from individual axles of 2- and 3-axle wagons will be merged into one pressure pulse, thereby permitting some increase in speed.

b. Resilience of elasticity

Resilience or elasticity is needed within limits to provide a smooth ride for cars and locomotives, to prevent the breakage of wheels, axles, wagon component, and to absorb shock, impact, vertical oscillations, and vibration. If the track is too stiff-rails on concrete slabs, for example-resilience must be introduced by inserting a wood, fiber, or rubberized pad under the rail. Greatly restrain track can lead to pumping and possibly to corrugations. There is, undoubtedly an as yet unspecified optimum resilience related to subgrade support, speed, and axle loads. Conventional ballast track normally provides too much rather than too little resilience.

c. Resistance to permanent deformation

Excessive deflection leads to permanent deformation. The greater the deformation, the more rapidly the permanent set will occur. Permanent deformation might be considered desirable if the track deformed or settled uniformly. Such is never the case. Differential rail settlement distorts cross level, creates warp and lateral deformation, and alters track alignment. The end result of permanent deformation is rough track.

d. Stability

The ultimate test of good track is stability, that is, its degree of permanence or ability to remain in the desired vertical and lateral position. Stable track requires a firm, well-drained subgrade, clean, well-compacted ballast, and sound sleepers supporting rail of adequate section and weight. Unstable track exhibits excessive deflection and degradation of track and roadbed materials, with a loss of surface, line, and gauge, lowered resistance to lateral deformation from thermal and braking forces, and traffic delays from slow orders.

e. Adjustability

Because track is never completely stable, a means of adjusting its geometric condition—cross level, gauge, and alignment-must be available. Tamping or surfacing and lining procedures restore surface and line to ballasted track. Spikes are pulled and the rails and plates reset to restore gauge. For non-conventional systems such as slab or beam track, the adjustment capability is usually included in the fastenings.

f. Goal

The goal in track construction and maintenance is a track that is safe and with a degree of excellence in life, stability, cross level, gauge, and line that is cost effective in terms of the traffic that moves over it

2.2 Rail

2.2.1 History

Developments in manufacturing technologies has led to changes to the design, manufacture and installation of rails, sleepers and the means of attachments.

The earliest use of a railway track seems to have been in connection with mining in Germany in the 12th century. Mine passageways were usually wet and muddy, and moving barrows of ore along them was extremely difficult, as shown in Fig. 2-4. Improvements were made by laying timber planks so that wheeled containers could be dragged along by manpower. By the 16th century the difficulty of keeping the wagon running straight had been solved by having a pin going into a gap between the planks, as shown in Fig. 2-4.

Fig. 2-4 Wooden track

Over the next few decades, other coal mines in England began to build this kind of wooden rails. In 1781, the whole northeast of England coal mine was covered with cobweb like wooden tracks. These are the private property of the owner of the coal mine, which is used to quickly transfer coal between the mine and the nearby river. Before being eliminated, this kind of wood track is constantly improved, for example, because of its poor durability, it will soon be damaged. In order to avoid touching the sleepers when replacing wooden rails, two wooden rails should be placed on the original wooden tracks, which will be very convenient to replace with bad. Later, in order to reduce the number of changes in the rail, the engineers also wrapped a layer of iron on the surface of the wooden rails to improve their service life. Cast iron rails laid on top of timber rails, 1.22 m long, began to be used in the 1790s and by 1820, 4.57 m long wrought iron rails were in use.

In 1789, William Jessop, a British civil engineer, designed for the first time the convex rail and the cast iron wheel with convex edges, and it was applied to the Mala railway in Loughborough Leicester. This is the rudiment of modern railway, as shown in Fig.2-5. Jie Thorpe later improved the wheel which was highlighted by the outside world, and developed the cast iron wheel and railway turnout with the inner flange protruding, becoming the standard form of modern railway wheel and rail. As an appendage of all kinds of mines, the railway has developed along with the continuous progress of mining and metallurgical industry.

Fig. 2-5 cast iron edge rail

The first steel rails were made in 1857 and standard rail lengths increased over time from 9.14-18.29 m. Railway sleepers were traditionally made of creosote-treated hardwoods and this continued to modern times, as shown in Fig.2-6. Continuous welded rail was introduced into Britain in the mid-1960s and this was followed by the introduction of concrete sleepers, as shown in Fig.2-7.

Fig. 2-6 steel rail

Fig. 2-7 continuous welded rail

2.2.2 The function of rails

All modern railways use steel rails which are specifically rolled for the purpose from steel which has the required qualities of strength, fatigue endurance and wear and corrosion resistance. Rails are continuous girders which carry the axle loads and serve the following functions.

(1) They provide a smooth, and uniform surface to bear the heavy wagon loads transmitted through the axles. The friction between steel wheels and steel rails is about 20% of the friction between pneumatic tyres and bituminous road surface.

(2) In addition to the vertical loads transmitted through axle, rails bear lateral stresses due to braking and thermal stresses as well.

(3) Because of the quality control exercised during the manufacture of the rails and rolling stock the wear and replacement cost is comparatively little and failure due to wear is rare.

(4) The rails transmit the load to the formation through sleepers and the ballast.

In order that the rails perform their function satisfactorily, they should have other properties detailed below:

(1) Should have adequate height so that the area provided to resist vertical shear is adequate.

(2) Should have adequate surface of contact with axle flanges and sufficient area of contact with the sleepers.

(3) The bottom of the head and top of the foot of the rail should be shaped so that the fish plates transmit the vertical load from the head to the foot of the rail joint satisfactorily.

(4) The centre of gravity of the section should be approximately the mid height so that the maximum tensile and compressive stresses are equal.

(5) The stress concentration should be avoided by having large radius of fillets.

(6) The rail section should satisfy the falling weight test as specified.

2.2.3 The length and weight of rails

1. The Length of Rail

From the consideration of maintenance cost and efficient functioning of the track, the longer the rail, the better it is. Long rails have less number of joints and hence lessen fittings which result in reduction in the cost of construction and maintenance. Longer rails also provide a better travel comfort to the passengers as the less number of joints results in smooth running of the train.

The length of the rail is therefore limited by the following consideration.

(1) Facility for economical length from the point of view of its manufacture.

(2) Facility for being transported by wagons.

(3) Facility for lifting and handling of the rail.

(4) Provision of expansion joints.

It is not possible to provide the required expansion joints for very long rails because the fittings which hold the two rails at the joints would not function effectively beyond a certain limit. This limit therefore governs the length of the rails. Different countries has different rail lengths, such as Russia 25 m, Germany 30, 45, 60 m, France 18, 24, 36 m, Italy 36 m, UK 18.4 m, United States 11.89 m, 23.96 m, Japan 25 m. Taking the above factors into consideration the Chinese convetional railways adopted 12.5 m and 25 m as standard rail lengths.

With the development of railway track towards high-speed and heavy-haul, long rail production has also become a trend in the world. For example, the French production of rail from the original 36 m into 72-80 m, Germany into 120 m, China is also stepping up the 100 m long rails.

2. The Weight of Rail

With the development of railway track toward the high-speed, heavy, long rail production has become a trend. The rail is designated by its weight per unit length (1metre length) in metric system. Heavier rail can support greater axle loads and higher train speeds without sustaining damage than lighter rail, but at a greater cost. Increasing the weight increases the moment of inertia (stiffness). The greater stiffness reduces rail deflection, while the heavier weight contributes to stability and to a bridging action over weak track support.

In North America and the UK, the usual range of weight is 57.0 to 69.9 kg/m. In mainland Europe, the usual range of weight is 40 to 60 kg/m. The heaviest rail mass-produced was 76.9 kg/m and was rolled for the Pennsylvania Railroad. A crude relation can be developed between rail weights and wheel load, whereby 0.5 kg/m (with normal wood sleeper spacing) will support 1,488 kg of concentrated wheel load. Thus a about 35 kg/m rail will support 10,416 kg of concentrated load, a 45 kg/m rail 13,608 kg, a 50 kg/m rail 15,649 kg, and 60 kg/m rail 17,962 kg.

At the beginning of the twentieth century the weight of rail worldwide is not more than 50 kg/m. As the annual transport volume is more than 30million tons and the maximum speed is more than 120 km/h , the 50 kg/m rail has been replaced by 60 kg/m. Although the increase of 18% steel, but the transport capacity can be increased by 50%, and the service life of rail can be prolonged to 70%. At present most countries adopt the rail above 60 kg/m. Thus, the heavy rail is an economical and effective means to prolong rail service life. The heavy rail weight used in American is 77 kg/m, the Soviet Union is 75 kg/m. States under specific conditions in different ways to improve the steel's wear-resistance, crushing-resistance, fatigue fracture properties.

In china, rails are in four types mainly: 75 kg/m, 60 kg/m, 50 kg/m and 43 kg/m. In order to meet the high-speed, heavy haul transportation requirements, there is a trend to develop heavy rail. 60 kg/m rail is widely adopted in high-speed railway, and 75 kg/m rail is used for heavy haul railway.

The choice of weight of a rail is governed by the following factors:

(1) Maximum permissible speed of the train.

(2) The gauge of the track.

(3) The heaviest moving or axle load.

(4) Depth of ballast cushion.

(5) Type of trails.

(6) Spacing of sleepers.

(7) Nature of traffic.

(8) Maximum permissible wear on the top of the rails.

2.2.4 Rail profile

1. The development of rail section

The rail profile is the cross sectional shape of a rail, perpendicular to the length of the rail. Early rails were made of wood, cast iron or wrought iron. All modern rails are hot rolled steel of a specific cross sectional profile. Because the rail is seen as supporting the continuous elastic infinite long beam, the cross section shape of I-section beam resists flexure best. So, typically the rail profiles on the basis of I-section beam include: Bullhead rail, double-headed rail, grooved rail, flat-bottomed rail.

1) Double-headed rail

Double-headed rail sections were used in the beginning. The head and foot of double-headed rail has the same profile and is supported by chairs. It was felt that if the top and bottom sections were kept identical, the life of the rails could be increased by inverting the rail and reusing it. It was however discovered that due to the impact of the wheels the lower surface in contact with the chairs got dented. This section was therefore modified so that only the minimum required section was kept at the bottom. Fig. 2-8 shows a typical double-headed rail section.

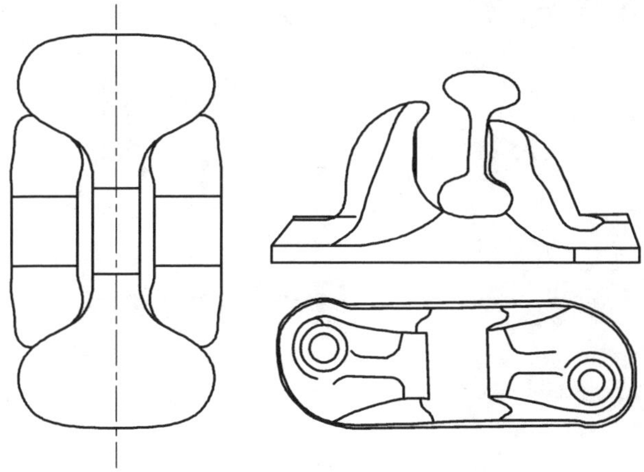

Fig. 2-8 Double-headed rail and chair

2) Bull-head rail

The double-headed rails were therefore replaced by bull-headed rails. These rails are made in lengths of 9.2 to 18.3 m and weigh from 29.8 kg to 49.60 kg per metre length. The rails are fixed to the sleepers by means of chairs. The head is larger than the foot and the foot is so shaped that it should hold the wooden keys with which the rails are secured to the cast iron chairs. Two cast iron chairs per sleeper are required with these rails. These rails are extensively used in England and other European countries Fig. 2-9 shows a typical bull-headed rail section.

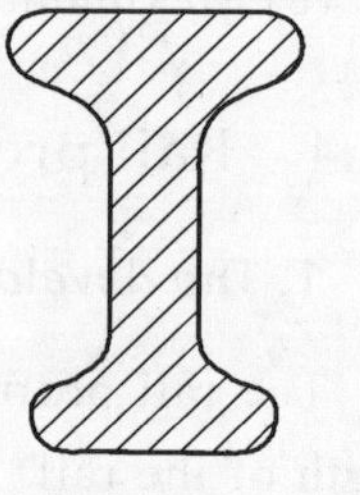

Fig. 2-9 Bull-head rail

3) Grooved rail

Grooved rail was invented in 1852 by Alphonse Loubat, a French inventor who developed improvements in tram and rail equipment, and helped develop tram lines in New York City and Paris. The invention of grooved rail enabled tramways to be laid without causing a nuisance to other road users, except unsuspecting cyclists, who could get their wheels caught in the groove. The grooves may become filled with gravel and dirt (particularly if infrequently used or after a period of idleness) and need clearing from time to time, this being done by a "scrubber" tram, as shown in Fig. 2-10. Failure to clear the grooves can lead to a bumpy ride for the passengers, damage to either wheel or rail and possibly derailing.

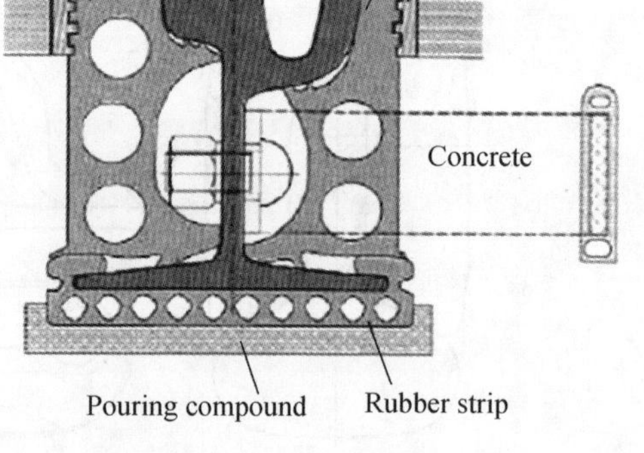

Fig. 2-10 Grooved rail

4) Flat-bottomed rail.

In 1836 a new section was invented by charles vignoles wherein the foot is spread out to form a base. Because of the advantage of this section it has been adopted all over the railway track in the world.90 percent of the railway track in the world is laid with this form of rails. Typical rail section is given in Fig. 2-11. Flat bottomed rail is the dominant rail profile in worldwide use.

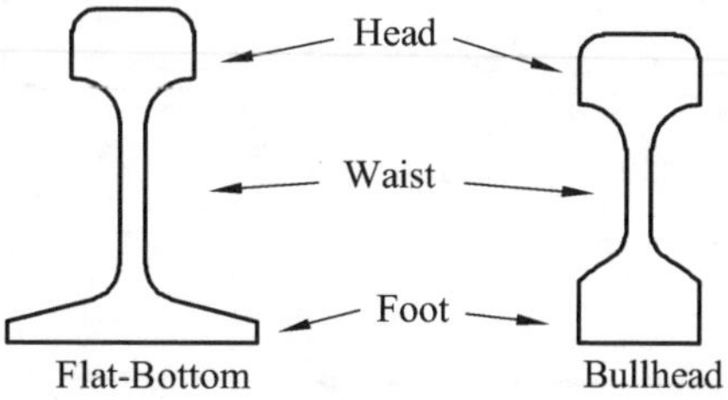

Fig. 2-11 Flat-bottomed rail And Bull-head rail

As compared to the bull-head rails, the flat-bottom rails have the following advantages.

- Better rigidity and stiffness to resist vertical and lateral forces.
- Simpler fittings. No chairs or keys are required.
- Turnouts are simpler as compared to bull-head rails.

2. Requirements of flat-bottom rail profile design

Rail section should be designed that every part of the rail material can bear the maximum allowable stresses, which would ensure that rail has minimum and the most economical cross-sectional area. Rail profile design should meet the following requirements.

1) Rail head design

The head of the rail is directly in contact with the wheel, and should have the ability to withstand crushing and wear resistance. Thus the rail head should be large and thick, and should have a shape adapt to wheel tread. The top surface of the rail head should be of sufficient width so that the wheel tread rolls on the top surface evenly. What's more, the top surface of the rail head should be rolled into a circular arc shape so that the pressure from the wheel can be concentrated on the rail axis. After long-term rolling of the rail by the wheel, the top surface shows the approximate 200-300 mm radius of the arc, so in China, the top surface of the light rail, often is rolled into a radius of 300 mm arc. And the top surface of the heavy rail is made up of 3 composite arcs with radius of 80 mm, 300 mm, 80 mm or 80 mm, 500 mm and 80 mm, respectively, as shown in Fig. 2-12.

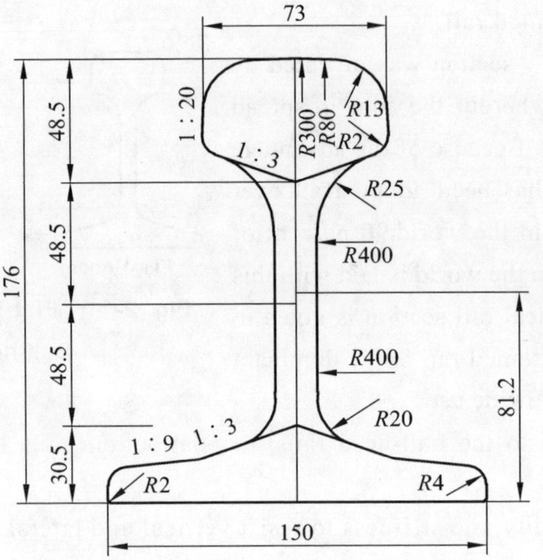

Fig. 2-12 60 kg/m rail profile

2) Rail waist design

Rail waist should have enough thickness and height to bear load and resistant bending stress. Both sides of the rail waist are curve. The connection between rail waist, rail head and bottom must ensure the clamping plate has enough bearing surface.

3) Rail foot design

As rail bearing directly on the sleeper, rail foot should have enough width and thickness to maintain rail section stability. In addition, rail foot should have necessary stiffness and resistance to corrosion.

Rail head width, rail waist thickness, rail height and rail bottom width is four main parameters of rail profile. Rail height should be as large as possible, in order to make sure there is enough inertia torque and section coefficient to withstand the vertical wheel load moment. But the higher the rail, the less stability under the action of horizontal force. Rail waist height and rail bottom width should have an appropriate proportion-about 1.15-1.20. For steel rolling and cooling even, there should be an appropriate proportion allocation among the area of rail head, rail waist and rail bottom. Tab. 2-1 shows the section dimensions of the rails of China railway.

Tab. 2-1 The section dimensions of the rails of China railway

Items	Rail type/ (kg/m)			
	75	60	50	43
quality per meter M/kg	74.414	60.64	51.514	44.653
cross section area F/cm^2	95.04	77.45	65.8	57
distance between gravity center and rail bottom y_1/mm	88	81	71	69
rail height H/mm	192	176	152	140
rail bottom width B/mm	150	150	132	114
rail head height h/mm	55.3	48.5	42	42
rail head width b/mm	75	73	70	70
rail waist thickness t/mm	20	16.5	15.5	14.5

2.2.5 Chemical composition and manufacture

1. Chemical composition of rail[2]

Rails are manufactured on steel and manganese alloy as base material, reducing the risk of breaking or cracking of its pearlitic structure by means of thermal treatments in modern lamination chains. The steel of the rails must fulfill several requirements, as the abrasion resistance, fragility, weld ability, etc. This capabilities are achieved by means of modification of the chemical composition of the steel. Below are explained some effects of the different components of the steel:

• Carbon: Improve hardness, wearing resistance and traction resistance. However, it also increases the fragility.

• Manganese: Improves hardness, wearing resistance, traction resistance and resilience. However, it influences negatively on weld ability.

• Silicium: Improves hardness, wearing resistance and allows the removal of gase during the pouring and rolling processes.

• Sulfur and Phosphorous: They make steel brittle and likely to break under impact, but regretfully are very difficult to remove, so it is just possible to limit their content.

• Chrome: Improves hardness, wearing resistance and resilience. However, it causes the formation of martensite, therefore increasing its fragility.

In addition, alloy rails are also produced in the world, that is, adding vanadium (V), chromium (Cr), molybdenum (Mo) and so on, in order to improve the quality of the rail, to meet the requirements of high-speed railway.

Concerning the tensile strength, rails are usually divided into three levels:

standard carbon rail steel (tensile strength is 70-85 kgf/mm^2), wear-resistant rail (tensile strength is 90-105 kgf/mm^2) and premium rail (tensile strength is 110-125 kgf/mm^2). Rail steels must reach the standards for chemical composition, strength and elongation, at the same time, must pass the tests for drop, metallography, low magnification, hardness and surface quality and dimensional deviation. Tab.2-2 shows the compostion of special type of steel.

Tab. 2-2 Composition of special type of steel

Carbon	0.3%-0.4 %
Manganese	Below 0.8%
Silicon	Below 0.15%
Sulphur and phosphorous	Below 0.06%

2. Manufacture of rail

In the beginning, carbon steel (C 0.3%-0.4%) is manufactured and used worldwide. At present, a large number of countries use carbon steel still, but carbon content of which has increased gradually (C 0.5%-0.8%). In some carbon steel, manganese content increase (Mn 0.6%-1%) too. Standard components of China heavy rail steel are C 0.67%-0.80%, Si 0.13%-0.28%, Mn 0.7%-1%, P$\leqslant$ 0.04%, S$\leqslant$0.05%. Facing the increase of vehicle axle load, vehicle speed and traffic volume, lots of methods have been used to improve rail such as:

- Improving rail weight per unit length.
- Using alloy rail.
- Improving the production process and product quality of rail.

For more service life of rail, some western european countries adapt alloying method: German Cr-V rail (C 0.55%-0.75%, Mn 0.8%-1.3%, Cr 0.8%-1.3%, V$\leqslant$0.3%) in German, Mn-Cr Rail (C 0.15%, Mn 1.25%, Cr 1.15%) in British. From 1965, China began to produce low alloy rail-copper rail (Cu 0.2%-0.4%), manganese rail (Mn 1.1%-1.5%). Medium manganese steel rail has good features such as abrasion resistance, rail integral reinforcement, uniform surface hardness, good weld ability. Its service life is 2 times higher than ordinary carbon steel and production process is simple, less investment, less energy consumption. Tab. 2-3 shows chemical composition of rail steel of China railway

Tab. 2-3 Chemical composition of rail steel of China railway

Steel type	chemical composition /%						Usage scope (rail type kg/m)
	C	Si	Mn	Cu	P	S	
U_{71}	0.64-0.77	0.13-0.28	0.60-0.90		≤0.040	≤0.050	50
U_{74}	0.67-0.80	0.13-0.28	0.70-1.00		≤0.040	≤0.050	50、60、75
U_{71}Cu	0.65-0.77	0.15-0.30	0.70-1.00	0.10-0.40	≤0.040	≤0.050	50
U_{71}Mn	0.65-0.77	0.15-0.35	1.10-1.50		≤0.040	≤0.040	50、60、75
U_{70}MnSi	0.65-0.75	0.85-1.15	0.85-1.15		≤0.040	≤0.040	50
U_{71}MnSiCu	0.65-0.77	0.70-1.10	0.80-1.20	0.10-0.40	≤0.040	≤0.040	50
PD_2*	0.74-0.82	0.15-0.35	0.70-1.00		≤0.040	≤0.040	50、60、75
PD_3	0.70-0.78	0.50-0.70	0.75-1.05	0.04-0.08**	≤0.035	≤0.035	50、60、75

Note: * is full length quenched rail for PD2; ** is micro vanadium content in PD3.

Since 1962, in France, USA, Japan and other countries, the oxygen top-blown converters are used to produce rail steel successively. In China, open hearth furnace and oxygen top-blown converter are used to produce rail steels. During the manufacture, rail is generally slow in cooling after rolling to eliminate the white spot. In order to shorten the cooling process, vacuum degassing process can also be used.

In addition, rail surface or full-length quenching after heat treatment are another mainly method to explore steel potential in the Soviet Union, USA, Japan. The service life of full-length quenched rail is 2-3 times higher than ordinary carbon steel. This method can not only make rail high strength and surface hardness, but also save alloy rails, suitable for mass production.

2.2.6 Rail life and maintenance

Rail represents a tremendous capital investment and a wide array of maintenance costs; safety is also involved. Hence the life and the proper selection and use of rail are matters of importance.

1. Rail Life and fatigue

Rail life is usually expressed in millions of gross tons carried. Total million gross tons divided by annual traffic density gives life in years. Life may be further identified as life in main track (first position) and as total life including main track, secondary tracks, yards, sidings, and side tracks.

The service life of rail will vary with traffic (tonnage, axle loads, and speed), the amount of curvature, gradient, subgrade and ballast support, and the standard of maintenance. A heavier rail normally outlasts a light rail, other conditions being equal. Rail may be removed early from main track for use in secondary track.

Rail life may be determined by wear-abrasion, rail-end batter, curve wear. It can also be determined by fatigue-extended repetition of flexure combined with the formation of contact- and shearing-stress-related defects such as detailed fractures.

Today, where high-capacity trains and unit trains predominate, and especially with CWR, fatigue has become a major rail life factor in tangent track, where new rail is subject to heavy loading before acquiring a work-hardened running surface. But on curves abrasion wears the rail so rapidly that fatigue stresses do not have time to develop, so it acts as a prime limit on rail life.

Rail life can be foreshortened by an unacceptably high incidence of rail failures, especially those associated with fatigue. As earlier noted, fatigue failures are assuming major proportions where new rail is subject to wheel loading from high-capacity cars and unit trains. Bending and thermal stresses combine with shearing and contact stresses to develop fatigue cracks where a weak spot exists in the metal or an intensified load is repeatedly applied. The number of such failures is likely to increase in terms of accumulated cycles of load application and the accompanying reversals of stress, hence in terms of accumulated tonnage.

A plot of failure incidence in terms of million gross tons of accumulated tonnage would reveal fatigue failures (and others) as occurring at an increasing rate. When the failure rate becomes intolerable, the rail is condemned and removed from track. The condemning point will depend on safety, economic considerations, and the stage in the cascade renewal cycle. Each railroad must set its own condemning point, because local situations vary widely and research has not yet established suitable.

2. Rail failures[6]

Aside from being a nuisance and an economic liability, broken rails are often the cause of disastrous derailments and wrecks. The immediate cause of a broken rail is usually an impact load beyond the strength of the rail. The ultimate source of the failure, however, can usually be traced to an imperfection in the molecular structure of the steel. This type of imperfection is particularly dangerous in that it is often inside the rail and therefore invisible. Obviously, some steps must be taken to prevent such imperfections from leading to rail failure. Many of the changes in rail form were adopted in an effort to reduce the occurrence of structural imperfections or flaws.

Rail failures include transverse and compound fissures, split and crushed heads, split waists, and broken bases. These and other failures, described in the subparagraphs following, are shown in Fig. 2-13.

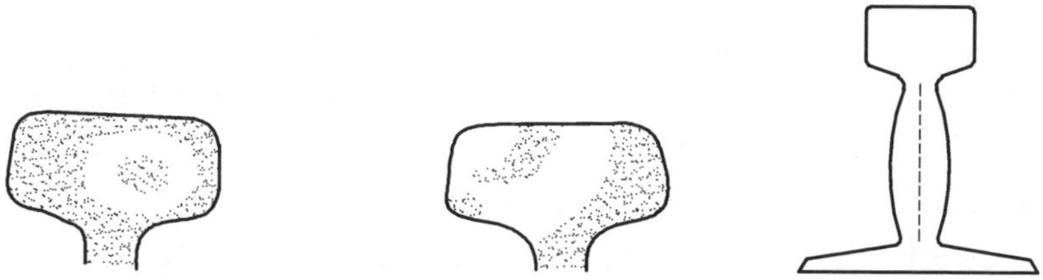

A. Transverse Fissure B. Compound Fissure C. Piped Rail

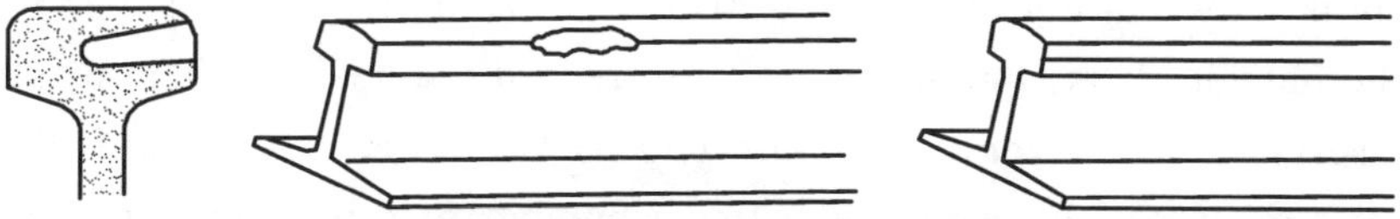

D. Horizontal Split Heads

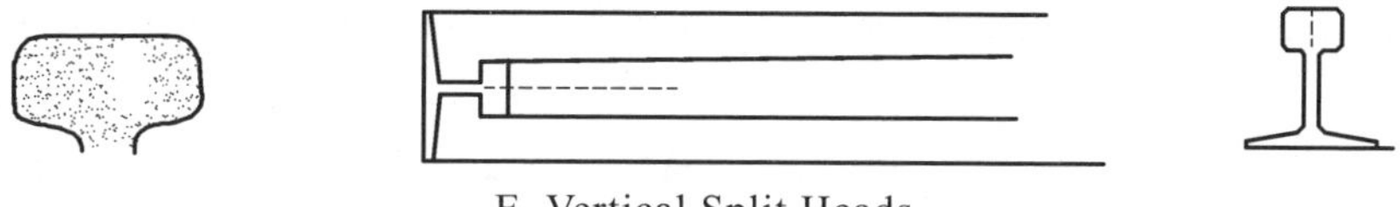

E. Vertical Split Heads

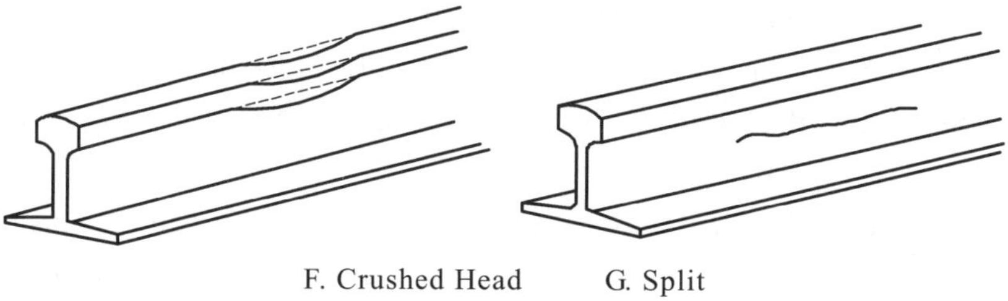

F. Crushed Head G. Split

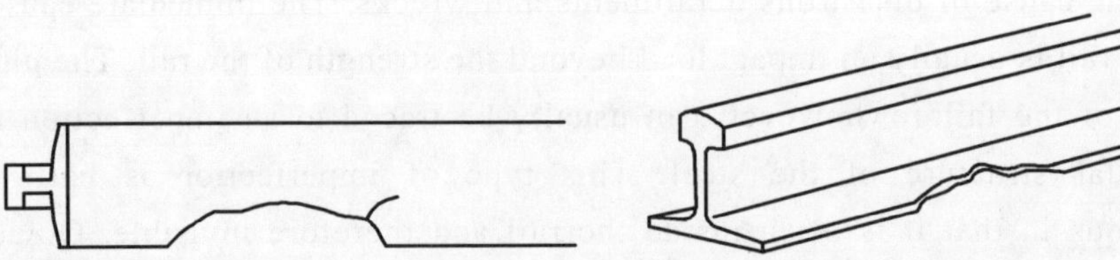

H. Broken Bases

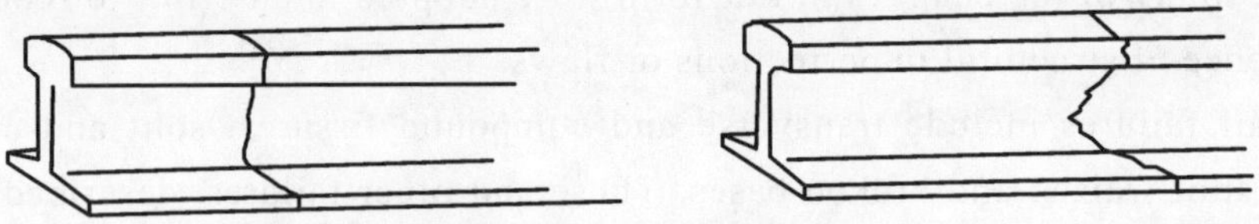

I. Square and Angular Breaks

Fig. 2-13 Rail Defects

a. Transverse fissure. The most frequent and aggravating of all the flaws is the transverse fissure, caused by hydrogen remaining in the rail after its manufacture. The fissure-crack is a crosswise break, starting from a nucleus inside the head of the rail and spreading outward. The failure can be recognized by either a bright or dark, round or oval smooth area around the nucleus. An example is shown in Fig. 2-13 (a). Until the rail actually fails, it appears sound from the outside. It is common practice to record the heat numbers of all rails put in service. Whenever a rail fails because of transverse fissure, the heat number is taken and kept on file. After a number of rails from the same heat have failed, poor steel is suspected. Often, all rails having that heat number are removed from service. Electronic detecting devices are used to spot transverse fissures in rails before they fail. When found, such rails are immediately removed from service. It is unlikely that such devices would be found in a theater of operations. In those localities, the track should be inspected closely to detect the more advanced cases of fissured rail visible to the naked eye.

b. Compound fissure. A horizontal split head which, in spreading, turns up or down in the head of the rail is called a compound fissure. An example is shown in Fig. 2-13 (b).

c. Piped rail. A vertical split, usually in the web, occurring because of the failure of the shrinkage cavity in the ingot to unite, is called a piped rail. See the example shown in Fig. 2-13 (c).

d. Horizontal split head. Horizontal breaks beginning inside the head of the rail and spreading outward are called horizontal split heads. They are illustrated in Fig. 2-13 (d). They are usually indicated on the side of the head either by a longitudinal seam or crack or by the flow of metal.

e. Vertical split head. Splits may run vertically through or near the middle of the head and extend into or through it, as shown in Fig. 2-13 (e). Such splits are called vertical split heads. A crack or rust streak may show under the head close to the web, or pieces may be split off the side of the head.

f. Crushed head. A flattening or crushing of the head, as shown in Fig. 2-13 (f), is called a crushed head.

g. Split waist. Cracks may run lengthwise along the side of the web and frequently extend into or through the waist. Such cracks result in what are called split waists. Fig. 2-13 (g) shows an example.

h. broken base. Any rail base with a crack or break in it can be said to have a broken base. Note in the two views shown in Fig. 2-13 (h) that pieces of the bases are missing.

i. Square and angular breaks. Any partial or complete break in which there is no sign of a fissure or any of the other defects discussed, is known as a square or angular break, depending on its shape. Examples are shown in Fig. 2-13 (I).

2.3 Sleeper

Railway sleeper (or cross-tie) is a rectangular support for the rails in railway tracks. Railway sleeper is a very important structural element of railway track. As well as pressure distribution and load transfer to the underlying layers, railway sleepers are in duty to maintain track gauge, grantee lateral stability of the track and contribute in better geometrical conditions of the track. Vertical, lateral and axial forces are applied to rail sleepers. These forces should be transferred to the underlying ballast layer within the admissible stress range with minimum disturbance of track quality and permanent deformation.

Railway sleepers were traditionally made of wood, but pre-stressed concrete is now widely used, especially in Europe and Asia. Steel sleepers are common on secondary lines in the UK.Plastic composite sleepers are also employed, although far less than wood or concrete.

2.3.1 Functions of sleeper

Sleeper forms a very important component of the track laid across the rails. It serves the following purpose:

- Hold the rail to the required gauge.
- Provide a firm and even support to the rails.
- Transfer load from the rails to a large area of the ballast.
- Absorb the vibration and blows of the moving loads by acting as an elastic medium between the rails and ballast.
- Provide stability to permanent way.
- Provide for easy replacement of rail fastenings.
- Permit track insulation for electrified section.
- Maintain track alignment.

The requirements of an ideal sleeper are:

- It should be able to maintain proper gauge.
- It should provide adequate bearing area for the rails.
- It should have weight for stability and at the same time, it should not be too heavy to pose handling and transportation problem.
- The area of contact between ballast and sleepers should be adequate.
- Its design should be such that tamping or packing below.
- It should be possible to fix and remove rails from the sleeper comparatively easily.
- The sleeper should have adequate strength to bear the heavy stresses.
- It should be possible to insulate the sleeper from rails if track circulating is required.

A first classification can be made regarding the material of which they are manufactured:

- Wood/Timber sleepers.
- Concrete sleepers.
- Steel Trough sleepers.

2.3.2 Timber sleepers

The traditional timber sleeper was accepted by most railways as standard up to about the middle of the twenties century, although its durability limitations were recognized. Even today there are still many railways using timber sleepers, where the advantages of good resilience, ease of handling, adaptability to nonstandard situations or electrical insulation are very important. Fig. 2-14 shows the size of timber sleepers.

Fig. 2-14 timber sleeper

1. Feature of timber sleeper

Timber sleepers have the following advantages:

- Easy to manufacture and cheap where locally available.
- It absorbs vibration and shocks.
- It is easy to handle.
- An ideal bearing surface for rails where the formation is yielding.
- It is suitable for track circuiting.

Meanwhile, the main disadvantages of timber sleepers are given below:

- Due to decay and vermin attack its life is reduced.
- It is difficult to maintain proper gauge.
- It is susceptible to get damaged by fire.

Timber sleepers and bearers are usually made of hardwoods. Oak has long been a favorite material, preferably white oak. Other hardwoods, including chestnut and gum, have been popular. Softer woods must of necessity be used when hardwoods are not available and may be deliberately specified for light traffic lines. All lines in deep tube tunnels or in locations where fire could be a risk are provided with sleepers and pit-blocks made from untreated hardwood such as Jarrah.

Timbers also are used on the surface for points and crossing work which is not protected from the weather can last up to 35 years. In the protected environment of dry tube tunnels, sleepers on the London Underground have been known to last in excess of fifty years before needing renewal.

All softwoods used in sleepers and bearers must be thoroughly seasoned and then impregnated under pressure with a suitable preservative before use. Traditionally this preservative has been hot creosote but other materials have been used successfully in recent years which may have less associated health hazards. Softwood treated sleepers on the surface can be expected to last between 15 and 25 years depending on location and traffic use. Renewal is usually required because bad splitting and/or rot has occurred.

Hardwood sleepers eventually usually need replacing after this long period not because the general condition of the timber has deteriorated but because it is by then not possible to get around fixing for chair screws.

2. Dimension of timber sleeper

A prime function of sleeper is load distribution. The sleeper load on ballast has a direct effect on required ballast depth. Unit load distribution in the ballast pressure equation is a function of sleeper bearing, sleeper spacing, and the portion of wheel load borne by each sleeper. These are closely related to sleeper size and design.

Sleeper section is generally rectangular, common wood classification according to China national standards GB 9221-1988. According to the usage, wood sleepers can be divided into three class: ordinary timbers leeper, turnout sleeper, bridge sleeper. Size of ordinary wood: standard length is 2.5 m, the cross-section shape is divided into Class I and Class II for different grade lines.. Class I: width 22 cm, thickness 16 cm. Class II: width 20 cm, thickness 14.5 cm. The turnout sleeper: used on the switch sleeper. Section size of two kinds of standards: 75 and 92. Standards 75: width 22 cm, thickness 16 cm, from 260 cm to 485 cm length, for each length is 15 cm, a total of 16 length specification. Standards 92: width 24 cm, thickness 16 cm; from 260 cm to 480 cm length, for each length is 20 cm, a total of 12 length specification. For the bridge sleepers, the section size for girder (or longitudinal) vary in size from center to center spacing. Fig. 2-15 shows the section and dimensions of timber sleeper.

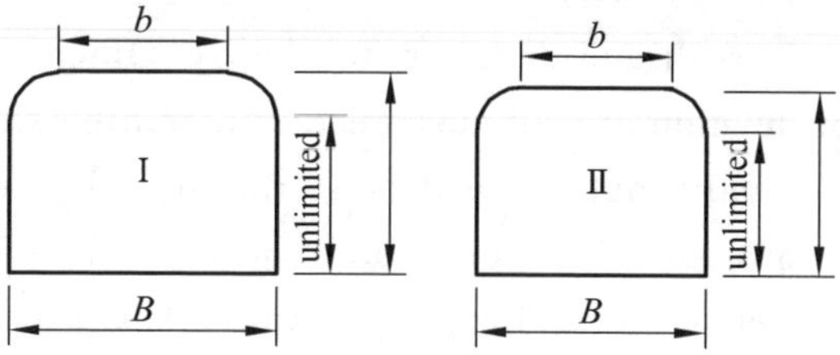

Fig. 2-15 Section and dimensions of timber sleeper (cm)

Tab. 2-4 shows the dimensions of timber sleeper

Tab. 2-4 Dimensions of Timber Sleeper

Classifications	size	Length/cm	Depth /cm	Width /cm	Thickness/cm	Usual Assignments
ordinary timber sleeper	I	250	16	22	16	Primary main lines
	Ⅱ	250	15	20	14.5	Yard tracks and side tracks
turnout sleeper	92	260-480 (by 20 step into)	18	24	16	
Bridge sleeper		300	20	20	22	
			20		24	
			22		26	
		320	22	22	28	
			24	24	30	
		340	24	24	30	
		420-480	20	20	22	
			20	20	21	
				22	26	
				22	28	
				24	30	

3. Life factors of timber sleeper

The following arbitrary catalog of principal factors that affect timber sleeper life includes general solutions to the problems each entails. Some solutions will merit additional comment.

a. Natural causes

Hard woods such as the oaks have an inherent resistance to wear and decay.

Soft wood fibers will crush and decay more readily. Other woods (some pines) will shatter, split, or develop dry rot more readily than others. Decay and rot will affect all woods eventually but proceed more rapidly when the wood is moist. Climate, therefore, has an effect on wood integrity, and so does drainage. Sleepers will last longer in a dry climate. In some areas insects such as termites and ants are destructive. The selection of good woods, creosote oil treatment, and drainage are corrective actions.

b. The dying process

The drying process might properly be included under natural causes. For natural drying freshly cut sleepers are stacked in the treating plant yard for about six months. sleeper-end splitting occurs during the drying begins offers restraint to splitting. Steel dowels in pre-bored holes have met with some success.

c. Service wear

Wheel loads concentrate crushing forces on the bearing area, and unprotected sleeper surfaces undergo a sawing action as rails "run" under load and temperature changes. These effects are intensified by heavy wheel loads, high-speeds, and dynamic impact. Gauge widening, occasioned by empty cars at high-speeds expands the need for regauging track and the accompanying redriving of spikes into the sleepers. Ballast particles in which the sleepers are embedded abrade the contact and bearing areas, especially on the bottom edges, as the sleeper rolls slightly under train movements. Sharp particles also penetrate the creosote seal in the wood, permitting the entry of moisture and hastening decay. In dirty, pumping track has been seen sleepers worn to half their original thickness, surrounded by fine wood fibers. Corrective measures include the use of sleeper plates and sleeper pads of adequate size between rail and sleeper, clean ballast and good drainage, and the adoption of car truck designs that provide better tracking characteristics and less need for regauging.

d. Abuse

Careless handling in loading, unloading, and installation and maintenance can reduce sleeper life. (Trackman should not beat the sleeper with a spiking hammer to set it square with the rails or poke it into place with a lining bar.) Any careless act that breaks the creosote seal permits moisture to penetrate the sleeper surface and hasten decay. Excessive bending moments at the sleeper center cause breakage at this point. Spiking and re-spiking for rail renewals or to correct poor gauge "spike-kills" the sleeper through which moisture can penetrate the sleeper. The insertion of sleeper plugs or filler compounds into the old spike holes does not entirely eliminate this hazard. An excessive number of spike holes also destroys the mechanical strength of the sleeper. This is considered by many to be a major maintenance problem. Research is in progress to develop a compound or procedure to restore the spike holding power and water resistance of such sleepers. Destruction of sleepers by derailment takes a large annual toll and some sleepers are lost to occasional track fires.

2.3.3 Reinforced concrete sleepers

A concrete sleeper is a railroad sleeper made out of steel reinforced concrete. With the decrease of forest resources and the enhancement of people's environmental awareness, of course, because of the development of science and technology, some countries began to produce steel sleepers and reinforced concrete sleepers at the beginning of last century to replace timber sleepers. However, because the metal consumption of the steel sleeper is too large, the cost is expensive and the volume is heavy, it is not popularized, only a few countries such as Germany are still in use. After the Second World War, the reinforced concrete sleepers were gradually used in the world because of the shortage of wood resources, and then they were improved to prestressed concrete sleepers. The Chinese railway has also used a large number of prestressed concrete sleepers. The concrete sleeper plays a great role in popularizing the seamless line.

1. Feature of concrete sleeper

Concrete sleepers have many advantages such as save high quality steel, long service life, and orbital stability, meeting requirements of high-speed, large-capacity. The main advantages of concrete sleepers are given below:

- Extra weight makes track more stable, particularly with changes in temperature.
- Free from fire hazard.
- Longer life than timber sleepers.
- Less maintenance means lower ongoing costs and fewer track closures.
- On account of flat bottom they are very suitable for modern tracks.

- Suitable for track circuiting.
- Suitable for mass production.

The drawback of the concrete sleeper is the stiffness, poor flexibility, resulting in pressure on the track bed and vibration acceleration and ballast powder, causing tracks to sink increases, adverse effects on locomotives and moving parts. For this reason, require hard and tough elastic layer set on the ballast and sleepers. In addition, many States also attach importance to the improvement of fastening performance. Timber sleepers were often manhandled into their final position and replacement of single defective sleepers (or "spotting" as it is sometimes known) was also done by hand. With concrete sleepers some form of mechanization is required for these operations. The main disadvantages of concrete sleepers are given below:

- poor flexibility, impact force under the same loads large (about 25% larger than timber sleeper);
- high requirements for the laying of the ballast bed, in addition to increasing the thickness of the bed, it is necessary to lay a cushion . Artificial replacement of concrete sleeper is inconvenient.
- Initial costs are greater.

2. Types of Concrete sleeper

There are two main types of concrete sleepers: twin-block sleeper, monoblock sleeper. Monoblock sleeper can be one piece of uniform or variable dimensions. Do twin-block sleeper can also consist of two separate blocks connected by a steel sleeper rod. Exceptionally, the concrete can be poured as two separate longitudinal slabs.

1) twin-block sleeper

The twin-block sleeper consists of two reinforced concrete blocks joined together with a steel sleeper bar cast into the blocks, as shown in Fig. 2-16. This type of sleeper is used extensively in Europe, particularly in France, The standard sleeper weighs 230 kg which is less than the mono-bloc equivalent. However handling and placing can be difficult due to the tendency to twist when lifted. Twin -block sleepers can be provided with resilient "boots" and

Fig. 2-16 Twin-block sleepers

can be incorporated into non-ballasted slab track or monolithic embedment in road surfaces for light rail street running.

Twin-block sleeper is suitable for urban transport, freight trains, passenger trains, high-speed trains and heavy haul trains, and boasts a vast array of advantages, include:

- High mechanical resistance of concrete
- High flexibility of sleepers, due to the steel sleeper bar's support of irregular loading and its ability to absorb shocks
- Avoidance of the undesired effect of negative bending
- High ballast center point, which means that there are no balancing sleepers
- High precision track gauges
- High lateral stability
- Lower weight and smaller dimensions for easier handling and transportation
- Suits all rail fastening systems and track types
- Easy set up of rail fastenings
- Simple maintenance
- Low investment on production equipment

2) Monoblock sleeper

Monoblock sleepers have an almost constant cross-section and are made of pre-stressed concrete. Fig. 2-17 shows pre-stressed concretes.

Fig. 2-17 Pre-stressed concrete diagram

In china, monoblock pre-stressed concrete sleepers is mainly used and referred as concrete pillow (PC pillow). The concrete sleepers are divided into three types: I type, II type and III type. I type and II type concrete sleepers is generally 220~250 kg, Ill type concrete sleepers is generally about 350 kg. The length of Ⅰ, Ⅱ type concrete sleeper is 250 cm, and the length of III is 260cm.

The cross section of concrete sleeper is trapezoidal, narrow top and broad bottom, which helps to increase the sleeper bearing area and set more steel bars in the bottom below the rail to resist positive bending moment. What's more, the shape of two ends of the sleeper bottom are double wedges, the middle part rectangular, and the sleeper bottom makes groove patterns to improve the resistance of the ballast bed. The thickness of sleeper is inconsistent in the whole length range, the thickness of part under rail is thick, and the thickness of middle part is thin. The purpose of doing so is as follows : for the reinforcement of concrete sleeper is straight-line, and the reinforcement of each cross sections of sleeper is the same, the shape of concrete sleeper can make the joint force line of the pre-stressed reinforcement go through under the cross section center of end part of sleeper below the rail, and above the cross section center of middle part of sleeper, which helps to make use of the eccentricity of the pre-compression stress formed by the reinforced concrete, so that the tensile stress of the concrete does not exceed the allowable limit and prevents the formation and expansion of the crack. Fig. 2-18 shows Ⅱ type concrete sleeper of China railway. Tab. 2-5 shows the dimensions of all type concrete sleeper.

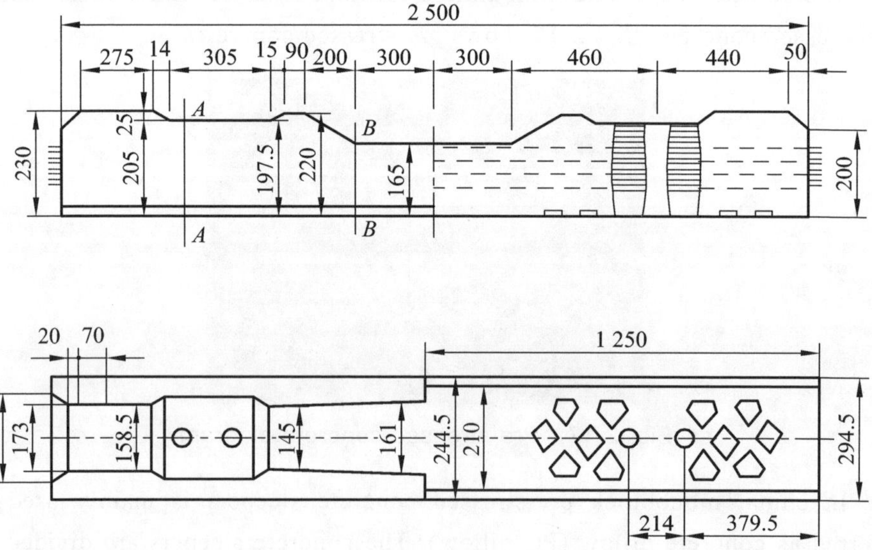

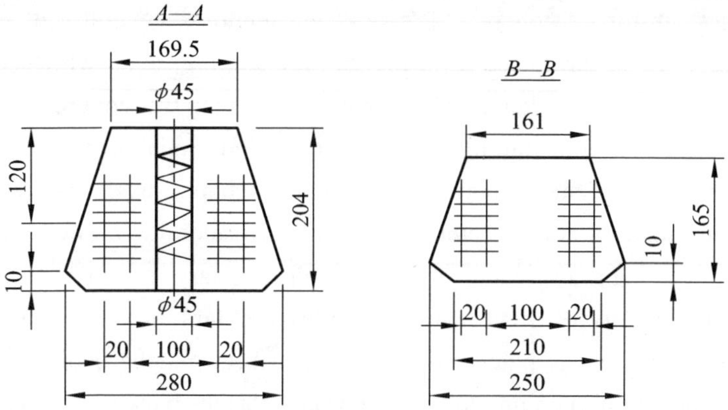

Fig. 2-18 Ⅱ type concrete sleeper of China railway

The following points should be attended to as a part of maintenance of the concrete sleepers:

- Not more than 30 sleepers should be opened at a time.
- Spacing of sleepers should be uniform.
- Compaction should be thorough and uniform.
- As far as possible laying and maintenance should be done by mechanical equipment.
- In case three consecutive sleepers are replaced at a time, speed of the train should be restricted to 15 km/h.
- The elastic fastening rubber pads and insulator should be inspected regularly.

Tab. 2-5 Dimensions of concrete sleeper

Classifications	steel wire number	Concrete type	depth/cm		width/cm			size /cm²	weight /kg	Length/cm
			Below rail	middle	End	Below rail	middle			
Ⅰ	36 ϕ3	C48	20.2	16.5	29.45	27.5	25	6 588	251	250
Ⅱ	44 ϕ3 4 ϕ10	C58	20.2	16.5	29.45	27.5	25	6 588	251	250
Ⅲ	10 ϕ7	C60	23.0	18.5		30.0	28.0	7 720	320	260

3.Manufacture of pre-stressed concrete sleeper

Pre-stressed concrete is a method for overcoming concrete's natural weakness in tension. It can be used to produce beams, floors or bridges with a longer span than with ordinary reinforced concrete. Pre-stressing tendons (generally of high tensile steel cable or rods) are used to provide a clamping load which produces a compressive stress that balances the tensile stress that the concrete compression member would experience due to a bending load. Traditional reinforced concrete is based on the use of steel reinforcement bars, rebars, inside poured concrete. Concrete reinforced by either pretensioning or posttensioning, allowing it to carry a greater load or span a greater distance than ordinary reinforced concrete. In pretensioning, lengths of steel wire or cables are laid in the empty mold and stretched. The concrete is placed and allowed to set, and the cables are released, placing the concrete into compression as the steel shrinks back to its original length. In posttensioning, the steel in the concrete is stretched after the curing process. Pre-stressing places a concrete member in compression; these compressive stresses counteract the tensile bending stresses of an applied load. The process was developed by the French engineer-Eugne Fressinet in the early 20th century. Tensioning and Unloading Machine (TUM) of pre-stressed concrete sleeper (PCS) is the core equipment in the process of sleeper production.

2.3.4 Sleeper spacing

Sleeper spacing as an important parameter of track has great influences on vibration of rail. Sleeper spacing type should be based on traffic volume, the driving speed and road conditions.

If spacing is small, the force involved to the roadbed, ballast, rails and sleepers in itself bears is small too, but it increases project costs and affect the tamping of ballast operations.

Generally the spacing is kept uniform throughout the length of the rail. Due to the impact of moving loads and weakness of the joint, the sleeper is about 5 cm apart at the joint. Generally two to three sleepers near the joint sleepers are spaced closer.

Sleeper spacing is usually 52-62 cm. For sleeper spacing has a relationship with the number of sleepers configured per kilometer, so in China, the number of railway sleepers laid per kilometer can show indirectly the sleeper spacing value. Chinese Railway stipulates that the number of sleepers can up to 1,920/km in wooden sleeper tracks, 1,840/km in concrete sleepers track, and less than

1,440/km. Increased sleeper numb every kilometer is 80.

Sleeper Spacing is dependent upon the following:

- Type and section of rail.
- Type and strength of sleeper.
- Nature of ballast.
- Axle load and speed.
- Nature of formation.

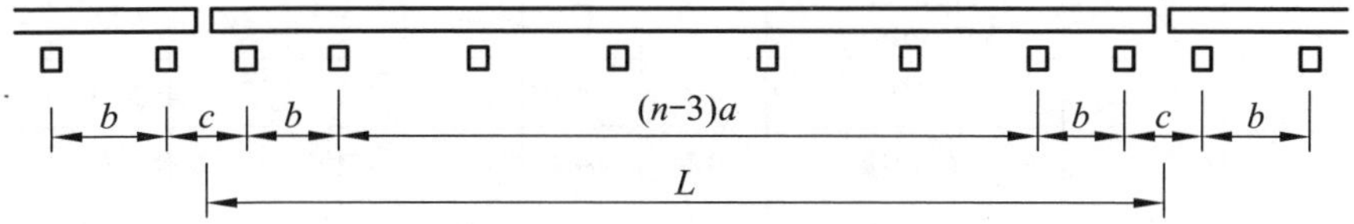

Fig. 2-19 Sleeper spacing

The relationship among *a*,*b*,*c*,*L* (Fig.2-19) meets the following formula:

$$L = c + 2b + (n-3)a \tag{2-2}$$

and *a*>*b*>*c*.

(1) c is fixed: when steel rails≥50 kg/m, *c*=440 mm(wooden sleepers), *c*=540 mm(concrete sleepers).

(2) calculation of *a*:

$$a = \frac{L-c-2b}{n-3} \tag{2-3}$$

put

$$b = \frac{a+c}{2} \tag{2-4}$$

into formula (2-3):

$$a = \frac{L-2c}{n-2} \tag{2-5}$$

(3) calculation of *b*:

put a (have taken the whole) into formula (2-3), then:

$$b = \frac{L-c-(n-3)a}{2} \tag{2-6}$$

Where *L*—length of rails,(included a Rail Gap Width, generally 8 mm);

n—sleeper numbers of a section of rail;

a—Middle sleeper spacing;

c—Joints sleeper spacing;

b—Transitional sleeper spacing.

For CWR, sleeper spacing should be arranged uniformly. Sleeper spacing dimensions according to the relevant provisions of "Maintenance Rule", as shown in Tab,2-6.

Tab. 2-6 Sleeper spacing dimensions of Standard rails

Type of rail /(kg/m)	Length /m	the number of sleepers configured per kilometer	*n*	Timber sleeper /mm			Concrete sleeper /mm		
				C	b	a	c	b	a
75,60,50	25	1,600	40	440	537	635	540	579	630
		1,680	42	440	487	605	540	573	598
		1,760	44	440	497	575	540	549	570
		1,840	46	440	459	550	540	538	544
		1,920	48	440	472	525	-	-	-
	12.5	1,600	20	440	594	640	540	587	635
		1,680	21	440	544	610	540	584	600
		1,760	22	440	525	580	540	569	570
		1,840	23	440	534	550	540	540	544
		1,920	24	440	469	530	-	-	-
43,38	25	1,440	36	500	622	705	500	622	705
		1,520	38	500	617	665	500	617	665
		1,600	40	500	599	630	500	599	630
		1,680	42	500	554	600	500	554	600
		1,760	44	500	564	570	500	564	570
		1,840	46	500	537	545	500	537	545
		1,920	48	500	509	522	-	-	-
	12.5	1,440	18	500	604	720	500	604	720
		1,520	19	500	604	675	500	604	675
		1,600	20	500	564	640	500	564	640
		1,680	21	500	559	605	500	559	605
		1,760	22	500	541	575	500	541	575
		1,840	23	500	504	550	500	504	550
		1,920	24	500	513	523	-	-	-

2.3.5 Other types of railway sleeper

1. Steel Sleepers

Steel sleepers are formed from pressed steel and are trough-shaped in section, as shown in Fig. 2-20. When France put forward the plan of steel sleepers in 1884, steel sleepers became the first opponent to compete with wooden sleepers, which was the fastest developing in Europe. The most steel sleepers are in Germany, France, Switzerland and South America. When Germany uses steel sleepers at most, the steel sleepers lines account for 40% of all lines, while the world's steel sleeper accounts for about 10% of the railway. Steel sleepers are lighter in weight than concrete and able to stack in compact bundles unlike timber. Steel sleepers are 100% recyclable and require up to 60% less ballast than concrete sleepers and up to 45% less than wood sleepers. However, steel sleepers cannot be used with track circuit based train detection, and easily corroded, and the amount of steel used is large and the maintenance cost is high,.

Fig. 2-20 Steel Sleepers

2. Y-shaped sleepers

An unusual form of sleeper is the Y-shaped sleeper, first developed in 1983, as shown in Fig. 2-21. Compared to conventional sleepers the volume of ballast required is reduced due to the load-spreading characteristics of the Y-sleeper. Noise levels are high but the resistance to track movement is very good. For curves the three-point contact of a Y steel sleeper means that an exact geometric fit cannot be observed with a fixed attachment point. The cross section of the sleepers is an I-beam.

Fig. 2-21 Y-shaped Sleepers

3. Broad sleeper

As shown in Fig. 2-22, the broad sleeper is made of reinforced concrete, similar to concrete sleeper, but wider and thinner than concrete sleeper, also known as sleeper plate. The concrete broad sleeper has a neat appearance, which is generally 2.5m long and 55 to 60cm wide, and the dense row is laid on the compact clean gravel bed.

The number of broad sleeper is 1760 kilometers per kilometer, and a pair of fasteners are installed on each broad pillow. Because of the large bearing area and compared with the concrete sleeper, the load of broad sleeper from rail is small and good for stability and the settlement of the track decreases obviously. It can slow down the accumulation of the permanent change of the road bed, and the maintenance work is reduced.

Because the elasticity, the section and the drainage of the broad sleeper are different from those of other type of sleepers, the transition section must be set up between the track with broad sleepers and other tracks with other type of sleepers.

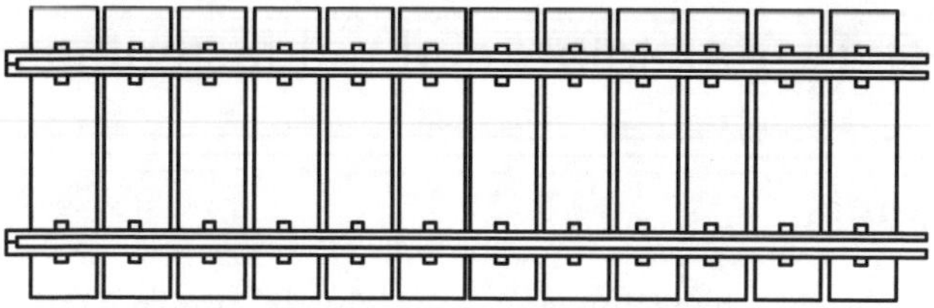

Fig. 2-22 Broad Sleepers

4. Ladder track

Ladder track is a type of railway track in which the track is laid on longitudinal supports with transverse connectors holding the two rails at the correct gauge distance, as shown in Fig. 2-23. Modern ladder track can be considered a development of baulk road which supported rails on longitudinal wooden sleepers. ladder track produces lower pressures on the road bed, both the maximum pressure and the amplitude of pressure pulses are smaller than transverse sleeper track, which can reduce maintenance costs in ballasted systems. An additional benefit in ballasted ladder track is increased resistance to ballast wash out and other forms of ballast degradation due the addition longitudinal support and rigidity in ladder track; the same structural rigidity also adds to buckling resistance.

Fig. 2-23 Ladder track

In the railway assembly, it must be taken special attention to ensure that the sleeper is well settled on the surface underneath, since otherwise, when having a vehicle passing over it, it could got broken.

2.4 Rail joints and rail fastenings

2.4.1 Rail joints

Due to the ease in handling and economy in transportation the rails are manufactured in certain fixed lengths. In order to make a long and continuous rail track, lengths are jointed together. Thus there is need of joints.

A rail joint is the weakest part of the track. In order to deal with expansion and contraction of rails due to variation in temperature, certain gap is provided at each joint. This gap causes break in continuity of rails in horizontal as well as in vertical plane, forming the weakest point of the track. This joint also causes severe blows to the passengers due to the moving of wheels over this gap. These blows may loosen the compaction of ballast under the sleeper and make the maintenance of joints difficult. Additionally, the fittings used to connect rails may become loose and cause heavy wear and tear of the track materials. It has been observed that joints need about 30% extra maintenance than the plain track.

It is now to understand that the rail joint must preserve insofar as possible the continuity of the rail by providing approximately the same strength, stiffness, flexibility, and uniformity as the rail itself. The joint must form a continuous girder with the rails, distributing over several sleepers whatever load is applied at the joint

1. Requirements of ideal rail joint

An ideal rail joint should possess the following characteristics:

- Should be as strong as possible. An ideal joint should have the strength of the original rail sections which it joins.
- Should be capable of maintaining two rails at the same level and should be capable to withstand lateral forces so that the gauge distance of the track is maintained.
- It should provide sufficient elasticity so that the vibrations and shocks caused by the moving loads are absorbed.
- It should provide resistance to longitudinal forces. These forces are developed due to acceleration, deceleration of moving loads and other miscellaneous forces. These forces are responsible for creeping of the rails.
- The joint fitting should be such that they may be readily fixed, easily

taken out and if required reused elsewhere.

- The number of parts should be standard ones and as few as possible. They should be easy to manufacture, and simple to be laid and maintained.
- It should be cheap and durable.

2. Structure of conventional rail joint

The rail joints are the weakest link of the rail track and therefore require careful attention both during and after construction. Even the best of joint has only about 50 percent of the rail strength. A conventional rail joint is made up of fishplates, fish bolt and spring washer. Fig. 2-24 shows some types of rail joint assembly Fig. 2-25 shows a conventional rail joint.

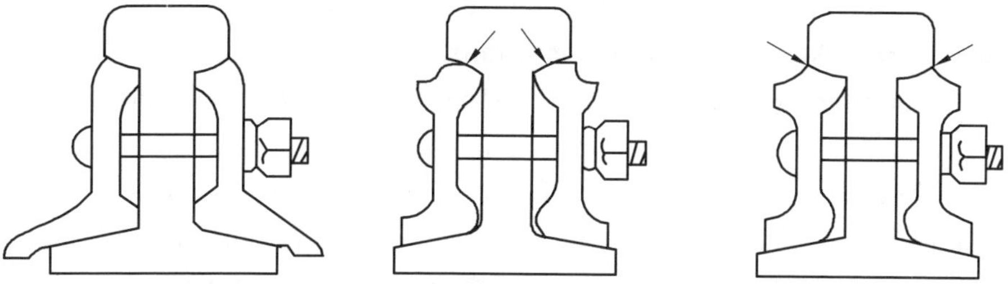

(a) Angle bar joint assembly (b) Head-free joint assembly (c) Head-contact joint assembly

Fig. 2-24 types of rail joint assembly

Fig. 2-25 Conventional rail joint

1) Fishplates

A fishplate is a flat metal plate used to join two wood or metal members by means of a number of bolts or nails passing through both the member and plate. Fishplates are generally associated with train track joints although they are also commonly used to connect other materials. Although fishplates are typically made of metal, other materials such as plastics and composites may add additional flexibility to their range of use[5]. The name is derived from fish, a wooden bar with a curved profile used to strengthen a ship's mast.

The essential requirement of the fish plate is to join the rails together in such a way that the joined rail may behave as one continuous rail. Fish plates are therefore designed for the following:

- Vertical and lateral forces that come on the joint.
- Free expansion and contraction of rails.
- Renewal and replacement of rails. The fish plates are manufactured from special type of steel having the following composition.

Fishplates are used in pairs either side of the rail ends and bolted together. The fish plates are so designed that they fit the underside of the rail head and the top of the rail foot. For free movement of the rails, these plates are occasionally oiled as part of maintenance. Fig. 2-26 shows a typical fish plate.

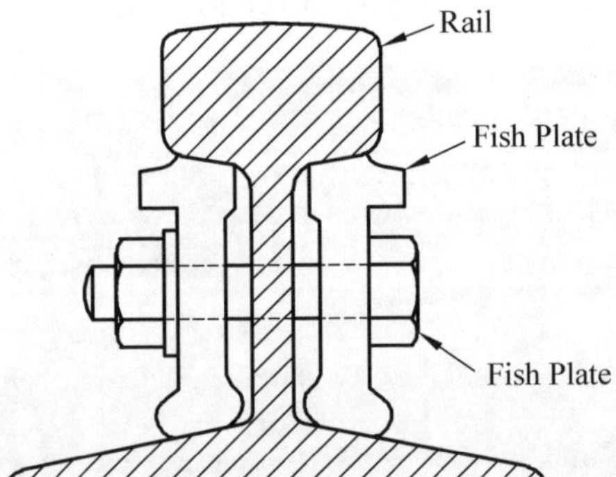

Fig. 2-26 Fish plate

In Chinese railways, generally 6 fish bolts are provided in a fishplate. In order to prevent the bolts from turning in the rails due to vibrations, alternate holes of the fish plate are made of oval shape or elongated, as shown in Fig. 2-27. Also bolts are provide inside and outside alternately to accommodate the expansion and contraction of rails due to variation in temperature.

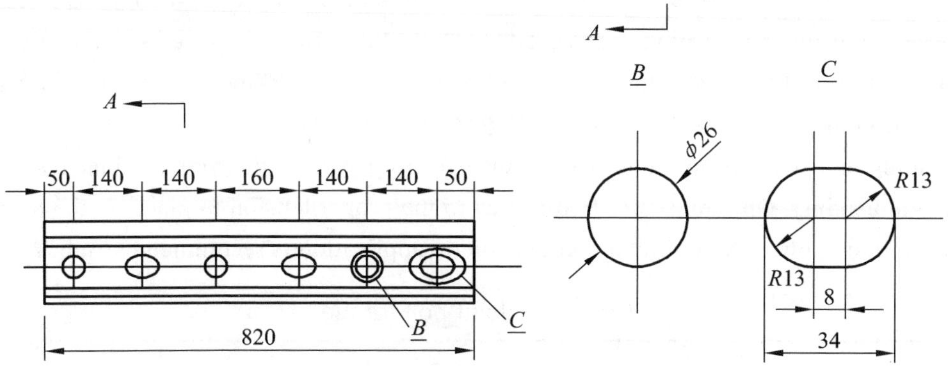

Fig. 2-27 The side and the hole of fish plate

2) Joint bolts, nuts and spring washers

Joint bolts, nuts are used to clamp the plate and rail accessories; spring washer role is to prevent the bolt loosening. Each pair of fish plate is joined by four or six bolts, two on either side of the joint. These bolts are very heavily stressed and hence they are made from medium or high carbon steel. Since they get due to vibrations, they are tightened from time to time. Over tightening however prevents the free expansion of rail is prohibited. To avoid over tightening at the end of complete tightening, nut is loosened by a quarter turn. Fig. 2-28 shows a typical fish bolt.

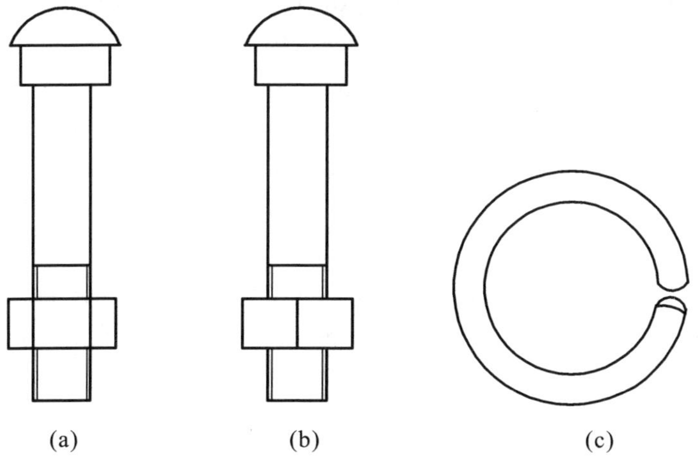

Fig. 2-28 Typical rail joint bolts, nuts, and spring lock washer

Bolt tension is an important element in rail joint design, installation, and maintenance. Sufficient bolt tension must be maintained to draw the fishplates as far as possible into the fishing spaces, effecting a closer fit and reduction in vertical play between the rail and the plates, and to prevent its working out under twisting and bending of the rail. Bolt tension may give lateral restraint, reducing the lateral bending and twisting in angle bars. It also forms a part of the moment that resists lateral bending. Opinion seems to differ as to the proper tension to place on the bars when first applied. A minimum bolt tension on application is recommend as tab. 2-7.

Tab. 2-7 Joint bolt torque

Items	unit	25 m-length rail						12.5 m-length rail	
		Highest and lowest rail temperature difference>85 °C			Highest and lowest rail temperature difference≤85 °C				
Rail type	kg/m	60 and above	50	43	60 and above	50	43	50	43
Bolt grade	-	10.9	10.9	8.8	10.9	8.8	8.8	8.8	8.8
Torque	N · m	700	600	600	500	400	400	400	400
CValue	mm	6			4			2	

A major problem of jointed track is cracking around the bolt holes, which can lead to the rail head (the running surface) breaking, so the new type joints are used.

3) Rail joint gap

In order to meet the requirement of rail thermal expansion and cold contraction, rail joint gaps should be deliberately reserved at rail joints. The rail joint gaps should meet the following conditions: when the rail temperature reaches the highest local rail temperature, the rail joint gap should be greater than or equal to zero, to allow for expansion of the rails in hot weather and to prevent the the temperature pressure of rail ends too large, the holes through which the fishplate bolts pass are oval to allow for movement with expansion. When the rail temperature reaches the local minimum rail temperature, the rail joint gap should be less than or equal to the construction joints, to prevent the joint bolts not to be bended or pulled apart.

The rail joint is the weakest section of the rail and is an unavoidable evil. Because of rolling difficulties rails were earlier rolled in short lengths. The lengths were increased but still the temperature effect resulting in large expansion joint and transportation difficulties limit the length of the rail.

Calculation of rail joint gap for traditional railroad:

$$a_0 = \alpha L(t_z - t_0) + \frac{1}{2} a_g \tag{2-7}$$

Where a_0——rail joint gap (mm);

α——Coefficient of thermal expansion of steel rails, α=0.011 8 (mm/°C);

L——Rail length (m);

t_z——Local intermediate rail temperature (°C);

t_0——Temperature of changing the rail or adjusting the rail;

a_g——Design joint gap value of rail joints. For 43 kg/m、50 kg/m、60 kg/m、75 kg/m Rails, a_g=18 mm.

$$t_z = \frac{1}{2}(T_{max} + T_{min}) \tag{2-8}$$

Among them,

T_{max}、T_{min} —Highest and lowest rail temperature(°C).The highest temperature is equals to the local history of the highest temperature of +20 °C, the lowest rail temperature is equal to the local history of the lowest;

To reduce the joint gap in winter when the temperature variety is less than 85 °C, the reserve rail can be reduced by 1-2 mm according to the formula (2-7).

3. Rail joint position

Depending upon the position of joints, rail joints may be classified as follows:

- Square joint(Fig. 2-29).When a joint in one rail is exactly opposite to the joint in the other parallel rail, it is called a square joint. It is very common in straight track.
- Staggered joints (Fig. 2-30). When the joint in one rail is exactly opposite the center of the parallel rail, then it is called staggered joint. It is used on curves.

Depending upon the position of sleepers, rail joints may be classified as follows:

- suspended joint

In the case of suspended joint the rail ends are joined between the two sleepers and by the time the stress is transferred to the sleeper it gets distributed. For this reason this type of joint is not only popular in China but also in other parts of the world. Fig. 2-30 and 2-31 show supported and suspended rail joints.

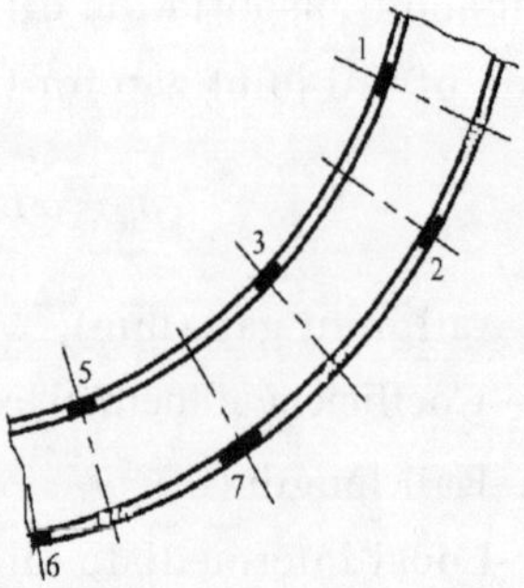

Fig. 2- 29 Staggered Rail Joint

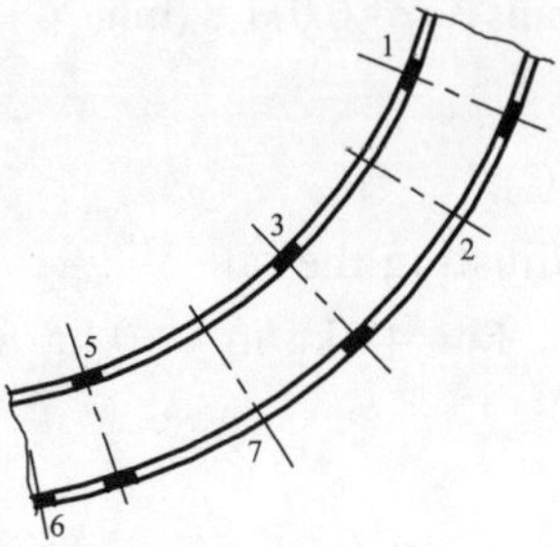

Fig. 2-30 Square Rail Joint

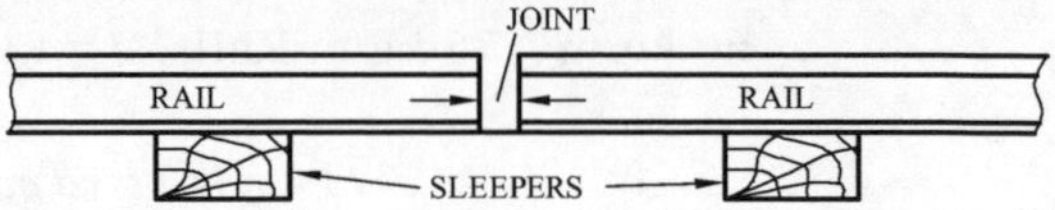

Fig. 2-31 Suspended Rail Joint

- supported joint

In the case of supported joint, the ends of the rail rest directly on the sleeper. This type of joint has large rigidity and difficult tamping. The sleeper is subjected to heavy stresses and wears out comparatively quickly. So, the maintenance of the joint is very difficult. It's used only under special circumstances.

- bridge joint

This joint is similar to suspended joint, with the difference that a length of metal is used to connect the ends of two rails so that bending stresses may not develop in the rails. The bridge end rest on two sleepers. In actual practice this joint is not preferred and seldom used.

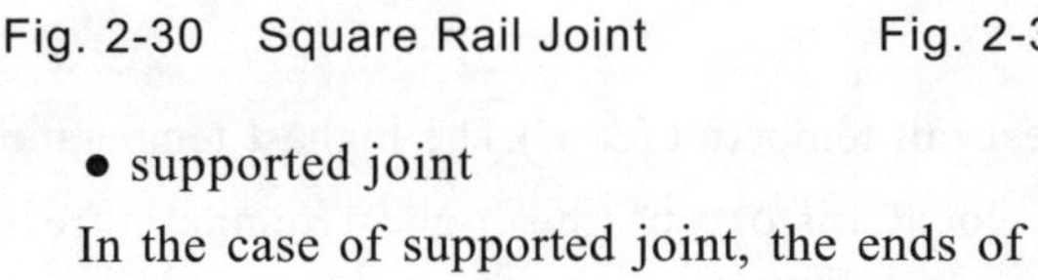

Fig. 2-32 Supported Rail Joint

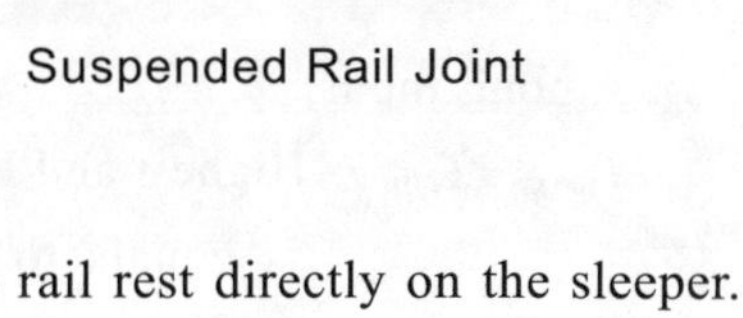

Fig. 2-33 Bridge Joint

4. Special rail joint

1) Compromise Joint

When rails of one section are being joined to rails of another section, differences in height of rail, width and depth of head, location of bolt holes, height of waist, and extent of fishing areas necessitate the use of so-called compromise, step joints, or offset bars. Each end of the bar is designed to fit the particular rail. In addition, by proper offsets of metal, the tops of the two rails and the gauge corners are brought into correct alignment. When ordering or specifying compromise bars, it is important to specify the weights and sections of the two rails to be joined and whether a "right-hand" or "left-hand" pair is required. To do this, face the joint from the center of track. When the higher joint is on the right, it is a right-hand joint, when on the left, it is a left-hand joint. When rails are of the same height, consider the heavier rail as indicating right- or left-handedness. Compromise bars, when vast rather than rolled, are more susceptible to breakage and should receive close routine inspection. Forged steel bars are less likely to break.

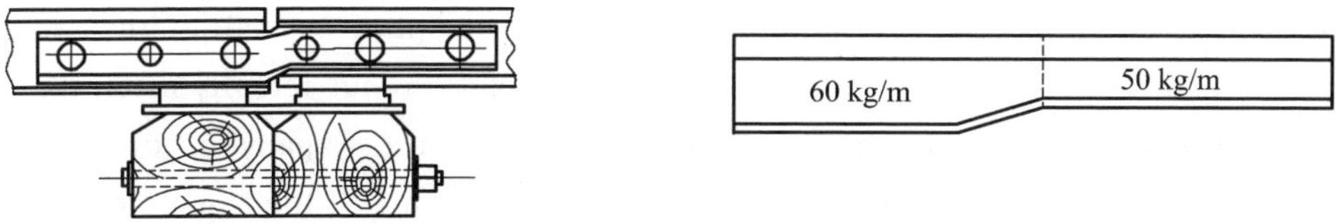

Fig. 2-34 Compromise fish plate

2) Insulated joint

Adjacent track circuits flowing through the rails must be isolated from each other by insulated joint. There are two type of insulated joint: ordinary insulated joints, glued insulation joints.

- Ordinary insulated joint (Fig.2-34)

Fiber impregnated with an insulating compound are placed between the rail and the joint plate. Bolts are inserted through fiber bushings in the bolt holes, and a fiber washer is placed back of the washer plates. Between the rail ends a fiber end post is installed. Where track circuits exist for signalling purposes, insulated joints are required. These compound the weaknesses of ordinary joints, so ordinary insulated joints are hard to maintain.

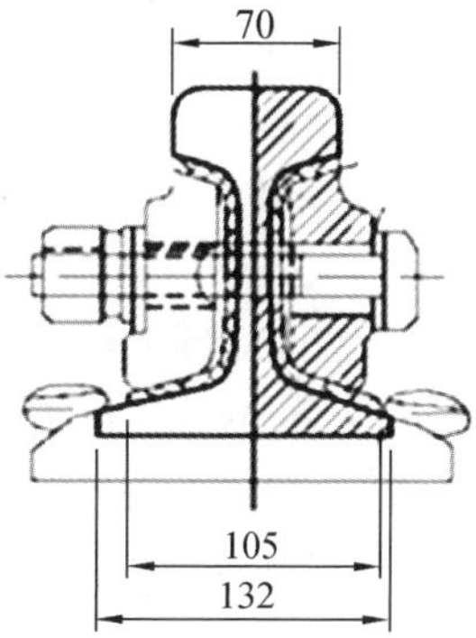

Fig. 2-35 Ordinary insulated joint

- Specially-made glued insulated joint (Fig.2-35)

Specially-made glued joints, where all the gaps are filled with epoxy resin, increase the strength again. As an alternative to the ordinary insulated joint, audio frequency track circuits can be employed using a tuned loop formed in approximately 20 m of the rail as part of the blocking circuit.

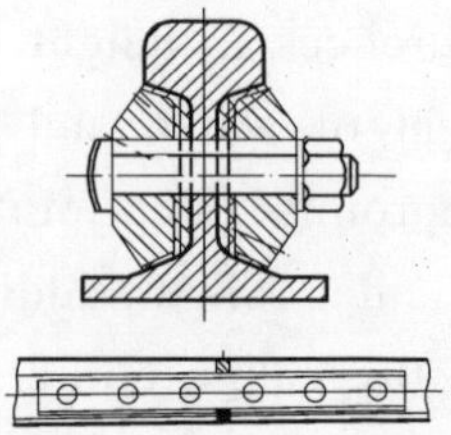

Fig. 2-36 Specially-made glued insulated joint

3) Expansion joint (Fig.2-36)

At certain locations it is desirable to provide for the free running and expansion of rails. Such a location is at the ends of movable span bridges, where an expanding rail might (and has) created a serious obstacle to closing the bridge. The usual form of such a joint is a half-section of rail on two adjoining and overlapping rail ends in a bed plate or chair, with spaces for expansion at the rail ends. Even though the rail ends do not actually meet, there is nevertheless a solid support for the wheels at all times. Expansion joints may also be used in connection with track scales, since the rails of track scale must be free of contact with adjoining rails.

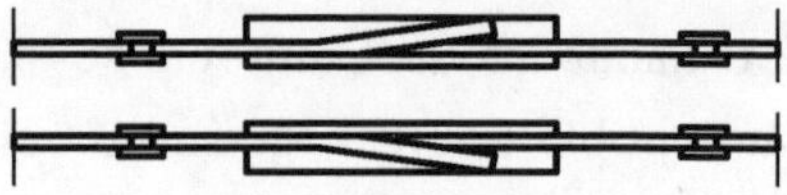

Fig. 2-37 Expansion joint

Expansion joints have found use in Europe at the ends of long CWRs. Such use in the United States has been limited to where CWR is laid across long open-deck bridges, and sometimes at approaches to railroad crossings at grade. Switch point-stock rail assemblies have also served as expansion joints.

4) Welded joint

Nowadays, thanks to the improvements of the design and construction of sleepers, fastening and welding methods, as well as to the better control of the dilatation with the use of the system of "tension release", the joint plates can be removed from the railway. Welded joint is an important and popular type of joint, removing joint plate.

The ends of the rails are joined by heating, high temperature or high pressure so as to eliminate the rail joint gap. This is an important and popular type of joint. This type joint will be described in details in Chapter 5.

2.4.2 Rail fastening

A rail fastening system is a means of fixing rails to sleepers. The terms rail anchors, sleeper plates, chairs and track fastenings are used to refer to parts or all of a rail fastening system. Various types of fastening have been used over the years.

1. Purpose of rail fastening

The rail fastening must permanenly and reliably transmit forces to the sleeper. These forces are generated by vehicles and by temperature changes. In particular, this involves: vertical forces, horizontal forces, longitudinal forces.

The magnitude of the vertical forces depends on the magnitude of the axle loads. As a rule, locomotives are the decisive factor here, since they have the heaviest axle loads because of their high friction weight. The wheel load is displaced on curves as a consequence of lateral acceleration. At high-speeds, beginning about 200 km/h, additional dynamical forces are expected, and these must likewise be included.

The magnitude of the horizontal forces depends on the magnitude of the velocity, the magnitude of the lateral acceleration, the magnitude of the radius of curvature, as well as the running characteristics of the vehicles. Quite generally, horizontal forces increase as the radius of curvature becomes smaller. The wheelbases of the vehicles here play an important role.

The longitudinal forces are a consequence of the inhibited longitudinal expansion of the rail as a consequence of temperature changes. The magnitude of these forces depends on the rail cross-section, the maximum rail temperature, and the respective difference with respect to the neutral temperature that was chosen when the rails were welded.

Because of the presence of vertical, horizontal, and longitudinal forces, rail fastenings have the following specific purposes:

- The fastenings must always provide a friction-tight lock between the rail and the sleeper.
- It must guarantee that the gauge between the rails always remains uniformly good.
- It must prevent torsional distortion of the rails.

In addition, these fastenings could satisfy the following requirements:

- Should be sufficiently elastic to absorb the vibrations and shocks.

- Should provide longitudinal and lateral rigidity to the track.
- It should be easy to insert and remove but at the same time it should not be readily taken out so that it is free from sabotage.
- Should be capable of being used on all types of sleepers.
- It should not be costly.
- Should be durable.

2. Types of rail fastening

The first rail-fastening nailed the rail directly to the sleepers by means of a hook. Currently there are many types of rail fastenings all over the world.

Regarding the type of anchoring to the sleeper and the way to fix the rail, rail fastenings have two types: rigid fastening, elastic fastening. The conventional rigid fastenings, used for fixing the rails to the sleepers is not able to meet the higher stresses due to increased loads and higher traffic of the present age. It was soon found that too rigid fastening became loose under vibration and that some degree of elasticity was necessary to resist both creep and buckling. There is therefore need for such fastenings which may protect track against the shocks and vibrations, so elastic fastenings are showed.

Regarding the type of anchoring to the sleeper and the way to fix the rail, rail fastenings can be divided into: direct fastening, indirect fastening and mixed fastening. Direct, indirect (separated) or mixed fastening can be rigid and elastic, depending on the elements used in the system[2]:

- Direct fastening: the same fastening fixes the rail to the base-plate (or base-sheet) and the base-plate to the sleeper. Direct fastenings can be seen in Fig. 2-38.

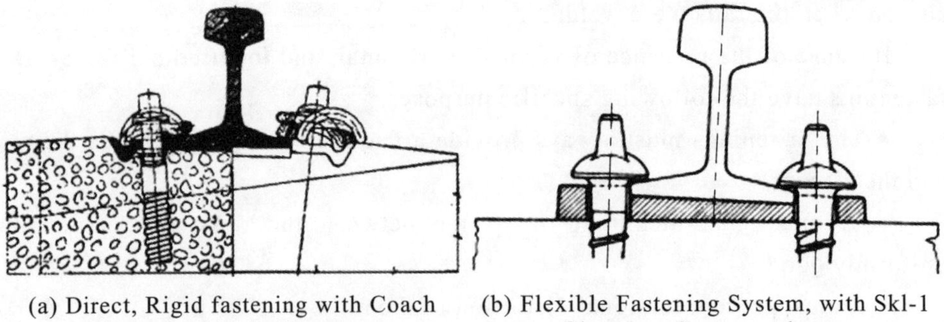

(a) Direct, Rigid fastening with Coach Screw on Timber sleeper

(b) Flexible Fastening System, with Skl-1 Clamp on Concrete sleeper

Fig. 2-38 Direct Fastenings

• Indirect (or separated) fastening: when the fastening fixes the base-plate to the sleeper, and an independent fastening fixes the rail to the base plate. Indirect fastenings can be seen in Fig. 2-39.

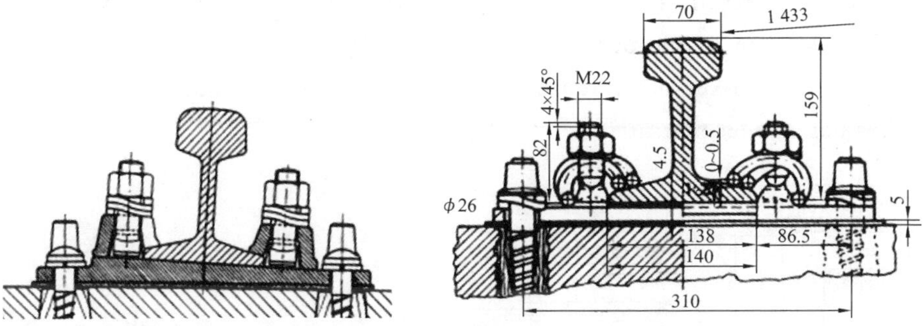

(a) Rigid Fastening system on concrete sleeper

(b) Flexible system with skl-3 clamp on concrete sleeper

Fig. 2-39 Indirect Fastenings

• Mixed fastening: when the fastening fixes the base-plate to the sleeper, and other base-plate fixes the rail to the sleeper. Mixed fastenings can be seen in Fig. 2-40.

3. Rail fastenings for timber sleeper

1) Spike and sleeper plate

Early railway, spike and plate is used directly fixed timber sleeper. There have been a variety of spikes, but its creep resistance is too low and not suitable heavy, high-speed railway.

Fig. 2-40 Mixed Fastenings

A rail spike (also known as a cut spike or crampon) is a large nail with an offset head that is used to secure rails and base plates to railroad sleepers in the track. There are various types of spike. Originally spikes were driven into wooden sleepers by hammering them with a heavy hammer by hand, such as dog spike, round spike etc. This manual work has been replaced by machines, commonly called "spike drivers" (A machine that removes spikes is called a "spike puller").Splitting of the wood can be limited by pre-boring spike holes or adding steel bands around the wood.

(1) Dog spike (Fig. 2-41).

The dog spike has a square section. This type of spike is popular as it is very cheap. It however requires more attention as it becomes loose due to vibrations of the moving train. The spike holds to the sleeper because of frictional force between the spike and the timber fibers of the sleepers. Two spikes are driven on one sleeper per rail. They are staggered. On curved track two spikes are fixed outside and one inside per rail. On joint sleepers, bridge sleepers and turnout sleepers, two spikes are fixed on either side of the rail making a total of four spikes per sleeper per rail.

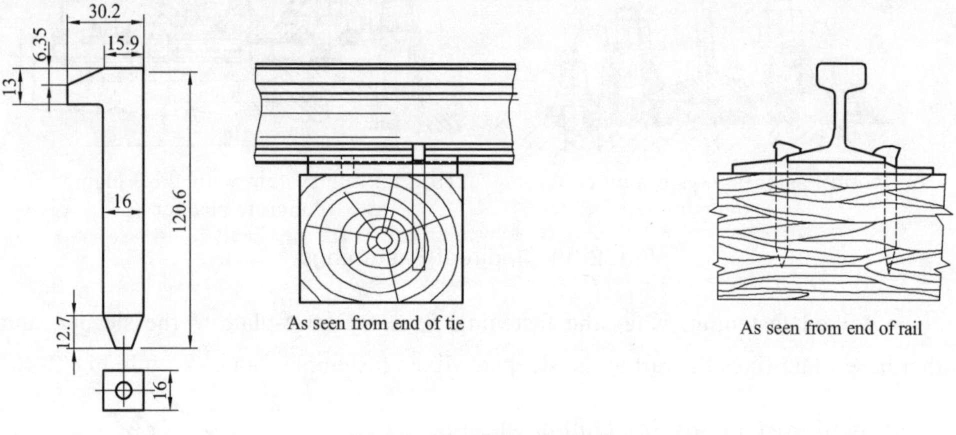

Fig. 2-41 Dog Spike

(2) Round spikes(Fig.2-42)

There spikes are fixed on timber sleepers where anti-creep bearing plates are used. The round spike has a round section of 19.05 mm diameter and is of variable length. These spikes are also used for fixing assembly of switches on timber sleepers. As they are not used with flat bottom rails, their use is very limited.

(3) Screw spikes(Fig.2-43).

To obtain better life from timber sleepers, screw spikes have been developed such as on main lines. The 18 mm diameter screw spikes are used for fixing anti-creep bearing plates in place of round spikes and are known as "Rail Screws". For direct fastening of rails to the sleepers 22 mm diameter screw spikes are used and these are known as "Rail Screws". These spikes are driven in the

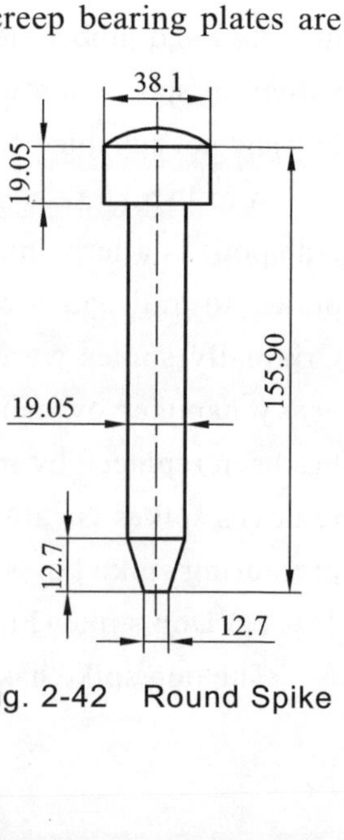

Fig. 2-42 Round Spike

sleeper first by boring a hole and then revolving it with the help of a spanner. The fixing and extraction of these spikes is time consuming. The cost is also high but they have better lateral rigidity than dog spikes. High cost and difficulty in operation are the disadvantage of them. The screw spike was first introduced in 1860 in France (French tire-fond), and became common worldwide.

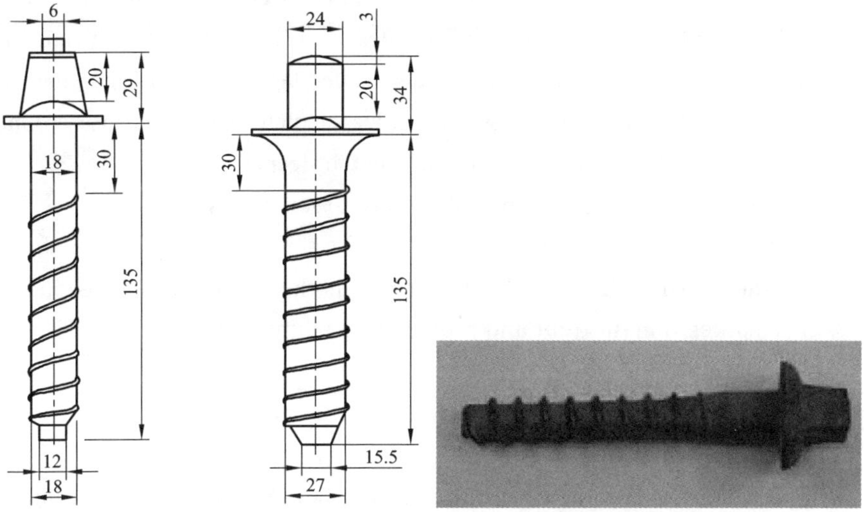

Fig. 2-43 Plate screw and rail screw

(4) sleeper plates(Fig.2-44)

A sleeper plate, baseplate or sole plate is a steel plate used on rail tracks between flatbottom rail and the sleepers. The sleeper plate increases bearing area and holds the rail to correct gauge. They are fastened to timber sleepers by means of spikes through holes in the plate. These plates are used for fixing rails to the sleepers. These plates distribute the load over a larger area, so that the pressure is reduced.

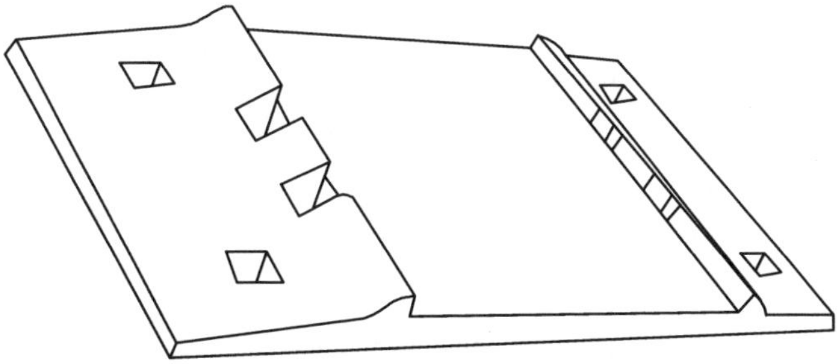

Fig. 2-44 Typical sleeper Plate

The part of the plate under the rail base is tapered, setting the cant of the rail, an inward rotation from the vertical. The usual slope is one in forty (1 : 40 degrees). The top surface of the plate has one or two shoulders that fit against the edges of the base of the rail. The double-shoulder type is currently used. Older single-shoulder types were adaptable for various rail widths, with the single shoulder positioned on the outside (field side) of the rails. Most plates are slightly wider on the field side, without which the plates tend to cut more into the outsides of the sleeper, reducing cant angle.

Many railways use large wood screws, also called lag screws, to fasten the sleeper plates (or baseplates) to the railroad sleepers. Sleeper plates came into use around the year 1900, before which rail was spiked directly to the sleepers.

The advantages of using sleeper plates are given below:

① The "adzing" of the sleeper for tilting the rail is not required as the tilt is provided in the bearing plate itself. The sleeper is therefore not weakened.

② The spikes remain tight and require less maintenance.

③ Maintain proper gauge.

④ Reduce the wear of the sleepers and hence increase their life.

⑤ Prevent crushing of sleepers.

However due to settlement of ballast, the plate gets loosened and moisture gets between the sleeper plate and the sleeper. Secondly if a spike is damaged, another spike may be required for which all the spikes have to be pulled out. This operation reduces the holding power of the spike.

2) K fastening (Fig. 2-45)

The sleeper plate with its respective cant is fastened on the sleeper by means of four sleeper screws through predrilled holes. A spring washer is placed between the sleeper screw and the sleeper plate to prevent the screw from loosening and to assure permanent tightness. The rail and the sleeper plate are tightened by means of a hook bolt, sleeper clip, spring washer and nut. The hook bolt is here anchored in the sleeper plate.

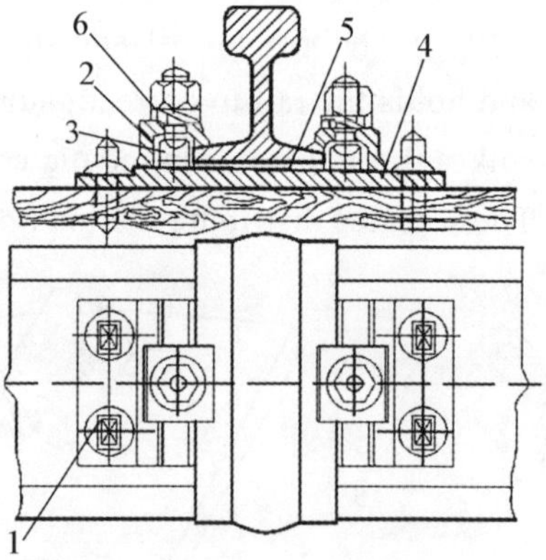

Fig. 2-45 K fastening on timber Sleeper

One advantage here is that the rail is adequately guided by the lateral sleeper plates even though the rail fastening may be loosened, and that the rails cannot move laterally when they are traversed at moderate speeds. Powerful coach-screwing machines are now available for tightening and loosening the rail fastenings. One disadvantage is the limited spring path of the spring washers, so that repeated tightening of the screws is unavoidable.

3) Mixed fastening

Mixed fastening as shown in Fig. 2-40, with spikes and a five-hole double shoulder iron plate. Mixed fastening is one of the most widely used fastening methods on railway track. It will, in addition to spike rail pad and sleeper fastening together, but also spike the plate and sleeper separately. This method can reduce the vibration of the fastening plate, and fewer parts, convenient installation; its drawback is that when the track is deflected upward by the load, it is easy to pull up the spike and reduce the buckling force.

4. Rail fastenings for concrete sleeper

1) Buckle Fastening (Fig. 2-46)

The buckle fastening is mainly composed of buckle plate, screw spike, spring washer, iron base and insulation cushion plate. Screw spike with sulphur cement mortar anchor in the concrete sleeper rail bearing reserved hole. Install a rigid plate in the spiral spike anchoring good, through washers and spring washers fastening nut fastening rail. One end of the buckle plate presses the bottom top surface of the rail, and simultaneously, the side of the rail bottom is resisted, so as to maintain the necessary gauge and transmit lateral thrust to the iron seat and the concrete pillow shoulder. An insulating cushion is arranged between the iron seat and the retaining shoulder, so as to reduce the impact effect of the lateral thrust, prevent the damage of the concrete pillow shoulder and form the insulation effect.

In order to meet the requirements of different rail types and gauge, 5 types of buckle plate with different size are designed respectively. The upper and lower sides of each buckle plate can be turned over. Buckle fastening has a simple structure and adjusts the gauge more conveniently, but the buckling pressure is low and easy to loose in use process. Buckle fastening is suitable for 50 kg/m and below rail line.

3) Spring clips fastening

At present, China's main fastening to concrete sleepers is I-type spring clip fastening. In recent years, China has successfully developed for heavy-duty, high-speed lines on the Ⅱ, Ⅲ type spring fasteners

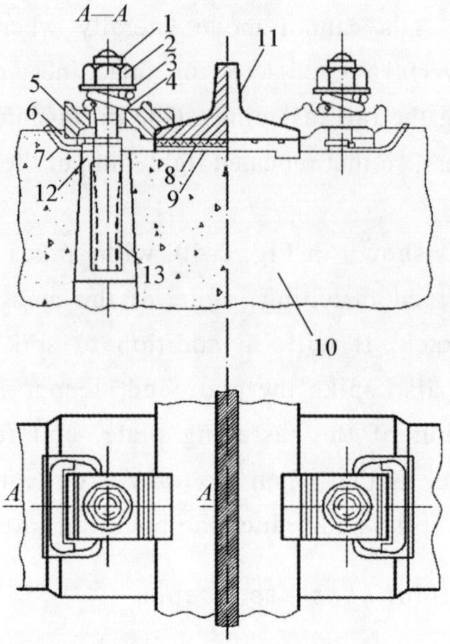

Fig. 2-46 Buckle fastening

1—screw Spikes; 2—nut; 3—flat washer; 4—spring washer; 5—buckle plate; 6—iron base; 7—insulation cushion shit; 8—insulation cushion plate; 9—Liner; 10—sleeper; 11—rail; 12—Insulation antirust paint; 13—sulphur cement mortar

(1) I-type spring clip fastening (Fig. 2-47)

This fastening includes the w-shaped clip, spiral spike, gauge apron, apron base, rubber pads and other components, as shown in Fig. 2-47. The clip is used to crimp the rail elastically, a certain buckle pressure and sufficient strength is required to maintain. The clip is made by a 60Si2Mn or 55Si2Mn rolled spring round steel whose diameter is 13 mm. The clip is divided into two types as A-type and B-type, in which A-type clip is longer. For 50 kg/m rail, A-type clip is installed except that the No.14 joint gauge apron is installed with the B-type. The rail of 60 kg/m is always installed with B-type. Gauge apron is used to adjust the gauge and pass lateral horizontal force of rail. There is a long hole in middle of gauge apron, and its size is constant. Apron base are used to support the apron, back inclined plane is supported on the sleeper shoulders. Apron base require certain strength to withstand and transmit lateral horizontal forces, and enough insulation properties to prevent leaking electricity. Two inclined plane thicknesses of apron base are different, and can be swapped using, and also play a role in adjusting gauge.

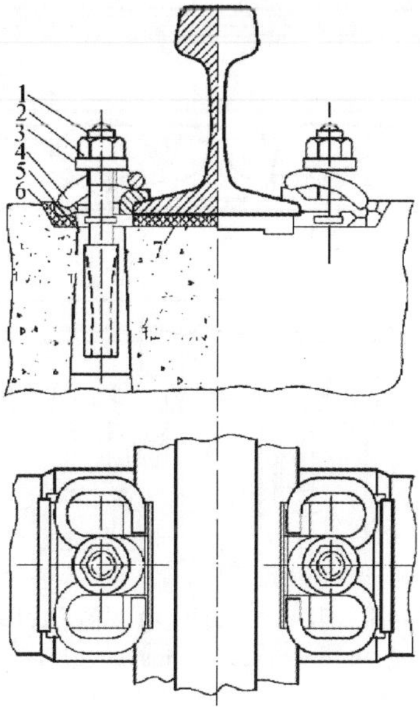

Fig. 2-47 I-type spring clip fastening

1—screw Spikes; 2—nut; 3—flat washer; 4—clip; 5—gauge apron; 6—apron base; 7—rubber pads

(2) II-type spring clip fastening

Except the clip is redesigned with new materials, the remaining parts of II-type spring clip fastening is in common use with I-type spring clip fastening, still with shoulders and screw fastening. The II-type spring clip fastening can replace the I-type where the I-type has been use initially. The clip of II-type is 60Si2CrVA to improve the strength and buckle pressure, and the yield strength and tensile strength are increased by 42% and 36%. The diameter of clip is 13 mm. Gauge is adjusted through the number configuration of gauge apron and apron base.

(3) III-type spring clip fastening (Fig. 2-48)

III-type spring clip fastening is without shoulder and screws. It is especially suitable for heavy large capacity and high-density transport conditions. III-type spring clip fastening is made of a clip, embedded iron base, insulated gage blocks and rubber pad, as shown in Fig. 2-48. Its advantage are below:

- Large buckle pressure and good elasticity.
- The concrete sleeper shoulder is cancelled, thereby eliminating possibility of gauge expanding caused by the lateral movement of rail bottom under the action of the lateral force.

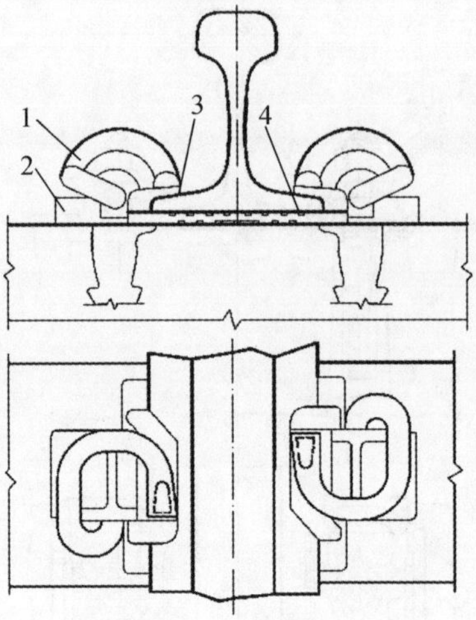

Fig. 2-48 III-type spring clip fastening

1—spring clip; 2—embedded iron base; 3—insulated gage blocks; 4—rubber pad

- The cancellation of screw connection greatly reduces the maintenance workload of fastenings.

The adjustment of the gauge is configured with a different number of insulated gauge blocks. The number of insulation gauge have two types: block 7-9 and 11-13. The configuration of the adjustment of different gauge and the number of the corresponding insulation gauge block is shown in table 2.8.

Tab. 2-8 Number of insulation gauge block in different gauge adjustment

Gauge adjustment	Left Rail		Right Rail	
	Outside	Inside	Outside	Inside
−8	13	7	7	13
−6	13	7	9	11
−4	11	9	9	11
−2	11	9	11	9
0	9	11	11	9
+2	7	13	11	9
+4	7	13	13	7

(4) Pandrol clip (Fig. 2-48, Fig.2-49)

Fig. 2-49 Flat Bottom (FB) rail and Pandrol clip fastening

The standard fastening used by Rail on all new FB track in recent years in UK or other Europe countries has been the 'Pandrol' clip. This clip is made from circular section spring steel bar by a process which involves heating the bar, hot pressing into shape and then quenching and annealing. The majority of plain line track is laid on concrete sleepers without base plates and in this case the anchorage shoulder is cast into the sleeper during manufacture. Where Pandrol rail clips are used in conjunction with base plates the latter are secured to the timber or sleeper by chair screws.

Fastenings require insulation both from electrical current and from vibration/noise. This is achieved by the introduction of resilient insulating pads at points of contact.

2.5 Track Ballast

The railroad term ballast (Fig. 2-50) is possibly a carry-over from the use in early track of sand and gravel that had been carried as ballast in ships. In railroad usage it refers to a layer of broken stones, gravel, earthen rocks or any other gritty material packed below and around the sleepers so that the load from the sleepers may be transmitted to the formation.

Fig. 2-50 Ballast

The track was originally laid direct on the ground, but this quickly proved unsatisfactory and some form of ballast was essential, to spread the load and to retain the track in its proper position. The natural ground is rarely strong enough to accept the loading from locomotives without excessive settlement, and a layer of ballast under the sleeper reduces the bearing pressure on the ground. The ballast surrounding the sleepers also tends to keep them in place and resists displacement.

Today the required depth of good quality ballast beneath sleepers varies depending upon the maximum speed of trains, the maximum axle loads carried and the gross annual tonnage expected. In general the absolute minimum depth of ballast needed beneath sleepers for even a lightly loaded railway should never be less than 150 mm

To ensure both lateral and longitudinal stability of the track, particularly when using continuously welded rail, it is essential that ballast is taken up to the level of the top of the sleepers between the sleepers and given a good "shoulder" at the sleeper ends. To achieve maintenance of this condition, regular inspection and periodic tamping is necessary.

2.5.1 Purposes of ballast

The ballast under the sleepers is thoroughly compacted and is primarily responsible for transmitting load from sleeper to the formation. Literature[4] gives the following purposes of ballast, which is complete relatively:

(1) It serves as a load transfer device from the sleeper to the formation in such a way that by the time the loading is transferred to the formation it spreads

over a large area and the final intensity of loading on the formation is within the bearing capacity of the soil.

(2) The track is anchored in place against lateral, vertical and longitudinal movement. Irregular-shaped ballast particles interlock with the sleepers and with each other to resist the disturbing forces of dynamic loads.

(3) Moisture is drained quickly away from the track and not allowed to accumulate around rails and sleepers. The shape of the section and the porous free-draining properties of ballast materials provide immediate drainage.

(4) Frost heaving of track is reduced. Ballast not only drains surface water but reduces capillary action by the relatively wide voids between ballast particles. Also, a certain elasticity in the ballast tends to absorb some of all of any heaving in the subgrade beneath.

(5) Maintenance operations are facilitated. Irregularities in surfaced can be corrected by tamping ballast under the sleepers and the track can be shifted to restore line. Sleepers do not have to be dug out of the mud when being renewed.

(6) The growth of vegetation is retarded. Drainage removes the moisture necessary for most plant growth. New ballast is presumed to be sterile, to contain little or no clay or silt in which vegetation can develop. When ballast does become foul with clay, silt, and plant life after a period of service, its sterile qualities are renewed by cleaning or replacing with new ballast.

(7) Resilience to absorb shock from dynamic loadings is found in ballast. The rough particles interlocked together will move a slight amount, giving to a limited degree a spring-like action to the ballast as it supports the imposed loads.

There are several types of ballast according to its hardness and cleanliness. The specific type will be selected subject to the type of railroad it will be used for.

2.5.2 Ballast materials

Good quality track ballast is made from crushed natural rock with particles. Angular stones are preferable to naturally rounded stones, to achieve the best interlock properties and resistance to longitudinal and lateral movement under dynamic loading. If ballast particles are too large, there may only be two or three stones between the underside of the sleeper and the sub-grade which will be insufficient to properly distribute the load. Too many small stones will however clog the ballast and reduce, in the longer term, its drainage properties. Samples of track ballast must be checked for grading by sieve analysis to make ballast particles into a reasonable match. Fig. 2-51 shows the sieve process of ballast particles. The ballast stone is a kind of granule, and its grain composition range means the match proportion of various size of the ballast particles, and has important effect on the physical and mechanical properties of the track ballast and the maintenance work. The current standard of grain composition range is graded according to the requirements, to ensure that the ballast products have the best particle composition. There are three sizes of gravel in China's railway ballast: 20-70 mm for the new track and track ballast refurbished; 15-40 mm for the ballast maintenance; 3-20 mm for the ballast mattress. The smaller size pieces are desirable because of the fineness of adjustment

Fig. 2-51 the sieving of ballast particles

Railway ballast is classified into up-ballast and sub-ballast. And Tab. 2-9 and Tab. 2-10 are the grain composition range standard of them in Chinese railway.

Tab. 2-9 the grain composition range standard of up-ballast particles

Side length of Square hole mesh/mm	16	25	35.5	45	56	63
The percentage of the quality of the sieving	0-5	5-15	25-40	55-75	92-97	97-100

Tab. 2-10 the grain composition range standard of sub-ballast particles

Side length of Square hole mesh/mm	0.075	0.1	0.5	1.7	7.1	16	25	45
The percentage of the quality of the sieving	0-7	0-11	7-32	13-46	41-75	67-91	82-100	100

The shape of the ballast particles has a great impact on the quality of the track bed, the general requirements of the ballast edge is roughly similar to the cube. Flat and needle ballast is easy to break. Ballast particles longer than thc average particle size of 1.8 times, is known as needle-like ballast, the thickness of which less than the average particle size of 0.6 times known as the chip ballast. As for China's ballast standard, needle and chip particle index are not greater than 50%

Ballast particles can suffer degradation due to the action of traffic and maintenance operations in broadly two ways. Either edges can become rounded and lose their interlocking effect or particles can break or crush under repeated loading. Some of the softer stones suffer badly from attrition in the presence of water. This deterioration, particularly at rail joints, can be associated with "wet spots" in the track, which can cause rapid deterioration of line, level and riding comfort.

Certain tests can be introduced to check the wet attrition qualities of ballast. Generally speaking limestones tend to have poor wet attrition qualities, and crushed granite being one of the best, although expensive.

The raw material for permanent-way ballast has to meet the following requirement:

(1) Resistance to weather influences (to be determined by the freeze-thaw test),

(2) High toughness(to be determined in the rotary drum grinder),

(3) No loam or earth content,

(4) The rocks should break into sharp-edged cubes.

The most suitable materials are hard ballast which meets the above requirements. Soft rocks are usually less suitable. Following are the common materials of ballast[1]:

(1) Broken stone.

It is produced from good quality stone like granite, limestone and hard trap rocks. Stone possesses strength, durability, stability, and can be cleaned readily.

(2) Gravel.

Gravel consists of rounded pieces of stones obtained from river bed. Larger pieces are broken to smaller sizes. To increase interlocking of stones rounded pieces are broken. On soft formation gravel ballast gives better performance.

(3) Sand.

It is suitable for in areas where intensity of traffic is low. It also causes excessive wear of top of rail due to grinding of sand particles which get deposited on the top of the rail head. On account of the above drawbacks sand ballast is used on branch line or on feeder railways. It has however good drainage properties and keeps yards dry during the rainy season.

(4) Coal ash or Cinder.

It is cheap and easily available and is used in the initial stages of new construction. It has however corrosive action on steel sleepers and its fittings and is therefore not used with steel sleepers. It has good drainage properties and holds the track to correct shape both longitudinally and laterally.

(5) Brick.

It has good drainage property but gets crushed under heavy load. It is therefore used on unimportant lines as a substitute for stone ballast.

(6) Earth.

It is used in the initial stages of a new line till the settling of the formation due to heavy loads is stabilized. Stones ballast is subsequently placed over consolidated and hardened earth.

2.5.3 Ballast cross section

The ballast cross section (Fig. 2-52) is the cross section of a track between and above the toes (the lowest points) of the ballast slopes. It may or may not include the sub-ballast. Deciding on the amount, thickness, and disposition of

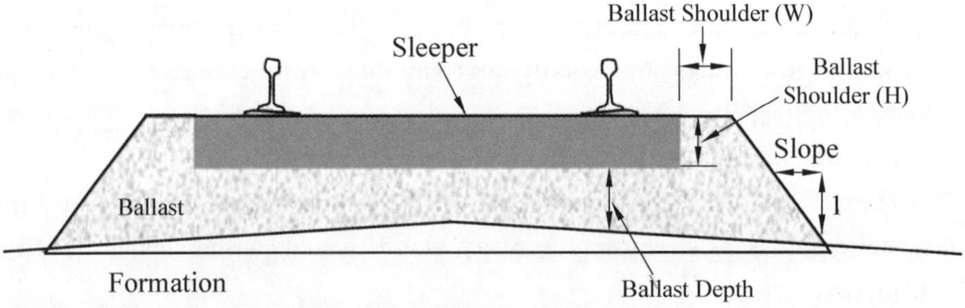

Fig. 2-52 Typical ballast cross section

Note: (1) H (the distance from sleeper soffit to under side of the rail) is determined by the sleeper design and therefore use of new and untried sleeper types will need special consideration with regard to ballast profile, in particular for the purposes of track lateral stability.

(2) Shoulder slope = 1 in slope.

(3) Depth of ballast (Z) is measured under the rail seat and does not include sub ballast where used.

ballast in a ballast cross section is no less a problem than that of picking the right material. Again, traffic and terrain govern the decision. In general, heavier, faster trains require a thicker ballast cross section than do others. Remember that ballast provides drainage, holds track in line and surface as permanently as possible, distributes train weight over the roadbed, reduces dust and weed growth, and provides a means for returning track to line and surface after passing trains move it. If these purposes are kept in mind, the specifications given below for thickness and the position of ballast will seem reasonable.

1. Ballast Thickness

The ballast thickness is the distance between the lower surface of the sleeper and the subsoil. Ballast thickness has been arrived at by theoretical and practical assessment of various loadings. Use of design ballast thickness with poor subgrades may still cause the subgrade to be over stressed. Detailed investigation and analysis of the whole track structure including the substructure condition may be necessary in these situations. It can equally be demonstrated that in areas with very good subgrades (natural or designed). It is possible to provide adequate support to the track structure with lower ballast thickness than those specified. In general the safety of the track is determined by factors other than ballast thickness. Some of these factors, such as track geometry, have a dependency on the ballast depth and subgrade support. Although ballast thickness is one factor that determines the effort required to maintain a safe track, it is only incidentally represented in these other factors which are monitored and maintained to ensure safety.

The required ballast thickness depends on:

- The sleeper spacing,
- The sleeper width,
- The angle of friction of the ballast.

The thickness of the ballasted should be at least 30 cm for axle loads of 220 kN, a sleeper spacing of 60 cm and sleeper width of 28 cm. For high-speed railway, a thickness of 40 cm is advisable. It is important to provide 45-50 cm of ballast at the sleeper ends. This guarantees a significant resistance to lateral displacement.

2. Ballast surface Tab. 2-11

The width of ballast surface should be adequate to provide necessary lateral stability to the track. The width of ballast surface is related to the length of the sleeper and the shoulder width of ballast. The length of the sleeper is basically fixed, so the width of ballast is mainly determined by the width of the shoulder. Ballast shoulder width is one factor that contributes to overall track lateral stability. Additional ballast shoulder may be necessary in areas of poor track lateral stability to provide adequate resistance to track buckling and movement, however detailed investigation and analysis of the whole track structure may be necessary in situations. The provision of additional ballast shoulder on sharp curves may also be necessary to maintain lateral stability. Height of the shoulder ballast is measured from the sleeper base and width of the shoulder ballast is measured from the sleeper end. Under normal circumstances, the shoulder width in the 450-500 mm has been able to meet the requirements, then no need to widen.

Ballast surface width at the sleeper ends:

- 0.4 m at $v \leqslant 160$ km/h,
- 0.5 m at $v > 160$ km/h,
- Ballasting up to the upper edge of the sleeper.

3. Ballast slope

The slope from the top of the ballast to the top of the roadbed is called ballast slope, and its size is very important to ensure the firmness and stability of track ballast. The stability of the ballast slope depends on the internal friction angle and cohesion of the ballast material, and also has a certain connection with the bed width. In the case of same shoulder bearing capacity, generally tend to use a larger shoulder and steeper slope, because it can reduce the width of the roadbed. But too steep slope is also unsuitable because the slope angle will be affected by the natural slope angle of the particles and the influence of the train vibration. The practice of operation shows that the 1 : 1.5 slope can not keep the ballast long-term stability, so the mainlines always use1 : 1.75 slope. According to the code for track design (TB 10082-2017) , ballast slope of main line and continuous welded railway should be 1:1.75..

Tab. 2-11 ballast section dimension

Railway grade	Designed train speed (km/h)	Ballast surface width /m	
		Ballasted track	Ballastless track
High-speed railway	$250 \leqslant V \leqslant 350$	3.60	-
Heavy-load railway	$V \leqslant 100$	3.50	-
Intercity railway Normal-speed railway	$160 < V \leqslant 200$	3.50	-
	$V \leqslant 160$	3.40	-
	$100 < V \leqslant 120$	3.40	3.10
Normal-speed railway	$V \leqslant 100$	3.40	3.00

It is advisable to provide ballast of high compactness and tension. This can be reached by inserting and compacting the ballast in layers. The best way to insert the ballast in layers is with the help of a tamping machine, sleeper end consolidators and a dynamic track stabilizer.

2.5.4 Phenomena occurred over the ballast[2]

There are some characteristic phenomena existing in the ballast: sleeper dance, easterly wave, ballast flying. The problems that these phenomena cause have different magnitudes: whereas the first two damage the very ballast, creating fine grains that compact the ballast and reduce its elastic functions, the third one damages the vehicles and the rail.

1. Sleeper dance

Sleeper dance is called to the phenomenon that appears through the time due to the very pass of vehicles and which is characterized by the loss of settling in some of the sleepers (“dancing sleepers”). This phenomenon causes the sleeper to be literally suspended over the ballast layer. When the train passes over these non-settled points, the load of the wheel applied to rail forces the sleeper to go down, hitting the ballast at a significant speed, therefore increasing the dynamic effect of the load on the structure and damaging the adjacent particles. Thus, with the continuous hitting fine grains are created, causing the compaction of the ballast and preventing it from carrying out its functions of shock-absorption and drainage.

2. Easterly wave

As the train advances, it lifts slightly the rail (and the sleeper to which it is fixed) from the front and from the back of the support-point of the wheels. The pass of the train through the point previously lifted forces the rail and sleeper to go back sharply to their original position, hitting the ballast placed below the sleeper. The impact speeds can be high, having the same negative effects as the above mentioned "dancing sleepers".

3. Ballast flying

With the pass of the trains at speeds near or even over 300 km/h, a turbulent flow is created (mainly behind the bogies) that can rise individual ballast particles. This raised particle is sufficiently displaced from the base to hit the wheels and the train-floor. In this moment when the particle shoots out again due to the impact of the train circulating at high-speed, therefore being charged with high kinetic energy. This first stone raised and hit by the train goes back to the ballast layer and hits the ballast, raising then more stones with its impact, which at the same time can hot again the train, creating what is called "ballast cloud", where the particles are ricocheting continuously between the railroad, wheels and train-floor.

The damages are significant in the train-floor, even causing perforation of the hydraulic-circuit conduits, breaking cables or other essential equipment, etc. The damages on the rail can be cause by direct hitting of the particles or by crushing of the ballast-grains over it with the pass of the train.

In spain, after carrying out aerodynamic studies of turbulences, it was suggested the change of the central section of the sleepers: virtual simulations proved that this section-change helped to drop substantially the turbulences caused with the pass of the train. They seem to be a very effective solution for the problems of the platforms in high-speed railways.

4. Ballast deformation and maintenance

Behavioral characteristics of ballast determine how well it will satisfy its functional requirements and affect its usefulness and economy as a material and the geometric design of the ballast section. Those characteristics must be known to permit a proper selection of material that gives overall economy. Two kind of behavior are important: the short-term elastic response and the long-term permanent deformation and degradation.

As the grain structure, under the action of load, elastic and plastic deformation will occur. Part load disappears, the elastic deformation was restored, and the plastic deformation part would become permanent deformation or residual deformation. Obtained from the residual deformation mainly has two reasons, one is in charge to carry ballast particles under the action of mutual displacement and deformation caused by the rearrangement structure; the other is due to particles of grain crushing, powder formed by deformation. In under repeated train loads, every load generated by tiny residual deformation will gradually accumulate, eventually lead to subsidence of the track.

The subsidence of the ballast is the gradual accumulation of the plastic deformation of the ballast with the load. The law of the subsidence has been studied by various countries, such as the United States, Japan, the Soviet Union and so on. The data of each country show that the relationship between the sinking of the ballast and the total weight is basically similar, as shown in Fig. 2-53.

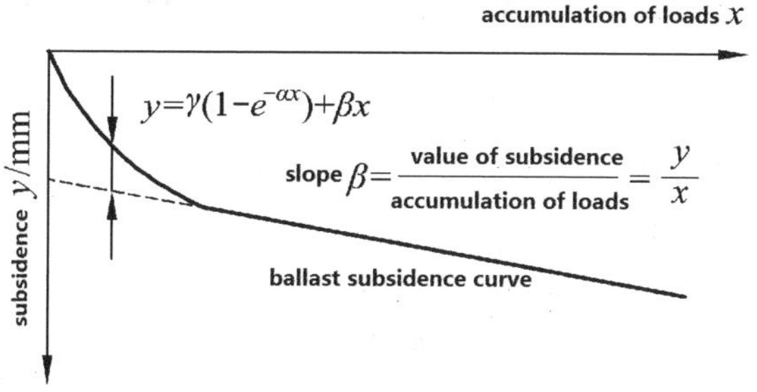

Fig. 2-53 Ballast Deformation Diagram

Roadbed subsidence is obtained from the plastic deformation with loads and gradual process of accumulation. Sinking of ballast is generally can be divided into two stages: early sharp sinking and lately slowly sinking.

Ballast is distributed in existing track structures (1) to fill the track as part of a track raise and surfacing operation (2) to restore ballast lost in plowing, sledding, or under cutting, (3) to restore ballast lost through abrasion and cleaning, and (4)to complete the ballast section following a profile revision.

2.6 Rail Creep

The longitudinal movement of rails in a track is known as rail creep (Fig. 2-54).

Fig. 2-54 Creep of rails

It varies, from almost negligible length to a few centimeters. A track may be affected by creep in two ways. Firstly the rails may move longitudinally with respect to sleepers; secondly, the sleepers may move longitudinally with the rails. The former is possible if the toe load of the fastenings on the rails is less than the force due to creep. The sleeper will move longitudinally with the rail if the resistance of the ballast to such movement is less than the creeping force.

The forces of creep under static and dynamic conditions are different as the toe load of the fastening on the rail foot and the ballast resistance get considerably reduced because of the high frequency vibrations caused by dynamic loading at high-speeds.

Other defects which may be developed due to creep are given below:

- As the sleepers are displaced, the gauge of the track gets disturbed.

• The opening out of joints results in development of heavy stresses in fish plates and bolts which may break and lead to accidents.

• Rail turnouts may be displaced which may lead to derailment.

• If one rail is removed for any purpose, the re-fixing causes much difficulty.

• The suspended joint may become supported joint which may result in the ends getting battered.

• Sleepers get out of square which result in distortion of the alignment.

2.6.1 Causes of creep

The causes of creep have been explained by the following theories: Wave Action or Wave Theory, Percussion Theory and Drag Theory.

1. *Wave theory*

As the rail gets depressed under the wheel shown as A in Fig. 2.56, a vertical reverse curve shown by B is formed. The wheels have a tendency to push the waves in the direction of traffic. With the successive forward motion of the wheel the creep is carried forward.

It has been found that pitch and depth of wave is governed by the following:

(1) Stiffness of track and stability of the formation. These two properties normally go together. Stiffness of track however, mostly depends on the type of rails and rigidity of joints and fastenings. The stability of the formation depends upon the character of the formation soil and packing of the ballast.

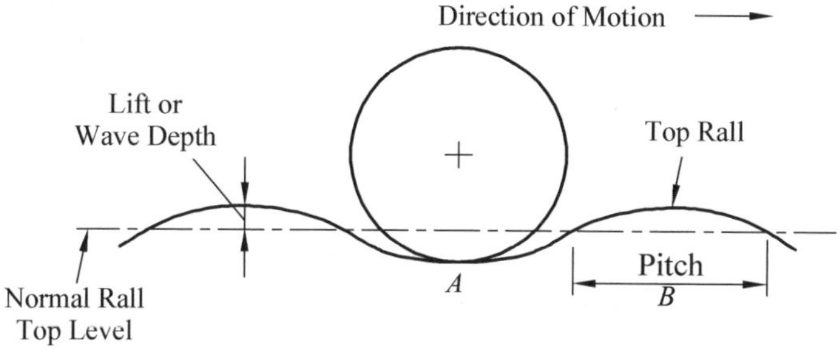

Fig. 2-55 Wave theory of creep

(2) Track modulus. Like modulus of elasticity, track modulus is an index of measurement of resistance to deformation. It is defined as the load in kg

percent of the rail length required to produce one cm depression of the rail table. The unit of track modulus is kg/cm^2 and the higher this value, the stiffer is the track.

2. Percussion theory

According to this theory the impact of the rail wheel ahead of the joints gives rise to creep in the rails. As illustrated in Fig. 2-56, the reaction “R” is normal to the surface of contact. Its horizontal component “H” causes creep and the vertical component “V” tends to bend the rail vertically which results in battering of the rail end. During the process of striking, the rail is pushed forward resulting in creep.

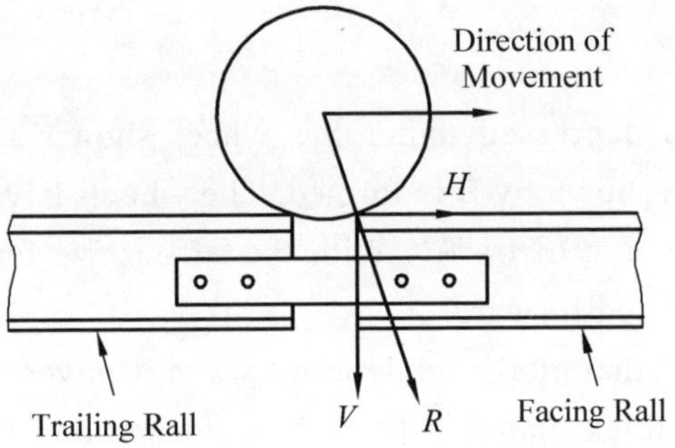

Fig. 2-56 Percussion theory of creep

3. Drag theory

According to this theory the rails are pushed off the track in the backward direction by the driving wheel of the locomotive of the train while the remaining wheels of locomotive and the train push the rail in the direction of travel. As a result of this, creep takes place along the direction of travel.

The other factors which give rise to creep are given below:

- Variation in temperature. The amount of creep in this case depends upon the range of temperature, location of the track and nature of adjoining area.
- Starting, stopping and change of speed. When the train is starting, or when it is being accelerated, the backward thrust tends to push the rails backward, on the other hand when the train is slowing down or when brakes are applied to bring it to a standstill the braking effect pushes, the rails in the forward direction:

• Track alignment. On curves creep is greater than on straight reaches.

• Track gradient. On sleeper gradients creep is higher.

• Poor maintenance results in larger creep.

• Old rail sections have greater creep.

• Unbalanced traffic. In single line, heavy traffic runs in both the directions and hence creep effect is negligible whereas in double line where the traffic is unidirectional, creep takes place in both the lines.

• Creep is more rapid during the hot weather.

• Rails usually creep more on embankments, especially newly made ones. On firm ground which has not been raised above the surroundings, there is little creep. In case of tracks laid over swampy or boggy land creep is the most.

The following five conditions govern all cases of creep in rails:

• Character of the ground or foundation of the track.

• Speed of the trains.

• Type of fastenings.

• Direction of heavier loads

• Character of ground.

2.6.2 Measurement of creep

Creep posts should be erected every kilometer on either side of the track and the position of joints should be marked on one side of the post. The arrangement of creep post or creep indicator is shown in Fig. 2-58.

A chisel mark is made at the bottom flange of the rail between the centers of the two sleepers. Two rail posts are fixed such that the line joining their centers passes through the chiseled marks on the rails. The top of these rail posts are at the top level of the sleeper as illustrated in Fig. 2-57. A tight string is stretched below rails on the marks of the indicator and horizontal displacement of the rails on the marks of the indicator and horizontal displacement of the rail marks from the stretched string gives thc amount of creep.

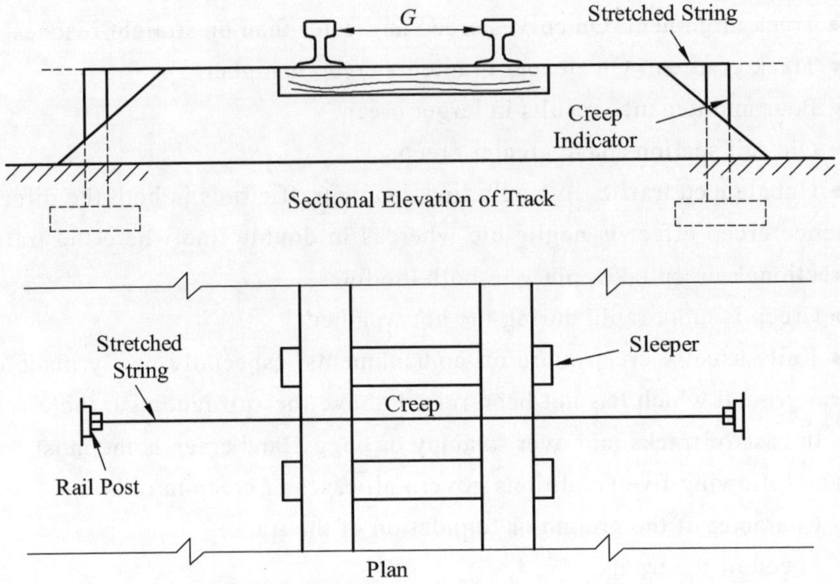

Fig. 2-57 Measurement of creep

2.6.3 Adjustment of creep

When the creep exceeds 10 cm, the rail should be adjusted by pulling back. A careful survey is carried out of the expansion gaps and the present position of the rail joints. Based on the survey thus carried out the following points are decided before the operation of actual pulling back is carried out:

- Total creep proposed to be adjusted.
- The correct expansion gap to be provided.
- Length of the track to be taken up in one operation.

The sequence of operation is as given below:

- Loosening of fish plates from one end and removing the same from other end of the rail.
- Removal of sleeper fittings such as spikes or keys.
- Pulling back of the rails one at a time with the help of rope attached to the hook.

Pulling back is carried out in such a way that the rail joints remain central over the joint sleepers. It is a slow process and can be done for a few isolated rails. When large number of rail lengths are to be adjusted by the pulling back method, the pulling back by rope is replaced by a below given by a 5 m cut piece of rail. By this method five rails can be pulled back at a time.

When a large number of rails have to be tackled, a creep adjuster is employed for adjusting the creep. The creep adjuster is set at the centre of the rail to be adjusted. The joints behind the adjuster are loosened whereas the joints ahead of the adjuster are tightened. Correct size expansion liners are then inserted in the expansion gaps. The creep adjuster is then allowed to operate in such a way that it pushes the rails forward and closes the gaps to the desired dimensions. The corrected rails are then keyed up. The operation is then repeated on the other side of the track. The above operation leaves some of the expansion gaps to be too big. These gaps are taken care of in the subsequent position of the creep adjuster.

2.6.4 Anti-creep devices

Where there is a tendency for rail to move longitudinally in track under one-way traffic or on high grade track, rail anchors are used to restrain the movement. The anchor is firmly attached to the base of the rail and bears against the side of the tie facing oncoming traffic. Anchors are always put on both rails of the track and are located opposite each other to prevent uneven movement of sleepers. Amongst these anchors, "dowelled anti-creep anchor"(Fig. 2-58(a)) and "spring anti-creep anchor"(Fig. 2-58(b)) have been standardized ,and The former is more widely used . To be fully effective, creep anchor should bear tight against the sleeper. Fig. 2-59 shows the proper installation locations. Anchors must bear directly on

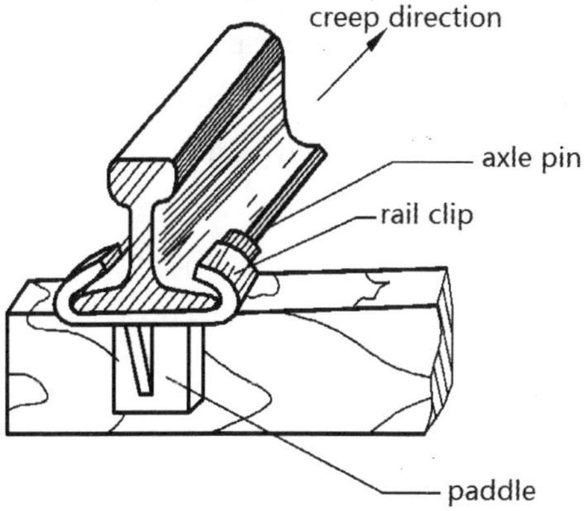

(a) Dowelled anti-creep anchor

(b) Spring anti-creep anchor

Fig. 2-58 Typical rail anchor

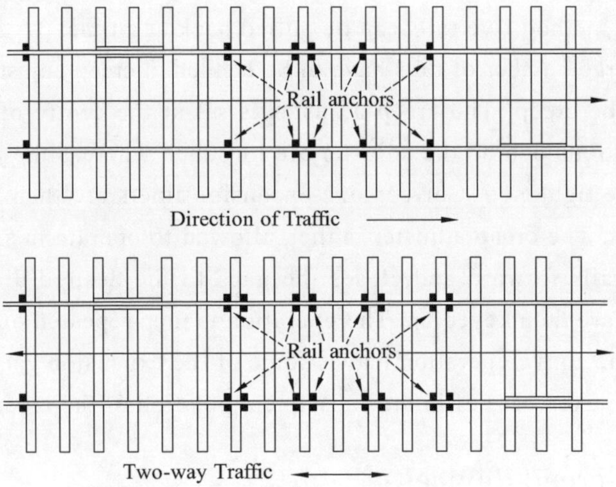

Fig. 2-59 Rail anchors correctly located

switches at all times for effectiveness. If the anchor loses contact for any reason, it must be removed and reset.

For satisfactory function of the anchors the following points need attention:

(1) The anchors should hold the sleepers firmly otherwise they would be ineffective.

(2) The anchors should be uniformly distributed along the defective rail.

(3) The anchors should be inspected at regular intervals and defective anchors should be replaced,

(4) The sleepers should be of good quality and free from defects.

(5) Creep anchors should not normally be provided on railway bridges.

(6) Where brake actions are normally expected the number of anchors should be increased. Examples of such locations are yards and approaches to yards, and level crossings.

The use of steel sleepers in locations which are prone to creep have been found to be very effective. In addition to the use of good quality sleepers, the number of sleepers, if increased, also act as creep prevention.

2.6.5 Gauge rods and rail brace

Gauge rods are used to hold track to proper gauge, like the one in Fig. 2-60. On very sharp curves or where sleepers are too weak to provide holding power for spikes in old and little used tracks, gauge rods are installed to hold the track against spreading by anchoring one rail firmly to the other. The jaws on one end of the rod are fixed and slip under and over the base of rail. Jaws on the other end are adjustable and may be drawn tight against the base of the opposite rail. Gauge rods are insulated or non-insulated, depending on whether or not they are used in track circuit territory.

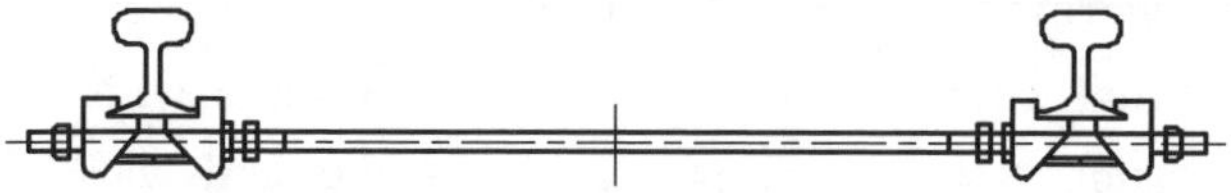

Fig. 2-60 Gauge rods

A rail brace, like the one in Fig. 2-61, is used on curves and switches to resist excessive lateral thrust on the rail. Placed outside the rail, the brace is spiked to the turnout and bears against the rail waist and head.

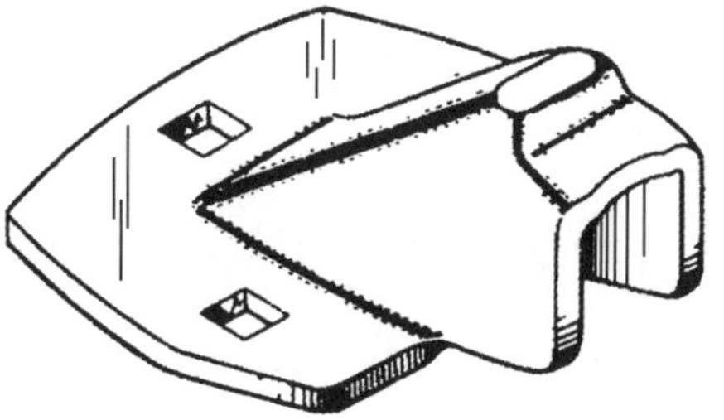

Fig. 2-61 Typical rail brace

2.7 Railroad level crossing

2.7.1 Overview

Railroad level crossing is an intersection where a railway line crosses a road or path at the same level, as opposed to the railway line crossing over or under using a bridge or tunnel. Other names include railway crossing, grade crossing, and road through railroad, railroad crossing and train crossing.

Fig. 2-62 Level crossings

Every year, more than 400 people are killed in over 1.200 accidents at road-rail level crossings in the European Union (European Railway Agency, 2011). Together with tunnels and specific road black spots, level crossings have been identified as being a particular weak point in road infrastructure, seriously jeopardizing road safety. In the case of railway transport, level crossings can represent as much as 29% of all fatalities caused by railway operations. [9]

In terms of warning systems, level crossings are either passive crossings which have warnings such as signs, or active crossings which have automatic warning devices such as boom gates, flashing lights and warning tones. Fewer collisions take place at level crossings with active warning systems. Today radar sensor systems for automatic level crossing free detection are a cheap way to improve safety of level crossings.

In china, speed-up campaigns have largely eliminated many crossings on heavily used trunk main lines though some still do exist. Most existed crossings in China are for smaller industrial spur and access lines which may or may not have crossing gates.

2.7.2 Protection arrangements of level crossings[9]

Level crossings present a significant risk of collisions between trains and road vehicles.The most common causes of accidents at level crossings are as followings

- Gatesmen's failure to close the gates well in time when the train is coming.
- Drivers of road vehicles are not vigilent for approaching trains.
- Clear view of road and rail traffic being obstructed by trees or bulidings.

The protection arrangements which are appropriate at level crossings will vary, depending upon the crossing location, for example proximity to road junctions, the level of use and the type of railway traffic.

An important factor in assuring the safety of level crossings is providing, so far as circumstances permit, a consistent appearance for road and rail users of any crossing. To help achieve this, several "standard" level crossing types have been developed over the years.

Types of level crossings include:

(1) Gated crossings operated by railway staff-this type of crossing is

protected by gates, on both sides of the railway, which complete the fencing of the railway when closed across the road or the railway.

(2) Barrier crossings operated by railway staff-this type of crossing is protected by road traffic light signals and lifting barriers on both sides of the railway. An audible warning to pedestrians is also provided.

(3) Barrier crossings with obstacle detection-this type of crossing is protected by road traffic light signals and lifting barriers on each side of the railway. An audible warning to pedestrians is also provided.

(4) Automatic half barrier crossings-this type of crossing is protected by road traffic light signals and a lifting barrier on both sides of the railway. Audible warning to pedestrians is also provided.

(5) Automatic barrier crossings, locally monitored-this type of crossing appears, to the road user, to be similar to an automatic half barrier crossing. It is protected by road traffic light signals and a single lifting barrier on both sides of the railway.

(6) Automatic open crossings, locally monitored-this type of crossing has no barriers but is protected by road traffic light signals and an audible warning for pedestrians.

(7) Open crossings-this type of crossing does not have barriers or road traffic light signals. Only road traffic signs are provided. Road users must give way to trains at the crossing.

(8) User worked crossings for vehicles-this type of crossing is normally protected by gates, or lifting barriers on both sides of the railway. The gates, normally closed across the road and hung so as to open away from the railway, are operated by the users.

(9) Foot crossings at stations-this type of crossing is found between platforms at stations and may be the only route between platforms or the only practicable route for people who cannot use steps.

2.7.3 Construction of level crossings

Roadways should cross railroad tracks in such a way that they can be clearly sighted from the highway. The surface of the roadway where it crosses the tracks should be level with the top of the rails. For a distance of 50 m on each side of the crossing rails, the highway approach should be 5 mm below the level of the rails.

This insures that approaches are on a smooth grade so that vehicles with low road clearance may pass over the crossing without their undercarriages touching either the rails or road surface, and no vehicles are jolted in making the crossing. Flange-ways, or passage-ways for the wheel flanges should be 70-100 mm wide, no more than 60 mm and no less than 45 mm deep, to provide the train pass away

Level crossings may be constructed of various materials and in different designs; the choice depends upon the amount and kind of highway traffic and the materials available. Materials include rails, wooden, asphalt, concrete, precast concrete, or prefabricated metal panels. Fig. 2-63 illustrates precast concrete slab level crossing.

Fig. 2-63 Panel of level crossings

A simple crossing may use wooden panel spiked to blocks on both sides of each rail. The outside ones are placed flush against the head of the rail, while those inside are set to provide the necessary flangeway between the panels and the gauge side of the head of the rail. The space between the inside panels may be filled with cinders, gravel, concrete, panels, or asphalt. A similar crossing uses rails instead of panels inside the running rails. The ends of the inside rails are bent toward the center of the track to provide a flangeway opening. The rails may be placed on their sides with their heads against the waist of the running rails, or they may be placed on their bases with separators to maintain the proper flange-ways.

2.7.4 Choice of crossing panel type

Panel is the most important component of level crossings, and there are different kinds of panel as below:

1. Stone crossing panel

The stone panel is mostly made of local materials. And it is not common now. Its advantage is to use stone locally, and price is low. The drawback is that the stone is brittle material and easily damaged. The stone panel is smaller in width, allowing only a few pedestrian and animal-drawn vehicles.

2. Wooden crossing panel

The wooden crossing is paved with wood sleeper, the advantages are simple, easy to lay, and easy to repair. As the wood sleeper has been soaked in oil, it also has a better durability. The drawback is that the timber resources are expended, and if the vehicle's traffic and the load are heavy the wooden panel will be obviously damaged, and its life expectancy will be shortened. Besides the maintenance volume will increase. Wooden crossing panel is used in the places where vehicle traffic and weight is not very large, or the temporary crossing. Wooden panel crossing is easier to lay and recycle, and that the wood sleeper can be used after recycling save material cost.

3. Reinforced concrete crossing panel

The advantage is easy to manufacture, low price, can be made in batches, laid fast and replaced easily. There is a longer service life compared with the former types of panel. The disadvantage is when the dosage is lower, the relative cost is higher. The life of the reinforced concrete panel in use is much shorter than that of the theory. The reason is that the influence of the processing technology, the panel between the panel or the contact between panel and other facilities are not very good. The vibration of the vehicle will cause the concrete to break. With the emergence of breakage, panel damage will greatly accelerate. So the service life of reinforced concrete panel is shortened. The reinforced concrete panel is used in the new circuit. It is used in large number panel, factory area, or on the road in factory area of no-heavy loading vehicle.

4. Steel crossing panel

The steel panel is made of steel plate welded, the thick of plate should more than 15 mm, and the plate and floor board can use 8-10 mm thin plate. Its advantage is firm, large load, smooth, beautiful and long service life. The drawback is the high cost of making and laying, difficult maintenance because of hard movement, easy to steal at the crossing of the unattended. It can be used in the intersection of important roads and railways, and its advantages will be fully utilized when it combined with the overall rail of the track.

5. Rubber crossing panel

The rubber panel is a new type of panel in the last few years. It is widely used. According to different requirements, different quality can be chosen. As laying simple, small maintenance quantity, long service life, it is in the promotion practical stage at present. The drawback is high cost.

2.8 Ballastless track

2.8.1 Introduction

A disadvantage of traditional track structures is the heavy demand for maintenance, particularly surfacing (tamping) and lining to restore the desired track geometry and smoothness of vehicle running. Weakness of the subgrade and drainage deficiencies also lead to heavy maintenance costs. This can be overcome by using ballastless track.

Ballastless track is designed such that no underlying ballast is required. The first such tracks were mountain railways (like Pilatus Railway, built in 1889) with rails attached directly to the mountain rock. From the late 1960s onwards, German, British, Swiss and Japanese railroads experimented with alternatives to the traditional railway sleeper in search of solutions with higher accuracy and longevity, and lowered maintenance costs.

This gave rise to the ballastless railway track, especially in tunnels, high-speed rail lines and on lines with high train frequency, which have high stress imposed on trackage. However ballastless track is very expensive in first cost. However, its whole life cost can be lower because of the great reduction in maintenance requirement.

Generally speaking the advantages of the ballastless track are the significantly reduced maintenance need in combination with its higher serviceability life, as well as its higher structural track stability.

Ballastless track systems have various disadvantages too. Suchas high investment costs, long manufacture and installation time, as well as the limited options in adjustments after construction, and the high air-borne vibration emissions.

2.8.2 Different ballastless track system

Some representative ballastless track systems are listed below:

1. Rheda system

The Rheda system in its various forms is one of the most commonly used ballastless track systems worldwide. This system is widely used due to its adequate performance and long experience comparing to other ballastless track systems. The Rheda design is free of any patent rights, thus, since its birth it has been under continuous development by various contractors and many different structural versions have been created to fulfill different specifications in various projects.

The first Rheda system to be constructed was in the Rheda-Wiedenbruck station (Germany) in 1972 (Lichtberger22). The Rheda system is very flexible allowing for design changes and enhancements in order to fit the demands of each project. Hence it can be found in tunnels, bridges, as well as on earth structures.

The latest developed version is Rheda 2000 as shown in Fig. 2-64. This system is flexible enough to allow for design adaptations according to the individual constraints of a project. The basic system structure, however, always consists of:

• Modified twin-block sleepers with untensioned braced girder reinforcement.

• The sleepers are securely and reliably embedded in a monolithic concrete slab.

• Highly elastic rail fastenings are used to ensure the required vertical rail deflection for load distribution and for smooth train travel.

• The Rheda systems rest on a hydraulically bonded layer (HBL) and a frost protection layer (FPL).

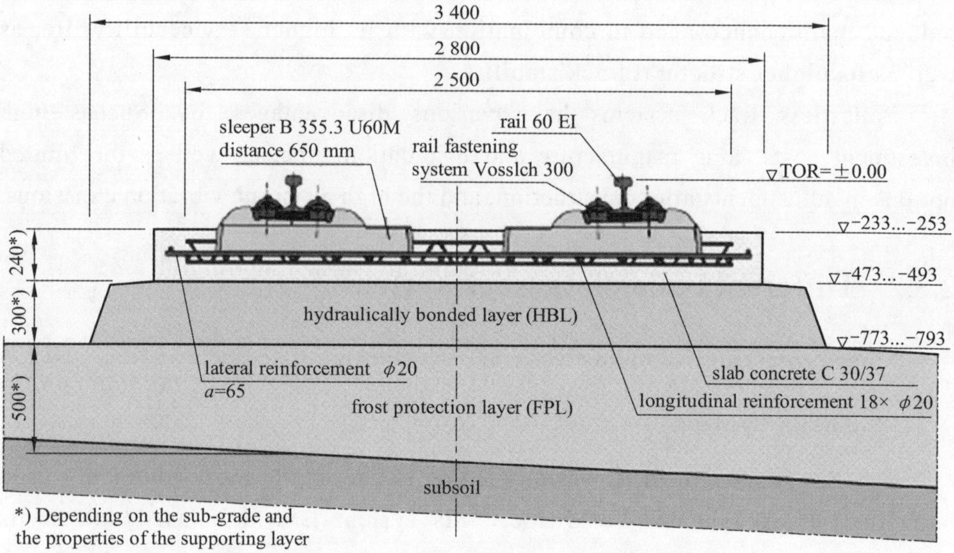

Fig. 2-64 Rheda 2000 on earthwork

2. ATD system

The systems with sleepers on top of asphalt-concrete layer perform adequately and that asphalt layers can provide a stable and supportive layer suitable to replace the conventional ballast layer. ATD system is a representativeness.

The ATD system consists of an asphalt roadbed set up over the cement stabilized support layer. The sleepers are placed on the asphalt layer and the ridge in the middle of track between them takes up the lateral forces. After the track grid horizontal adjustments, the free space between the ridge and the sleepers is cast in a synthetic material. The construction of these includes the use of twin-block as well as mono-block sleepers which are equipped with a groove on their lower surface which can resist all the lateral forces, see Fig. 2-65 (a). The ATD system is consisted by the following basic elements:

- Hydraulically-bonded layer .
- Asphalt supportive layer.
- Twin-block sleeper or mono-block sleeper.
- Elastic rail fastenings and the UIC 60 rail.

To provide extra support and greater resistance of the sleepers to survive sudden breakings of the continuous welded rail, ballast is placed around the sleepers or heavier sleepers maybe used. The asphalt is applied with ±2 mm accuracy and is laid in three or even four different layers. The asphalt mix can guarantee a 50 to 60 year life span under extreme weather conditions.

(a) mono-block

(b) twin-block sleepers

Fig. 2-65 ATD system sleepers

3. Shinkansen system

This ballastless track system was first developed and used in Japan in 1972. It consists of a sub-layer stabilized with cement, and assembly plates of 4.95 m×2.34 m×0.19 m and 0.16 m thick in tunnels with low pretension are used in longitudinal and lateral dimension. These slabs weigh approximately 5 tons each and are adjusted on top of a hydraulically bonded surface, under the slab is injected a minimum 4 cm thick bituminous mortar, except few cases where a rubber mat in some anti-vibration versions is used. The slabs are hold longitudinally and laterally by concrete cylinders (dowel) which are rigidly connected with the structural concrete of the bearing plate. Details on the shinkansen slab track system can be observed in Fig. 2-66.

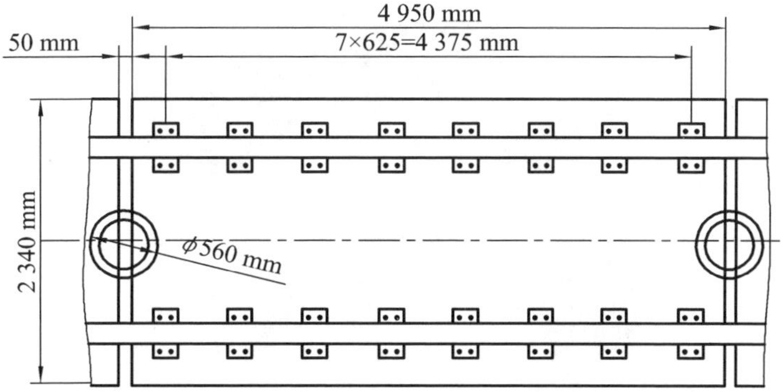

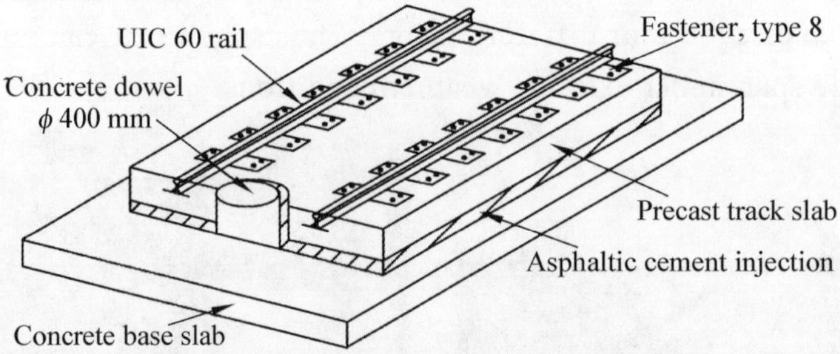

Fig. 2-66 Shinkansen slab track system

Special attention must be paid in the bituminous injection under the prefabricated slab due to its weakness in fulfilling the expected technical performance. The Shinkansen slab track system has influenced other systems that have been used around the world, using similar design and construction principles.

4. Monolithic designs

These designs are consisted of only a continuous monolithic concrete layer and direct rail fastenings adjusted on it. The sleeperless designs are established either as monolithic concrete layer produced by a concrete paver or as prefabricated slabs connected together. The direct rail fastenings used for this system are very effective in bridges making them lighter and eliminate problems associating the sleepers. The monolithic designs are stiff and rigid enough to behave structurally as a continuous supported elastic beam under traffic loading. The rigidity of this system makes it suitable for use in soft soils. The loads are distributed across a much longer and wider area. Attention must be paid to the crack formation of the concrete bearing layer (CBL) and proper measures have to be taken to prevent cracking caused by the rail fastenings. Fig.2-67 shows a momolithic slab track.

Fig. 2-67 An example of a monolithic slab track design with direct rail fastenings

5. Embedded rail structures

The embedded rail structure is a continuous elastically supported rail by means of a compound such as cork and polyurethane. The rail fixation is established by an elastic compound surrounding the whole rail profile except the rail head. This system includes the full range from high-speed tracks to light rail. What characterizes this concept is the absence of additional components to secure track gauge.

The characteristic principles of the rail fixation in this concept are the following:

- An elastic strip provides continuous support under the rail.
- The rail is guided in a groove by elastic fixation.
- Top-down alignment of the rail.
- The rail profile is fixed by an elastic compound.
- Optimization of the elastic compounds, the groove dimensions and strips for specific elasticity.

The advantages of this concept are the following:

- Absence of dynamic forces due to secondary bending between single rail points.
- Less noise emissions.
- Increases rail life span.
- Overall reduction of maintenance.
- The embedded rail construction height can be reduced (e.g., in case of road crossing where a smooth obstacle free surface is needed).

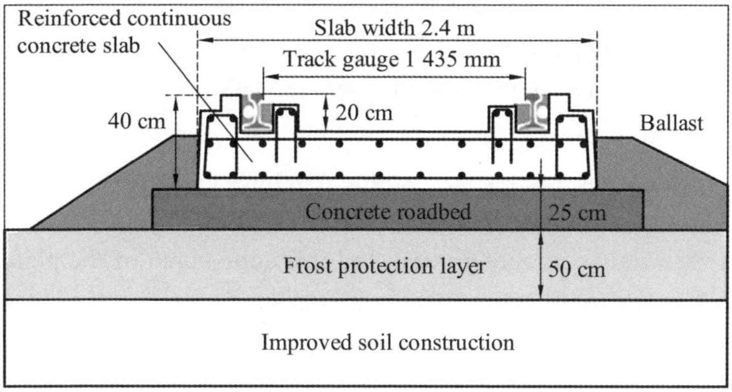

Fig. 2-68 A embedded rail construction

2.8.3 Ballastless track of Chinese high-speed railway

Nowadays, there are five types ballastless track in China, forming a series of

CRTS ballastless track system: CRTS-I slab track, CRTS-II slab track, CRTS-III slab track, CRTS-I bi-block sleepertrackk, CRTS-II bi-block sleepertrack.

CRTS-I slab track (Fig.2-69) comes from the Japanese Shinkansen slab track system . Prefabricated track slab is laid on the reinforced concrete base slab cast-in-place. Under the track slab is a cement asphalt mortar adjustment layer. Concrete cylinders (dowel) can hold the slab longitudinally and laterally.

Fig. 2-69 CRTS- I slab track

CRTS- II slab track (Fig. 2-70) comes from the Germany Borg slab track system. The reinforced concrete bearing plates are laterally prestressed and longitudinally normally reinforced by the so called "GEWI" bars. Prefabricated track slab is designed with special breaking points arranged between the supporting points in order to prevent random crack formation in the slab. This design is turned to be a system of many wide sleepers joined together due to these specifically designed cracking points. Special screw-jacks (spindles) integrated in the slabs reassure an easy and fast adjustment of the plates.

CRTS- III slab track (Fig. 2-71) comes from China's independent research and is the development of CRTS-I and CRTS-II slab track, which advantages have been kept and shortcomings removed. The track structure adopts the modular block structure. Prefabricated track slab is designed with shoulder. The base plate is provided with two limiters (groove structure) within each track slab, and an intermediate isolation layer (geotextile) is provided between the base plate and the self-compacting concrete layer.

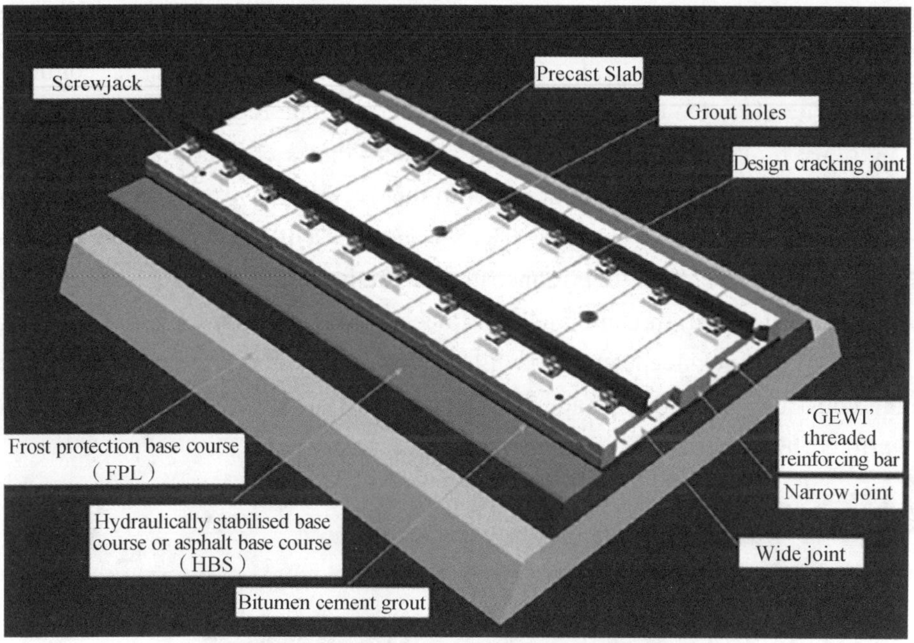

Fig. 2-70 CRTS-II slab track

Fig. 2-71 CRTS-III slab track

For bi-bocksleeper ballastless track, bi-bocksleeper is prefabricated in a precast concrete factory. It is characterized in that the sleeper is connected together with concrete blocks through a steel truss. The regulator will be used as an auxiliary tool to adjust double block sleepers into a correct plane position on bearing base, finally pouring concrete into the overall construction of the sleeper to complete the double block track. CRTS-I and CRTS-II bi-bocksleeper track are similar in structure, but their construction methods are different. The higher degree of mechanization can be used in mechanical vibration embedding method for CRTS-II bi-bocksleeper track, while CRTS-I can only be constructed by rail frame construction method. Tab. 2-13 shows the type of CRTS ballastless track in various HSR lines.

Fig. 2-72 CRTS-I double-block track

Tab. 2-12 CRTS ballastless track in HSR Lines

Type	HSR Lines
CRTS-I slab track	Shijiazhuang-Taiyuan, Guangzhou-Shenzhen-Hongkong, Guangzhou-Zhuzhou, Shanghai-Nanjing
CRTS-II slab track	Beijing-Tianjin, Beijing-Shanghai, Beijing-Shijiazhuang, Shijiazhuang-Wuhan, Tianjin-Qinhuangdao, Shanghai-Hangzhou
CRTS-III slab track	Chengdu-Mianyang-Leshan(Leshan section),, Wuhan-Xiaogan, Wuhan-Huangshi, Wuhan-Xianning, Panjin-Yingkou, Chengdu-Dujiangyan, Shengyang-Dandong, Beijing-Shengyang
CRTS-I bi-bocksleeper	Wuhan-Guangzhou, Hefei-Wuhan, Wenzhou-Fuzhou, Fuzhou-Xiamen, Xiangfan-Chongqing
CRTS-II bi-bocksleeper	Zhengzhou-xi'an

Professional Words and Expressions

rail 钢轨
sleeper (or cross tie) 轨枕
fastening 联接零件
ballast 道床
turnout 道岔
subgrade 路基
ballasted track 有砟轨道
ballastless track 无砟轨道
load transmission 荷载传递
track stresses 轨道应力
vertical Bending stress 垂直弯曲应力
lateral Bending stress 横向弯曲应力
shearing stress 剪切应力
longitudinal stress 纵向应力
length of Rail 钢轨长度
weight of Rail 钢轨重量
rail profile 钢轨轮廓线
double-headed rail 双头钢轨
bullhead rail 牛头钢轨
grooved rail 槽轨
flat-bottomed rail 平底轨
rail head 轨头
rail waist 轨腰
rail foot 轨底
rail Life and fatigue 钢轨寿命及疲劳
rail failures 钢轨失效
timber sleepers 木枕
concrete sleepers 混凝土枕
monoblock sleeper 整体轨枕
sleeper spacing 轨枕间距
rail joints 钢轨接头
fishplates 鱼尾板
joint bolts, nuts and spring washers 接头螺栓、螺母和弹簧垫圈
rail Joint gap 轨缝
square Joint 对接式接头
staggered Joints 错接式接头
suspended joint 悬空式接头
supported joint 承垫式接头
bridge joint 桥式接头
compromise Joints 异型夹板联结
insulated joint 绝缘接头
expansion Joints 伸缩接头
welded Joint 焊接接头
direct fastening 直接联结扣件
indirect(separated) fastening 间接联结扣件
mixed fastening 混合式联结扣件
spike 道钉
K fastening on timber Sleeper K 型木枕联结扣件
indirecting K fastening with spring clips on timber Sleeper 间接 K 型木枕弹条联结扣件
I-type spring clip fastening I 型弹条式扣件
ballast material 道床材料
ballast section 道床断面
subsidence of ballast 道床下沉
plastic deformation 塑性变形

steel sleepers 钢枕

sleeper plate 轨枕垫板

Y-shaped sleepers Y 型轨枕

broad sleeper 宽轨枕

ladder track 梯型轨枕

twin-block sleepers 双块式轨枕

elastic deformation 弹性变形

sieving of ballast particles 道砟筛分

rail creep 钢轨爬行

anti-creep devices 防爬设备

rail anchor 钢轨放爬器

gauge rods 轨距拉杆

rail brace 轨撑

railroad level crossing 铁路平交道口

panel of Level crossings 平交道口铺面板

CHARPTER 3 TRACK GEOMETRY

【Primary Contents】

(1) Concept, features and significance of track geometry

(2) Features and setters of basic track geometry elements: rail gauge, cross level, alignment, surface, rail cant, gradient etc.

(3) Features, calculation and setters of track super-elevation

(4) Features, calculation and setters of track transition curves

(5) Features, calculation and setters of gauge widening on curves

3.1 Introduction

Track geometry is three-dimensional geometry of track layouts and associated measurements used in design, construction and maintenance of railroad tracks. For the convenience of design, the three-dimensional track geometry are usually expressed in horizontal layoutsandvertical layouts. Horizontal layout is the track layout on the horizontal plane and involves mainly three geometric elements: straight line, horizontal curve, and transition curve (also called easement line) which connects between a tangent and a curved track. Vertical layout is the track layout on the vertical plane and involves mainly three geometric elements too: straight line, vertical curve and gradient. Furthermore, two rail of a track should maintain geometric standards such as rail gauge, cross level, alignment, surface etc. For the smooth and safe operation of vehicles, other geometric elements such as super-elevation, gauge widening of curves, vehicle limited speed on curves, should be determined. Track geometry is very important for the behavior of vehicles.

In this section an introduction to the most common elernemts of track geometry will be presented and ensure the purposes below:

• The construction and maintenance of tracks is carried out within safe geometric limits.

• The geometry of the track must be closely matched with the geometric size of the locomotive wheel set. Therefore, the control of the track geometry is very important to ensure the safety of the train operation.

• With the progress of high-speed railway, excessive acceleration forces on rolling stock shall be limited and hence ensure passenger comfort and safety are not compromised. Track forces which may cause excessive track maintenance are limited.

To achieve above purposes, should meet the following requirements in details:

• The gauge of the track should be correct and uniform.

• The alignment should be correct. There should not be kinks and irregularities in the track.

• In straight line there should be the same rails level, while on curves there should be proper super-elevation.

• Gradient should be even and uniform. Any change of gradient should be followed by vertical curve.

• Special attention should be given for the design of radius and super-elevation on curves. They should be properly maintained.

3.2 Basic track geometry elements

Track shall be laid and maintained with correct gauge and level of the rails to ensure safe driving.

3.2.1 Track gauge

The nominal track gauge is the distance between the inner faces of the rails. In current practice it is specified at a certain distance below the rail head as the inner faces of the rail head (the gauge faces) are not necessarily vertical. The definition of track gauge is shown in Fig. 3.1.

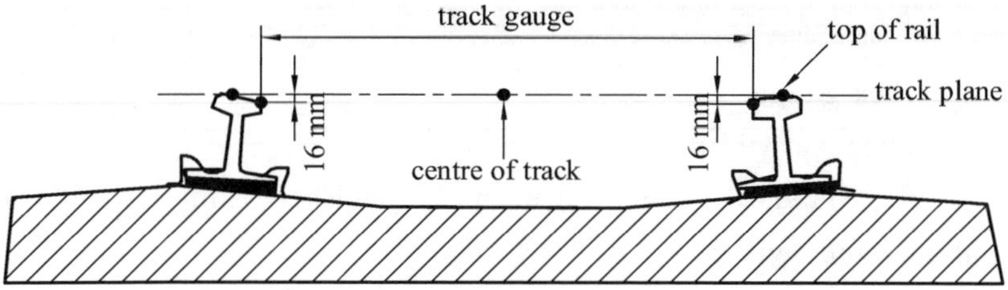

Fig. 3-1 The definition of track gauge

Rolling stock on the network must have running gear (wheel sets) that are compatible with the gauge, and therefore the gauge is a key parameter in determining interoperability. Due to historical reasons, different countries adopt different track gauge. In general, there are three types of track gauge including standard gauge, wide gauge and narrow gauge. The size of the standard gauge which was developed by Stephen George with the original mail coach's gauge in 1,825 is 1,435 mm. At present, United States, Canada, most of Europe countries and some Asia countries are using the standard gauge. Gauge wider than 1,435 mm is called wide gauge. Usually, wide gauge that consists of 1,524 mm, 1,600 mm and 1,670 mm are used by Soviet Union, India, and Australia. Gauge narrower than 1,435 mm is called narrow gauge including 1,067 mm, 1,000 mm and 762 mm. Besides a few countries have adopted size of 1,067 mm and 1,000 mm for main line gauge, narrow gauge is mainly used in industrial and mining enterprises. Sixty percent of the world's railways use standard gauge.

Track gauge is measured by track ruler or other suitable means. The error in track gauge should not be 6 mm wider or 2 mm narrower. That is to say, the track gauge on straight track should not be greater than 1,441 mm, nor smaller than 1,432 mm. The change of track gauge should be smooth enough and not exceed 2 mm in 1m. Otherwise it will cause excessive vibrations of the rolling stocks even when the error is within its allowable limit.

Since the track gauge is greater than the wheel set width, there will be a gap between the rail and wheel flange, called clearance. In Fig. 3-2, when one flange of the wheel is closely contact with the rail, then the clearance between the other wheel flange and the rail will be got as below:

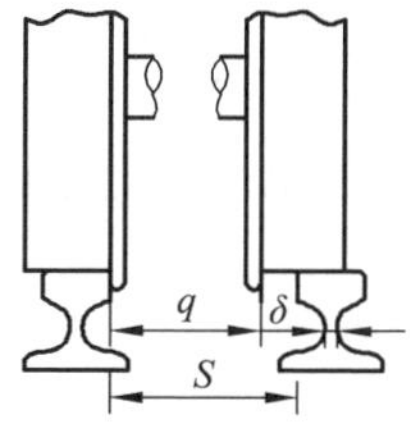

Fig. 3-2 The clearance between rail and wheel flange

$$\delta = S - q \tag{3-1}$$

Where S—track gauge;

q—Wheel set width.

Let S_0, q_0—Standard gauge and normal wheel set width respectively, then the normal clearance will be

$$\delta_0 = S_0 - q_0 \tag{3-2}$$

Let S_{max}, S_{min}—Maximum and minimum track gauge respectively, then the maximum and minimum clearance max, min will be

$$\delta_{max} = S_{max} - q_{min} \tag{3-3}$$

$$\delta_{min} = S_{min} - q_{max} \tag{3-4}$$

Since, on straight tracks, the values of maximum, minimum and normal clearance are calculated as shown in Tab. 3-1.

Tab. 3-1　The value of clearance

Wheels	δ_{max}	δ_0	δ_{min}
Locomotive wheel	45	16	11
Vehicle wheel	47	14	9

The clearance between rail and wheel flange is not only necessity, but also an objective reality. It has its advantages and disadvantages as regard to the train operation. Its advantages are to prevent the wedging of the wheels in the track, thus alleviating the train resistance and wear between wheel and rail. Nevertheless, it should not exceed certain allowable limit, otherwise the effect will be even worse. This is because of the larger clearance, the greater will be the hunting motion of the train, also the greater will be the attack angle between the wheel and rail and the force acting on the rail. The higher the train speed is, the more serious will be the effect of the clearance.

3.2.2 Track alignment(or profile)

Marking the position of center line on the ground and giving direction to track is known as alignment of the railway track. The term alignment is used in both horizontal and vertical layouts to describe the line uniformity of the rails. The alignment or location of the railway track comprises of the following two components:

• Horizontal components. It includes the straight path, its width, curves and deviations in width and curves.

• Vertical components. It includes changes in vertical curves and gradients.

Both these components play a vital role in determining the alignment of a railway track. The alignment of a new railway track should be done after careful study of the area. The improper alignment would either prove uneconomical in initial cost of construction or in maintenance of the track and vehicle operations or both. Once the track aligned and constructed, it becomes impossible to change it due to increase in cost of adjoining land and high cost of construction etc.

1. Basic requirements of a good alignment

In case of a railway alignment the profit is not the only criterion, but the needs of the area for its development it is going to fulfill. More stress should be given to the convenience and comfort of the passengers. An ideal alignment should fulfill the following requirements.

(1) Purpose of opening the new track. Need the purpose of opening a new track, such as transportation services, military defense purposes, connecting industrial centers, shorting the existing distance etc.

(2) It should be feasible to construct and maintain. The alignment should be such that it is easy to construct and maintain the track. The alignment also should be easy for the operation of vehicles with easy gradients and curves and it completed within stipulated resources.

(3) It should be economical. The alignment could be considered economical if the total cost including initial cost, maintenance and operation cost is minimum.

(4) It should be safe for the traffic. The alignment of the track should be such that it is safe for the traffic and it can be constructed and maintained safe. This can be achieved by selecting stable slopes, and foundations of the embankments etc. The foundations should be maintained properly.

2. Factors controlling the alignment

For an alignment, to be economical it should be straight between the two terminal stations, but it is not always possible due to various practical difficulties such as intermediate obstructions, steep gradients and topography etc. between the shortest routes. Due to steep gradients the operations of vehicles will not be easy. There may also be construction and maintenance problems along the shortest route. Hence a railway track often has to be deviated from the shortest route in order to cater for the needs of the intermediate stations.

An alignment which is economical in the initial construction cost need not necessarily be the most economical in maintenance cost or vehicle operation cost or both. It may also happen that the shortest and easiest alignment for vehicle operation may prove to be costliest of different alternatives from construction point of view. Thus it may be concluded that all the requirements cannot be met simultaneously and judicious choice has to be made considering all the factors.

3. Alignment measurement

The horizontal alignment is done by using a predefined length of string line (such as 20 m in Australia and 10 m in China) to measure along the gauge side of the reference rail. It is the distance (millimeters) from the midpoint of the string line to the gauge of the reference rail. The design horizontal alignment for tangent track is zero (perfect straight line on the horizontal layout). The design horizontal alignment on the curved track in China is 4 mm for main lines, and 6 mm for sidings and spurs for each degree of curvature. Any other readings indicate deviations.

The vertical alignment (not to be confused with rail profile) is the surface uniformity in the vertical plane. The measurement of uniformity is done using a predefined length of string line (normally the same length used in horizontal alignment) along the track. If the midpoint of the measurement has higher elevation, it is called hump deviation. On the other hand, if the midpoint has lower elevation, it is called dip deviation. These deviations from design alignment are used as parameters to assign speed limits.

3.2.3 Cross level

Cross level (Fig. 3-3) is the measurement of the difference in elevation (height) between the top surfaces of the two rails at any point of railroad track. The two points (each at the head of each rail) are measured at by the right angles to the reference rail. Since the rail can slightly move up and down, the measurement should be done under load.

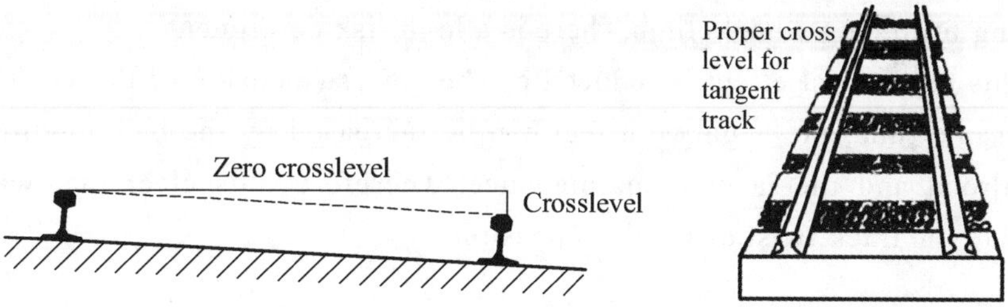

Fig. 3-3 Cross level

.In straight track, it is said to be zero cross level when there is no difference in elevation of both rails. In curved track, however, the outside rail is raised. The condition of cross level where one rail is purposely raised is known as superelevation and is discussed fully in later chapter.

The cross level is measured by a ruler or other tool. The allowable error of the cross level shall not exceed 4 mm at the main line and departure line of the maintenance line, and the other lines shall not exceed 6 mm. The change of the cross level can not be too large. Within the distance of 1 m, the change is not more than 1 mm; otherwise, even if the horizontal error of the two rail is not more than the allowable range, it will cause the strong vibration of the locomotive and rolling stock.

3.2.4 Track twist(or warp)

As Fig. 3-4 shows, within a distance, the left rail has higher elevation than the right rail, then the right rail has higher elevation than the left rail, and the distance between the two maximum horizontal error points is less than 18 m. According to this phenomenon, the rails are not in the same plate, and only 3 out of the 4 wheels of a vehicle or boogie will be leaning on the rails, and therefore one wheel will be "free". The wheel that is not leaning on the rail causes likewise the reduction of the height of the flange of the wheel that is in contact with the rail. when operating a train along such track, the motion will be rocking left and right that may result in the trains rocking back and forth and

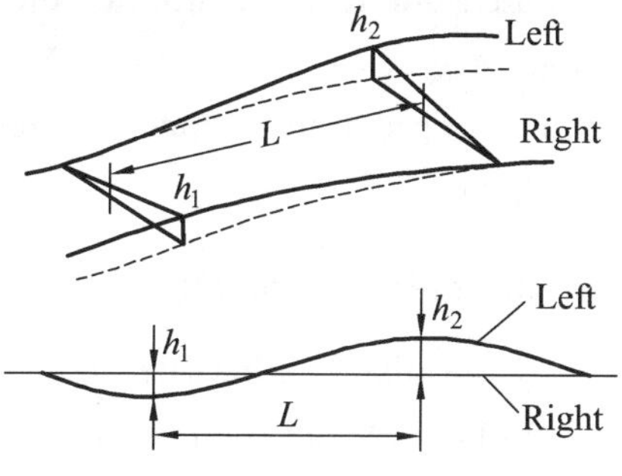

Fig. 3-4 track twist

derailing following wheel climb.There is a high risk derailment.

This track twist effect is reduced by the very suspension of the vehicle, but at the same time, the negative effect can be increased by the bad conditions of the railroad and the lack of maintenance. Therefore it is clear that we must eliminate the track twist as much as possible.

3.2.5 Rail cant

1. Theory of bicone[2]

The BICONE is a geometrical element composed of two solid cones, linked by their common base.

If we throw this solid element through two guides of fixed width, we will notice that it will roll with a rocking transversal-movement and a loop longitudinal-movement, always trending to center in the guides' axis. In order to produce such rolling effect, then following conditions have been fulfilled:

- Rolling along parallel guides.
- Coning of Rolling movement.
- Very low gravity center.

The railway rolls along parallel guides, the wheels are truncated cone-shaped, and the gravity center is very low. All these features provide the ensemble a significant stability.

The axles circulate along the straight line tracing a loop movement: the axle oscillated due to the coning of the wheel and the existing play between rail and flange, necessary to prevent excessive friction. The rail is placed with a tilt in order to improve the contact between wheel and rail and to adapt to the coning of the wheels.

2. Coning of wheels

If the distance between the inside edge of the flanges is kept equal to the gauge distance, the flanges of the wheel would rub against the inside face of the rail. To prevent this, the distance between the inside edge of the wheel flanges is kept less than the gauge distance.

If the rim of the wheels rests flat on the rails there would be lateral movement of the axle resulting in damage to the inside edge of the rails. This is prevented by sloping the wheels at a slope of 1 in 20. This sloping of the wheel from the vertical axis is known as "Coning of wheels".

When the wheel negotiates a curve, the outer wheel has to cover a greater distance than the inner wheel. The axils therefore shifts laterally towards the outer rail increases and that at the inner rail decreases. The outer wheel therefore is able to cover the additional distance without any "slipping" taking place.

One of the undesired effects of "Coning of wheels" is that the pressure of the wheel is always towards the inner edge of the rail which tends to wear out quickly. To reduce this wear of the rail, the rails are also placed at an inward slope of 1 in 40 as illustrated in Fig. 3.5. The cutting of the sleeper to provide tilting of the rail is known as rail cant.

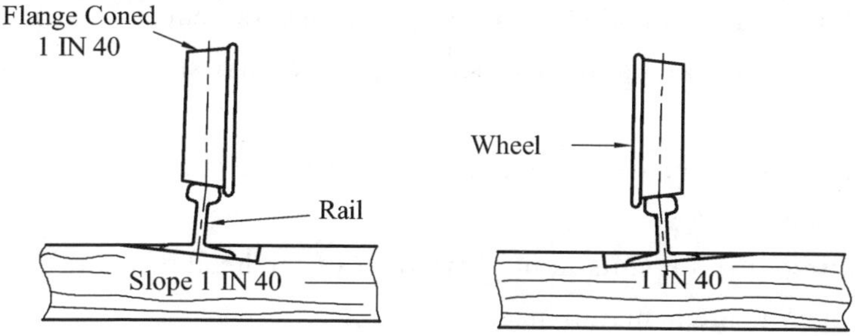

Fig. 3-5 rail cant

3. Rail cant

The load on the rail is a resultant of vertical and lateral wheel load forces. Ideally, the resultant should pass vertically downward through the center of the rail head and waist. Because the wheel load is applied eccentrically, that is, offset by a small amount from the center of the rail head, and because of lateral thrust, the resultant will pass outside the centerline, with the lateral component forming an overturning moment. The rail tends to rotate about its outer base corner (field side) and the field side of the sleeper plate tends to dig into the sleeper. To lessen these overturning and sleeper-destroying tendencies, rail cant is introduced into the sleeper plate to tilt the rail inward and bring the rail load resultant closer to the centerline of the rail. Note that in so doing, a greater area of wheel tread is in contact with the rail head, there by lessening the contact pressures.

The amount of cant to be introduced is subject to debate. High-cant advocates claim a reduction in contact stresses, shelly defects, and gauge corner abrasion, as well as a reduction in plate cutting and gauge widening as the resultant is brought closer to the vertical. Low-cant advocates cite increased torsion in the rail, with possible waist failures and head and waist separations, accompanying high cants, also crushing of the low rail and possible overturning can occur. Some even advocate a flat rail bearing surface with no cant.

Talbot's committee experimented with several cants, including a 1 : 20 cant to match geometrically with the 1 : 20 coning of wheel treads. The wheel coning, however, rapidly wears away in service, rendering a geometric match irrelevant. A 1 : 40 cant, found to give the most favorable results, is recommended and is in almost universal use in China. More recently, in USA, plates with cants of 1 : 14 and 1 : 30 have been available, usually for use on curves, with the 1 : 30 receiving especially favorable comment. Japanese high-speed lines use a 1 : 60 cant.

The advantages and disadvantages of rail cant are summarized below:

(1) Advantages:

① Tilting of rail results in uniform wear of the head of the rail.

② Proper gauge is maintained.

③ Life of sleeper and rail is increased.

(2) Disadvantages:

① This horizontal thrust tends to turn the rail outwardly. Sometimes this results in the increase in the gauge distance.

② Sleepers under the outer edge of the rail are likely to get damaged. This effect is reduced either by having "Rail cant" of sleepers or by providing inclined base plate as illustrated. According to American practice, the wear on rails is reduced by reducing the slope from 1 in 20 to 1 in 40, which is the same in China.

3.2.6 Gradients

The topographical conditions usually require some kind of vertical-longitudinal gradients, along the way. Building bridges and tunnels is a very expensive way to manage the topography constraints. In particular heavy railway traffic has problems to overcome large longitudinal gradients. Therefore restrictions for the amount of gradient are needed. This rise or fall of the track level per unit length of the track is known as gradient, as shown in Fig.3-6

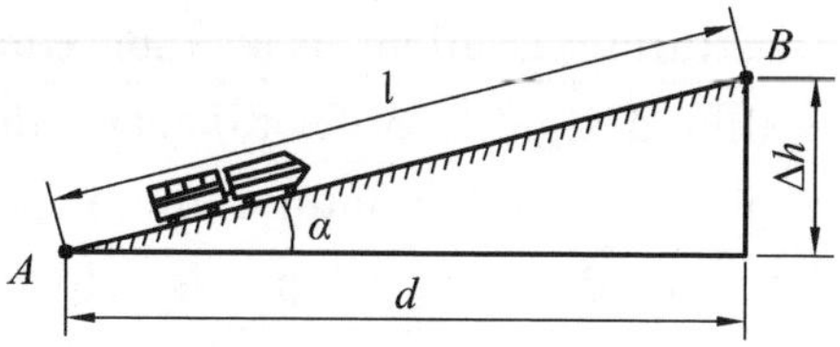

Fig. 3-6 gradients

The track is normally divided into sections such that the gradient between these sections is the same. It is not practicable to have the same gradient along the entire track for the following reasons:

(1) The natural longitudinal slope of the country is not uniform.

(2) The track alignment is not based on the consideration of direct construction between the starting and the terminating points, but the intermediate obligatory points have necessarily to be considered.

(3) In mountain, railways in particular unstable portion of the hill or in areas where excessive rock cutting over considerable length is involved normal gradient has to be varied.

(4) In bridge approaches, to avoid heavy embankment over a considerable length of the approach steeper gradients are adopted.

So the following requirements need to be considered because they have an effect on railway traffic[11]:

① The power supply and energy consumption will increase with large gradients.

② Heavy freight trains with an ordinary locomotive may have problems to climb up the gradient.

③ Braking distances increase for high-speed and freight trains in an ascending gradient.

Thus, large gradients result, principally, in heavier locomotives, increased locomotive, power, and/or less freight train weight, and/or reduced speed and line capacity, and/or requirement of higher braking capacity, and/or larger signaling distances.As compared to the gradients on the roads, much flatter gradients have to be provided on railways so that the speed and load carrying capacity of the trains is not sacrificed.

Gradients on railways may be classified into the following types: Ruling gradient, Momentum gradient, Pusher gradient, Station yard gradient.

1. Ruling gradient

Ruling gradient is the maximum longitudinal gradient allowed in the railline design. In order to ensure that all the uphill sections of the vehicle and train can pass smoothly, the ruling slope of roads and railways must be determined.Ruling slope is closely related to the engineering quantity, transportation capacity and operation expenditure, and sometimes even affects the direction of the line. It should be noted that it is the steeper gradient along the track which governs the maximum load carrying capacity of the train. For short stretches, however, slightly steeper gradient do not have any appreciable effect on the load carrying capacity, because a load which is designed to be carried at the design speed on a track can still be carried at steeper gradients by imposing speed restrictions.

2. Momentum gradient

The ruling gradient along a given section of the track may be exceeded without reducing the speed or load carrying capacity of the train if a falling gradient is followed by a rising gradient. While the train goes down the falling gradient, it gains momentum. This gain in momentum is utilized in negotiating a stretch of the track along which the gradient is steeper than the ruling. The steeper gradient provided in such cases is termed as "Momentum Gradient". Usually, when the train enters the gradient, it slows down under the action of large resistance, and uses locomotive traction and kinetic energy to break through the top of the slope no less than the calculation speed of the locomotive.

3. Pusher gradient

In undulating areas or in hilly terrain, it is very often not possible to restrict the gradient to the ruling one. The normal gradient would mean increasing the length of the track considerably resulting in heavy excavation. Gradients much steeper than the ruling are provided in such cases. In such cases if the locomotive designed for normal ruling gradient were to be used, the load would have to be reduced drastically or speed of the trains would have to be very much slowed down. This difficulty is overcome by providing one more locomotive to help in negotiating the steep gradient as if by "Pushing" from behind. The stretch along which this pushing engine or additional locomotive is employed to help negotiate the steep gradient is said to be having "pusher gradient"

4. Station yard gradients

As for as possible the track along the stations and yards should be level. This however would create drainage problem of the station complex and hence. On platforms however, the gradients are completely avoided. The reasons for decide the gradients along platform and yards are as below: a) An engine which is to start would require additional force during the starting of the train if it is to pull the train along up gradient. b) Bogies, standing on yard would start moving if the wind blows along the direction of the down gradient.

3.2.7 Surface (or longitudinal level) [6]

The concept of surface is somehow difficult to differentiate from gradient and cross level. As commonly used, surface describes the smoothness of track. Technically, it is the height relation of successive points along one rail of a track. Proper track surface is attained when the rail is at the same height throughout its length or when its elevation changes evenly. Proper and poor surfaces are compared in Fig. 3-7. Although gradient is also a height relation of successive points along track, this term should be used in referring to large changes occurring over long distances. The term gradient should be reserved for changes of elevation purposely made when the line was constructed. Surface, on the other hand, refers to irregularities of elevation occurring because of faulty maintenance.

Fig. 3-7 Proper and poor surface compared

The irregularity data is based on the measurement of a 10 m chord- versine. The principle of this technique is to assess the gap corresponding to the observed roughness of a straight-line in the center point of the track in the 10 m distance measurement. This gap is then defined as track geometry irregularity. The Fig. 3-8 illustrates how the track geometry parameters are measured.

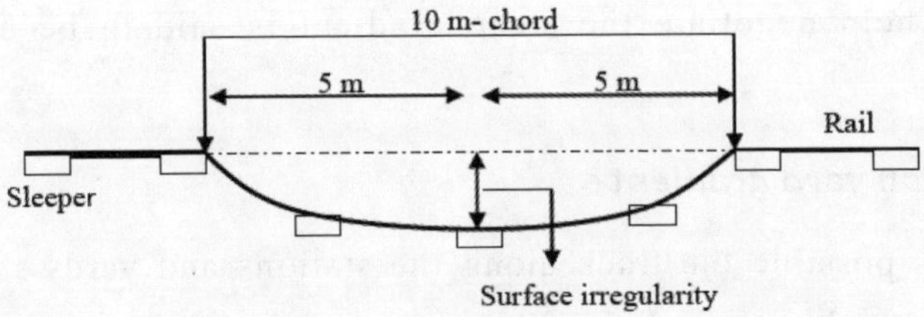

Fig. 3-8 Track surface irregularity and measurement

3.2.8 Irregularity [11]

In general, the geometric deviations mentioned above all belong to track irregularities. Track irregularity is the main cause of train vibration and wheel rail action force increasing. It has an important influence on driving comfort and safety, and is a major factor restricting the speed of trains directly. The two important parameters of track irregularities are wavelength and amplitude. On main lines, in particular on high-speed lines, less irregularities are permitted than on lines for lower speeds. Track irregularities can be represented by the following description:

(1) Vertical irregularity, deviation from the designed vertical alignment (center line).

(2) Lateral irregularity, deviation from the designed lateral alignment (center line).

(3)Gauge irregularity, deviation from nomial gauge.

(4)Cant irregularity, deviation from designed cant.

The four different irregularity types are illustrated in Fig.3-9.

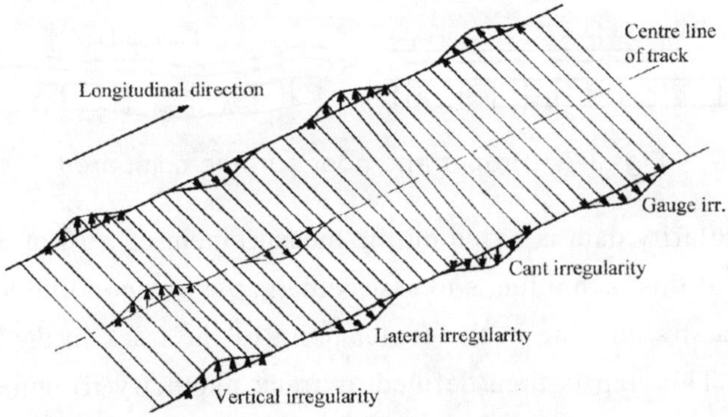

Fig. 3-9 track surface irregularities

3.3 Track Super-elevation[11]

On the curve, due to the action of inertia centrifugal force, the running locomotive and vehicle are push to the outer rails, thus the friction of the outer rails increase and make passengers discomfort , goods displaced. Therefore, raising the outer rail of the curve properly helps to achieve the uniform force of the inter and outer rails, to minimize friction and wear, to improve the stability and safety of the line. The measurement of the difference in elevation between the outer rail and the inner rail is called super-elevation in most countries (also referred to as track cant, cross slope, cross fall, or camber), as shown in Fig. 3-10. Sometime the super-elevation is measured in term of angle instead of height difference. In China, it is measured in height difference.

When the outside rail is at higher elevation than the inside rail, it is called positive super-elevation. This is normally the desired layout for curved track. Most countries achieve the desired level of positive super-elevation by raising the outside rail. In some countries (such as Swiss railroad), the super-elevation is done by rotating at the track axis (center of the two rails) to have outside rail elevated (raised) at the half rate of the desired super-elevation and the inside rail under elevated (lowered) at the same half rate of the desired super-elevation. When the outside rail is at lower elevation than the inside rail, it is called negative super-elevation (or reverse cross-level in the United States). This is not usually a desired layout but it may be unavoidable in some situations such as curves involving turnouts. There are regulations which limit the maximum super-elevation. This is to control the unloading of the wheels on the outside rail, especially at low speeds.

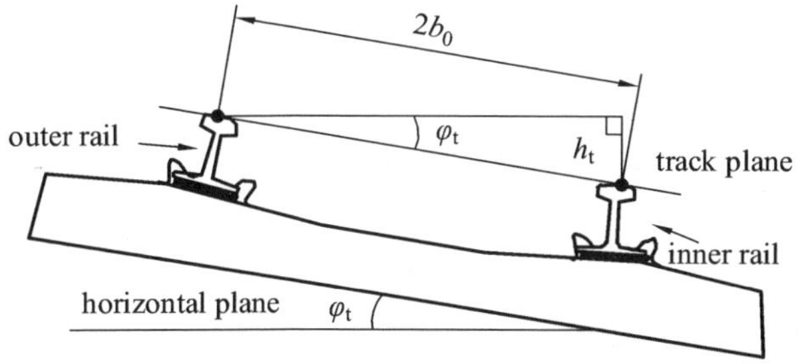

Fig. 3-10 Super-elevation

3.3.1 Track plane acceleration[11]

In case of quasistatic curving (i.e. curving at constant speed, radius and cant on perfect track geometry) the vehicle is exposed to two acceleration: horizontal centrifugal acceleration and gravitational acceleration, see Fig. 3-11. The resultant of the acceleration vector can be split up into two components: a_y is parallel to the track plane, and a_z is perpendicular to the track plane, see Fig. 3-11.

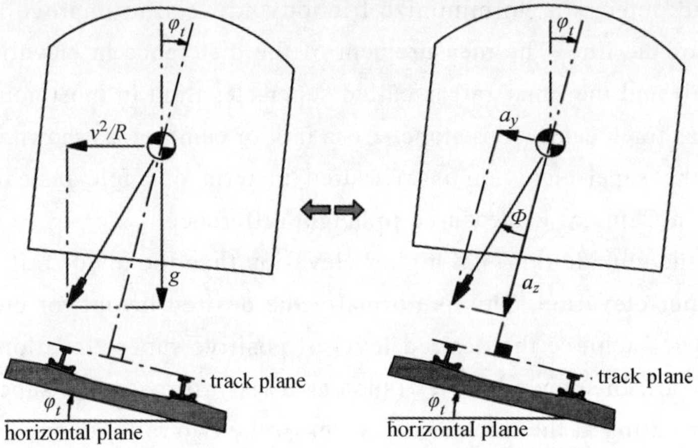

Fig. 3-11 Definition of track plane acceleration a_y and lateral force angle φ

The acceleration a_y is called track plane acceleration or, simply, lateral acceleration. The equations can be written as follows:

$$a_y = \frac{v^2}{R} \cdot \cos\varphi_t - g \cdot \sin\varphi_t \tag{3-5}$$

$$a_z = \frac{v^2}{R} \cdot \sin\varphi_t + g \cdot \cos\varphi_t \tag{3-6}$$

Where, $2b_0$=1,500 m (on standard track gauge),

v is the vehicle speed running on curve,

h_t is the super-elevation of curve.

Assuming φ_t is small angels, the equations can be approximated by:

$$a_y \approx \frac{v^2}{R} - g \cdot \sin\varphi_t = \frac{v^2}{R} - g \cdot \frac{h_t}{2b_0} \tag{3-7}$$

$$a_z \approx g \tag{3-8}$$

The lateral force angel ϕ in Fig. 3-11 are related to the acceleration a_y and a_z in accordance to the following equation

$$\phi = \arctan \frac{a_y}{a_z} \tag{3-9}$$

3.3.2 Equilibrium super-elevation and balanced speed

1. Equilibrium super-elevation

The super-elevation which gives $a_y=0$,for a given vehicle speed is called equilibrium super-elevation, h_{eq}. The equilibrium super-elevation can be got from equation3-7, thus

$$h_{eq} \approx \frac{2b_0}{g} \cdot \frac{v^2}{R} \tag{3-10}$$

Equation(3-10) are based onSI-units. In Practice it is useful to express speed v in "km/h" and super-elevation in "mm" shown in Equation(3-11)

$$h_{eq,mm} \approx \frac{2b_{0,mm}}{g} \cdot \frac{v^2}{3.6^2 \cdot R} \tag{3-11}$$

The equation can be simplified further if the values $2b_0$ for standard track gauge and the gravitational acceleration g are used

$$h_{eq,mm} \approx \frac{1,500}{9.81} \cdot \frac{v^2}{3.6^2 \cdot R} \approx 11.8 \cdot \frac{v^2}{R} \tag{3-12}$$

2. Equilibrium speed.

The amount of super-elevation which is provided depends on not only the speeds of fastest trains but also on the slow goods trains using the track. Therefore super-elevation provided with a view that fast trains travel safely without discomfort to passengers and slow trains may run safely without fear of derailment. The suitability of the super elevation used depends greatly on the selection of the average speed. There are different ways for selecting the average speed v_{eq} among which are:With consideration to the speed and mass of the trains, for a given curved track, the super-elevation h_{eq} and the distance between rail centers $2b_0$ are constant and unchangeable, but the mass of train and its speed and centrifugal force are different for different trains. We must have:

$$v_{eq} = \sqrt{\frac{\sum mv^2}{\sum m}} = \sqrt{\frac{\sum NPv^2}{\sum NP}} \tag{3-13}$$

Where, P is the mass of the train. v is the train speed and N is the number of trains passed daily with the same mass and speed.

Without consideration of the mass of train, calculate v_{eq} according to the trains with different speeds.

$$v_{eq} = \sqrt{\frac{\sum Nv^2}{\sum N}} \tag{3-14}$$

Where, N is the number of trains passed daily with the same speed.

Empirical formula for calculating v_{eq} for new line,

$$v_{eq} = 0.8v_{max} \tag{3-15}$$

In which, v_{max} is the maximum speed designed (km/h).

3.3.3 Super-elevation deficiency and super-elevation excess

For several reasons, fully compensated track plane acceleration can not be achieved in all cases according to:

- It is a possibility that a train stops or runs slowly in a curve. Therefore, the maximum super-elevation has to be limited. It is then desirable to allow a super-elevation deficiency, i.e., a certain amount of uncompensated lateral acceleration a_y remains in the track plane.
- Not all trains have the same speed. Therefore, it would not be possible to achieve fully compensated lateral acceleration for all trains anyway.

1. Super-elevation deficiency

When the super-elevation is less than the equilibrium super-elevation aso called deficiency arises. super-elevation deficiency h_d is the difference between equilibrium super-elevation h_{eq} and actual super-elevation h_t and is thus determined by the following equation:

$$h_d = h_{eq} - h_t \tag{3-16}$$

With equation (3-10) substituted into (3-16)we get :

$$h_d = \frac{2b_0}{g} \cdot \frac{v^2}{R} - h_t \tag{3-17}$$

A common way to write the formula is shown in equation(3-18).The speed v is expressed in km/h and super-elevation and super-elevation deficiency is expressed in mm.

$$h_{\mathrm{d,mm}} = 11.8 \cdot \frac{v^2}{R} - h_{\mathrm{t,mm}} \tag{3-18}$$

An additional way to express super-elevation deficiency is to solve equation (3-7) for v^2/R and substitute the expression into equation (3-17) and relate super-elevation deficiency to the track plane acceleration which gives.

$$h_{\mathrm{d}} = \frac{2b_0}{g} \cdot a_{\mathrm{y}} \tag{3-19}$$

Where $a_{\mathrm{y}}>0$.

2. super-elevation excess

If the actual super-elevation is higher than the equilibrium super-elevation, something called super-elevation excess will be introduced. super-elevation excess is the difference between actual super-elevation and equilibrium super-elevation and is defined as:

$$h_{\mathrm{e}} = h_{\mathrm{t}} - h_{\mathrm{eq}} \tag{3-20}$$

Super-elevation excess is achieved when the vehicle is running at a lower speed than the design speed of the track. Super-elevation excess can be related to lateral acceleration in the same way as super-elevation deficiency shown in Equation (3-20)

$$h_{\mathrm{e}} = -\frac{2b_0}{g} \cdot a_{\mathrm{y}} \tag{3-21}$$

Where $a_{\mathrm{y}}<0$ and $h_{\mathrm{e}}>0$.

3. Maximum value of unbalanced super-elevation

The super-elevation is maximized with respect to stationary conditions and slowly running trains. A maximum value is set for super-elevation because of the following problems which arise if a train is forced to stop or run slowly in a curve:

- Passenger discomfort at standstill or low speed;
- Risk of derailment of freight trains in sharp curves due to the combined effect of high lateral and low vertical load on the outer wheel at low speed;
- Possible displacement of wagon loads;

The unbalanced super-elevation is another means of expression for the unbalanced centrifugal or centripetal acceleration a_y. We can get the formula (3-22).

$$\frac{v_{\max}^2}{R} - \frac{gh_{\text{eq}}}{2b_0} < a_y \tag{3-22}$$

Then $11.8\frac{v_{\max}^2}{R} - h_{\text{eq}} \leqslant 153a_y$, and the maximum value $h_{\text{d,lim}} = 11.8\frac{v_{\max}^2}{R} - h_{\text{eq}}$

Then $h_{\text{d,lim}} \leqslant 153a_y$

In China, it is specified that the unbalanced centrifugal acceleration should not exceed 0.4-0.5 m/s^2, under special circumstances, not exceed 0.6 m/s^2. So,

If a = 0.5 m/s^2, then $h_{\text{d,lim}}$=76 mm

If a = 0.6 m/s^2 时, then $h_{\text{d,lim}}$ = 92 mm

We also specify that the allowable deficient super-elevation should not exceed 60-70 mm, under special circumstances, not exceed 90 mm.

3.3.4 Permissible speed with respect to radius, super-elevation and super-elevation deficiency

On any curved tracks, the super-elevation is fixed in accordance with the average speed; therefore the maximum speed for trains negotiating the curved tracks will be limited by the allowable unbalanced super-elevation as specified.

With a given horizontal curve radius and permissible lateral acceleration $a_{\text{y,lim}}$, or permissible super-elevation deficiency, $h_{\text{d,lim}}$, an expression for permissible speed, v_{lim}, can be expressed in many different ways:

$$v_{\text{lim}} = \sqrt{R\left(\text{a}_{\text{y,lim}} + \text{g}\cdot\frac{h_{\text{t}}}{2b_0}\right)} = \sqrt{\frac{R\cdot g}{2b_0}(h_{\text{d,lim}} + h_{\text{t}})} = \sqrt{\frac{R\cdot(h_{\text{d,lim}} + h_{\text{t}})}{11.8}} \tag{3-22}$$

In equation (3-23) permissible speed, v_{lim}, is given in km/h while super-elevation h_{t} and permissible super-elevation deficiency $h_{\text{d,lim}}$ are given in mm. Radius is always given in meters. Standard gauge is assumed.

With maximum super-elevation as 150 mm, the relations between the maximum allowable speed and the radius of curve are as follows equation (3-23) and equation (3-24):

If $h_{\text{d,lim}}$ = 75 mm, $$V_{\text{lim}} = \sqrt{\frac{(150+75)R}{11.8}} = 4.3\sqrt{R} \tag{3-23}$$

If $h_{\text{d,lim}}$ = 90 mm, $$V_{\text{lim}} = \sqrt{\frac{(150+90)R}{11.8}} = 4.5\sqrt{R} \tag{3-24}$$

Under ordinary conditions, the maximum allowable speed may be calculated by the following:

$$v_{\lim} = 4.3\sqrt{R} \tag{3-25}$$

If we limit the maximum train speed on curved tracks according to the unbalanced super-elevation allowed, the safety of train operation can be guaranteed.

3.3.5 Rate of super-elevation and rate of super-elevation deficiency

In the railway, in transition curve, the variation of the curvature is proportional to its length, so the super-elevation will also be proportional to the length. Namely, when a vehicle passes through the transition curve, the transversal acceleration with regards to the time ("over acceleration",) must be kept within acceptable limits.

1. Rate of super-elevation (super-elevation gradient) as a function of time

The following relationship are used for super-elevation gradients with linear superelevation deficiency, where Δh_t is the super-elevation variation over the transition length L_i:

$$\frac{\mathrm{d}h_t}{\mathrm{d}t} = \frac{\Delta h_t \cdot v_{\max}}{L_t} \tag{3-26}$$

2. Rate of super-elevation deficiency as a function of time

Rate of super-elevation deficiency describes the change of lateral acceleration (in the track plane) as a function of time. Another word for rate of cant deficiency is lateral jerk.

For transition curves with a linear change of curvature and super-elevation deficiency with linear variation:

$$\frac{\mathrm{d}h_d}{\mathrm{d}t} = \frac{\Delta h_d \cdot v_{\max}}{L_t} \tag{3-27}$$

3.3.6 Tilt technology

Several trains with tilt technology are today operating in large scale at maximum speeds 200-250 km/h(Italy, Sweden, Finland, Germany and also in the UK). Trains with tilt technology have the opportunity to operate at a higher super-elevation deficiency and hence at higher speeds in curves. The possible percentage of overspeed is among other things, limited by:

(1) Possible lateral accelerations and roll motions with respect to passenger comfort. This is an issue of suspension and carbody tilt control.

(2) Possible tilt angel within the vehicle (in particular between bogies and carbody).

(3) Permissible track forces. This is mainly an issue of track design and maintenance, as well as suspension in the running gear. For vertical track forces also the unsprung mass, axle load and location of centre of gravity are important factors.

3.4 Track transition curves

A track transition curve, or spiral easement, is a mathematically calculated curve on a section of highway, or railroad track, where a straight section changes into a curve. It is designed to gradually change the curvature and super-elevation of the track, so as to prevent sudden changes in lateral (or centripetal) acceleration, as shown in Fig. 3-12.

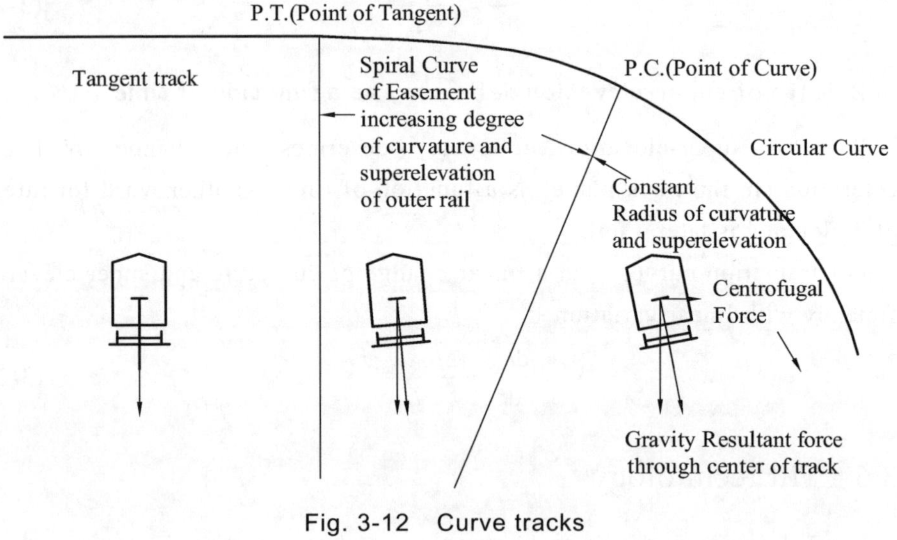

Fig. 3-12 Curve tracks

3.4.1 Curves

Curve tracks usually create more problems than do straight tracks. Problems of line, gauge, cross level, sleeper wear, rail life, and ballast are intensified on curves.

Train speeds and safety are directly related to the degree of curve and super-elevation carried. Spiral approaches contribute to smoothness of ride. Horizontal and vertical curves have to be introduced along the track alignment for the following reasons :

(1) To join obligatory points. The two stations to be connected by the track should as far as possible be joined by straight track. However if towns, villages and places of interest lie along the alignment, the track alignment has to be diverted. Similarly suitable sites for important bridges necessitate the deviation from straight alignment. This deviation from the straight is done by introducing horizontal curves so that the train may change its direction without causing discomfort to the passengers or without appreciable reduction its speed.

(2) To avoid certain locations. Sometimes swampy or marshy areas fall in the straight alignment. At other times scenery places like temple, protection zone or church may fall on the straight alignment. In order to avoid track along these places, deviation from the straight has to be introduced.

1. Horizontal curves

The most distinguished parameter for a circular curve is the radius, R=constant, which is inverse proportional to curvature, $k=1/R$. The radius is related to the center of the track. A vehicle running at a speed v in a curve with a radius R undergoes a centrifugal lateral acceleration $a=v^2/R$ which results in a number of undesirable effects. These effects can be:

- possible passenger discomfort;
- possible displacement of wagon loads;
- risk of vehicle overturning in combination with strong side winds;
- risk of derailment caused by flange climbing of a wheel on the outer rail or by loosening of rail fastenings;
- high lateral forces on the track.

Calculation of horizontal curve elements, the parameters shows in Fig.3-14:

$$\text{Tangent distance} = T = R\tan\alpha/2 \tag{3-28}$$

$$\text{Long chord} = L = 2R\sin\alpha/2 \tag{3-29}$$

$$\text{Midordinate} = M = R(1-\cos\alpha/2) \tag{3-30}$$

$$\text{External distance} = E = R(\sec\alpha/2 - 1) \tag{3-31}$$

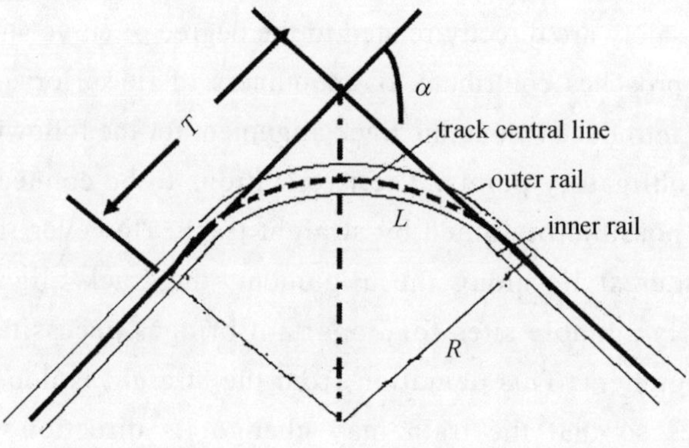

Fig. 3-13 The definition of horizontal circular curve radius R

2. Vertical curves

A vertical curve provides a smooth transition between successive tangent gradients in the railway profile. In charges of gradients a suitable radius must be used. If the vertical acceleration on a crest is too great, the loads on the vehicle wheels can cause the wheels to climb the rail and thus cause a derailment. Furthermore, the resistance against vehicle overturning at side-winds will be lower. It is also important that passenger comfort is being ensured. How two adjacent gradients are related to the vertical curve radius and the profile elevation is shown in Fig. 3-14.

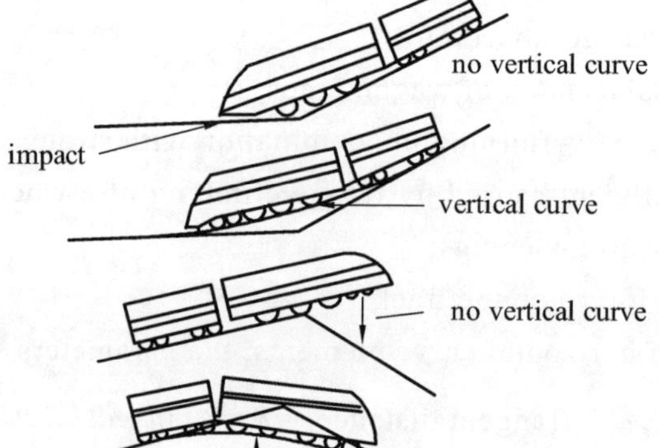

Fig. 3-14 Need for vertical curves.

and shows in the Fig.3-15:

$$\omega = |i_1 - i_2| \tag{3-32}$$

$$L = R \times \omega \tag{3-33}$$

$$T = L/2 \tag{3-34}$$

$$E = T^2/2R \tag{3-35}$$

$$y = x^2/2R \tag{3-36}$$

Where i_1, i_2—two tangent grades;

ω—algebraic difference in grades;

R—radius of the vertical curve;

L—length of the vertical curve;

T—tangent length;

E—external distance;

x—cross distance;

y—offset.

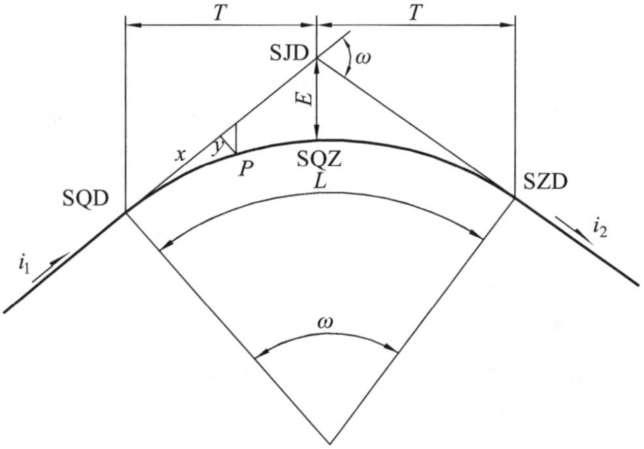

Fig. 3-15 The definition of horizontal circular curve radius R

3.4.2 The function of transition curves

A train travelling over a curve at uniform speed, produces centrifugal force of certain magnitude depending upon its weight and speed. As long as this force remains uniform or increased or decreased at a uniform rate no discomfort is felt by the passengers inside the train. A train travelling on a straight track with uniform speed has no radial acceleration, but as soon as the train enters a circular curve from the straight, the full radial acceleration is transferred to the vehicle.

The radial acceleration is countered by the raised outer rail on the curve. The change from the straight to a circular curve is instantaneous at the tangent point and therefore full radial acceleration exists at the tangent point. The outer rail can not be raised suddenly above the inner rail at the tangent point. This results in unbalanced forces over a length required for obtaining full super-elevation. These unbalanced forces, if excessive will be detrimental to the vehicle, and track due to lateral thrust. If the radial acceleration is attained suddenly or above a certain rate, it will cause great discomfort to the passengers. Sometimes even derailment may occur. Therefore it is essential that curvature and super elevation in the outer rail and the curvature in the inner rail is attained gradually by the use of transition curve. During the transition curve the centrifugal force is built up gradually by running out the super elevation slowly at a uniform rate.

Transition curves should achieve the following objectives:

- To attain the gradual rise of the outer rail. It helps in attaining the desired super elevation in the track gradually.
- To decrease the radius of curve gradually from infinite at the straight end of the track to that of the circular curve at the junction with the circular curve of the selected radius.
- To provide smooth running of vehicles and to provide comfort to the passengers.
- To reduce the chances of derailment. The provision of transition curves reduce the chances of derailment to a great extent.

An ideal transition curve should satisfy the following requirements.

- It should be truly tangential to the straight part of the track.
- The length of the transition curve should be such that full super-elevation is attained at the junction of the transition and the circular curve.
- The rate of increase of curvature should be equal to the rate of increase of super-elevation.
- The curvature of the transition curve should conform with that of the circular curve. The transition curve should join the circular arc tangentially.

3.4.3 The geometric features of transition curves

Assume that the purpose of a transition curve in between a straight section and a circular curve section is to provide a linear change of curvature. A typical transition curve is shown in Fig. 3-16. In this curve, "r" denotes the radius of curvature of the transition curve. The radius of curvature at the intersection of the transition curve and the tangent is infinitely large (R=∞), and the radius of curvature at the intersection of the transition curve and the circular curve is the same as that of the circular curve itself ($r = R$). In general, the transition curve and the super-elevation ramp have the same start and end points, i.e., the curvature and the super-elevation in transition curves correspond to each other, as shown in Fig. 3-17.

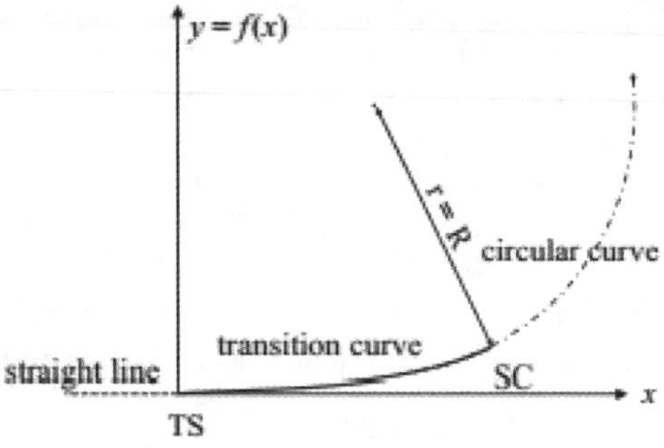

Fig. 3-16 Transition curve

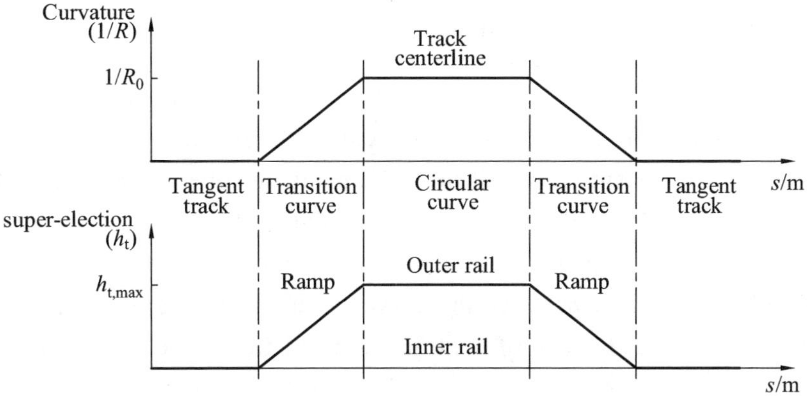

Fig. 3-17 Super-elevation ramps of transition curve

Super-elevation ramps shall be formed in straight line, as shown in Fig. 3.19 (a), and in curve, as shown in Fig. 3.19 (b). Using straight line super-elevation ramp, when the train passes through the transition curve, it will have impact on the outer rail at the start and end point of the curve, thus, the train speed can not be too fast. For high-speed train, in order to eliminate the impact of the train on the outer rail, super-elevation ramps should be treated as curve, and the ramp angles of the start and end of the transition curve are zero, $\gamma=0$.

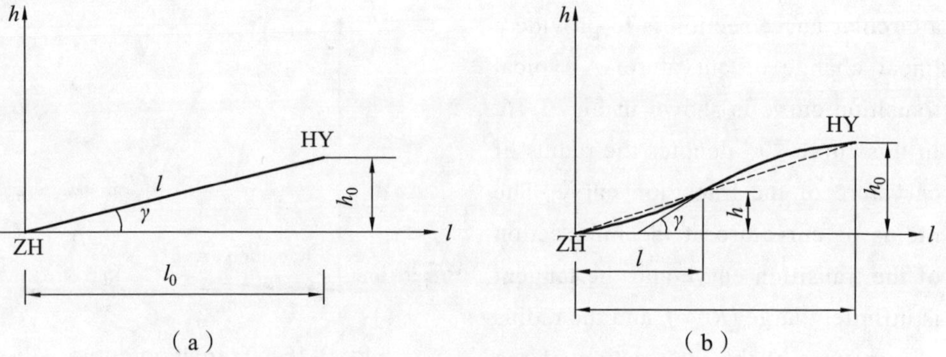

Fig. 3-18 Super-elevation ramp

When the transition curve connects a circular curve with a radius less than 350 m, within the entire transition curve length, the gauge widens linearly from zero to the value of circular curve widening.

3.4.4 Shapes of transition curves

The "main" elements in railway transition curve are: The radius of curvature at the end of transition, the length L of the curve, the length l of its projection on x axis and the coefficient k. Two of these elements must be given in order for the curve to be defined, the other two can be calculated. The secondary elements of the curve are: the coordinates R_x and R_y of the center of curvature at the end of the transition, the shift f between the curve R and the x axis, the angle τ of the tangent to the curve at the end of the transition and and y_l, the y coordinate of the curve at length l. When the "main" elements are known, the "secondary" elements can easily be calculated (Fig. 3-19).

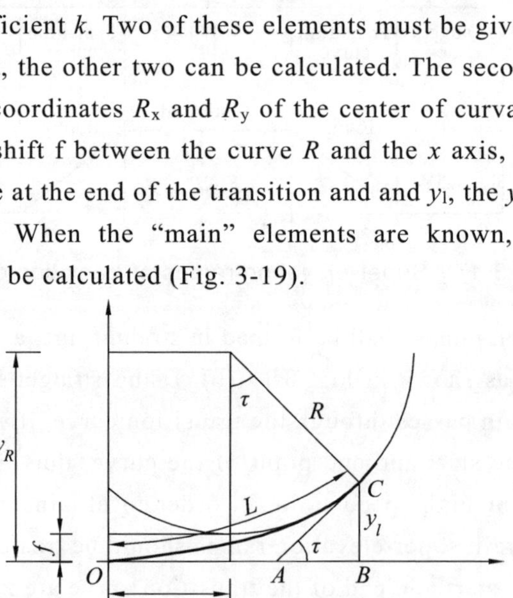

Fig. 3-19 Elements of transition curve

Following types of transition curves can be adopted:

(1) Spiral curves (or clothoid). It is an normal curve for transition and fulfills all the conditions of an ideal transition curve. The radius varies from infinity at the tangent end of the spiral to the radius of the circular arc at the circular curve end. The radius of the spiral is inversely proportional to the length of the curve and the rate of change of centrifugal acceleration is uniform throughout the length of the curve. The radius of curvature *R*=1/length of curve. The formulas of spiral curves is equation (3-37):

$$R \times L = A^2 \tag{3-37}$$

Where *R*—radius of any point of the spiral;

L—length of spiral from O to any point along the spiral;

A—Parameters of Spiral curves showing the change level(sharp or gentle) of the spiral curvature.

(2) Cubic parabola. the radius of curvature of the circular curve as well as the start and end point of the tangent can be treated as constants. The curvature of the transition curve, which connects the tangent and the circular curve, increases linearly. The advantage of cubic parabolic transition curve is that it is easy to lay and maintain, and the length of transition curve is short. The drawback is that there is an angle between the start and end points, which affects the operate stability. The formulas of cubic parabola is

$$y = \frac{x^3}{6RL} \tag{3-38}$$

Where *y*—vertical ordinate at a distance x from the commencement of curve;

x—distance of any point on the tangent from the commencement of the curve;

L—total length of transition curve;

r—radius of curvature of the circular curve.

(3) High order transition spirals. With the train speed increase, cubic parabola transition curve is difficult to fully meet the travel comfort requirements, orbital stability conditions also affected. In order to improve this situation, some countries adopts curve super-elevation ramp on transition curve. Within the transition curve range, super-elevation ramp changes according to the curvature of transition curve. When trains pass these shape transition curves, all kinds of force does not suddenly appear and disappear, adapt to the needs of the

high-speed driving. Therefore, higher order transition curves are general used in high-speed railway. The correct choice of transition curves generates an interaction between the vehicle and the railway track, resulting to protect each other and the interaction to be controlled. Some high order transition spirals are listed in Tab.3-4

Tab. 3-2 High order transition spirals

Transition spirals	Basic equations	Equations
Zhao's seventh power equation	$\frac{d^2K}{dl^2}=Bl\left(l-\frac{l_0}{2}\right)(l-l_0)$	$y=\frac{l_0^2}{R}\left[\frac{1}{7}\left(\frac{l}{l_0}\right)^7-\frac{1}{2}\left(\frac{l}{l_0}\right)^6+\frac{1}{2}\left(\frac{l}{l_0}\right)^5\right]$
Salmonella sinusoidal	$\frac{d^2K}{dl^2}=B\sin 2\pi\frac{l}{l_0}$	$y=\frac{l_0^2}{R}\left[\frac{1}{6}\left(\frac{l}{l_0}\right)^3-\frac{1}{4\pi^2}\left(\frac{l}{l_0}\right)+\frac{1}{8\pi^3}\sin\frac{2\pi l}{l_0}\right]$
the Japanese high-speed railway Half wave sinusoidal	$\frac{dK}{dl}=B\sin\pi\frac{l}{l_0}$	$y=\frac{l_0^2}{6R}\left[\frac{3}{2}\left(\frac{l}{l_0}\right)^2+\frac{3}{\pi^2}\left(\cos\frac{\pi l}{l_0}\right)-1\right]$

3.4.5 Length of transition curves

The length of transition spiral is influenced by many factors, among which the safety requirement of train operation and comfort requirement of passengers are the most important ones.

1. safety requirement

With the rolling stocks negotiate the curved tracks, neglecting the influence of the track elasticity and coil spring of cars, the two wheels at one end of the bogie will be in contact with rail surface, while at other end of the bogie, the outer wheel will be and the inner wheel will not be in contact with the rail surface. In order to ensure safe operation of trains, the wheel flange should not climb over the inner rail surface. Let i_0 be the slope of the super-elevation, L_{max} be the maximum length between wheel axis of the bogie, then the gap between the inner wheels tread and the rail surface will be $i_0 \cdot L_{max}$. In case this gap is greater than the minimum wheel flange height K_{min}, there will be the danger of derailment.

$$i_0 L_{max} \leqslant K_{min} \tag{3-39}$$

$$i_0 \leqslant \frac{K_{min}}{L_{max}} \tag{3-40}$$

The length of spiral l_0 should be

$$l_0 \geqslant \frac{h_0}{i_0} \tag{3-41}$$

Where h_0—super-elevation of the circular curve.

For transition spirals with curved super-elevation slope, its maximum slope must also fulfill the requirement of equation (3-40), and calculated by the following formula,

$$i = \frac{\mathrm{d}h}{\mathrm{d}l} = \frac{S_1 v_p^2}{g} \frac{\mathrm{d}K}{\mathrm{d}l} \tag{3-42}$$

When $\frac{\mathrm{d}i}{\mathrm{d}l} = 0$, or $\frac{\mathrm{d}^2 K}{\mathrm{d}l^2} = 0$, $i = i_{max}$

For curved super-elevation slope, this will be located at the middle of the transition spiral where $l = \frac{l_0}{2}$.

According to Chinese practice, in order to ensure the safety against derailment, the slope of the straight super-elevation should not exceed 2‰.

2. comfort requirement

1) the rate of rise of wheels on translation curves is not too rapid

Knowing the actual super-elevation, the spiral length can be computed. Let l_0 be the length of spiral, then $l_0 = v_{max}\, t$ and $t = l_0 / v_{max}$, where v_{max} is the train speed in meter per second and t is the time in seconds to travel l_0. Also, during time t, the outer wheel of the train are rising a distance h, the actual super-elevation in millimeter, so that $h = ft$, where f is the rate at which super-elevation is increasing in mm per second. From this, $t = h / f$. The times t are the same in both situations, so that the rate of rise of the wheels on the outer rail is calculated as follows,

$$f = \frac{h v_{max}}{l_0} \ (\mathrm{mm/s}) \tag{3-43}$$

Where h—super elevation on circular curves(mm);

v_{max}—maximum train speed(m/s);

l_0—length of circular curves(m).

In order to ensure the travelling comfort of the passengers:

$$l_0 \geqslant \frac{h}{f} v_{max} \tag{3-44}$$

or

$$l_0 \geqslant \frac{h}{3.6f} v_{max} \tag{3-45}$$

Where v_{max}—maximum train speed(km/h);

1/3.6—conversion factor.

According to the long term practices in China, under ordinary conditions, f=32 mm/s, that is $l_0 \geqslant \frac{h}{100} v_{max}$; under extraordinarily difficult conditions, f=40 mm/s and is used instead, that is $l_0 \geqslant \frac{h}{144} v_{max}$.

In china, the length of the circular curve between two transition spirals should not be less than 20 m. While reconstructing or double tracking the existing lines, it is allowed that this should not be less than 14 m under difficult conditions.

2) the transversal acceleration of wheels on translation curves do not exceed standards

When a vehicle passes through the transition curve, the variation of the transversal acceleration with regards to the time ("over acceleration", da_t/dt) must be kept within acceptable limits.

$$l_0 \times R = \frac{dl_c}{d(1/r)} \tag{3-46}$$

$$a_t = \frac{v^2}{r} \tag{3-47}$$

$$da_t = v^2 \times d(1/r) \tag{3-48}$$

$$l_0 \times R = \frac{dl_c \times v^2}{da_t} \tag{3-49}$$

$$\frac{dl_c}{dt} = (l_0 \times R / v^2) \times \frac{da_t}{dt} \tag{3-50}$$

$$\frac{dl_c}{dt} = v \tag{3-51}$$

$$\frac{da_t}{dt}=\frac{v^3}{l_0\times R} \tag{3-52}$$

Where l_0—length of translation circular curves;

R—radius of the translation circular curve;

l_c—length from the tangency point with the straight line to any other point of the spiral;

r—radius of the transition curve in this point.

Knowing that for the transversal acceleration we have allowed as acceptable the value of 0.65 m/s^2, for the over-acceleration (da_t/dt), we will set a maximum value of 0.4 m/s^3.

3.5 Gauge Widening of Curves

Due to the rigidity of the wheel base, sometimes the rails are titled outwards due to the impact of outer wheels of the front axle against the outer rail. This impact results in greater actual gauge than the theoretical gauge. If this tendency is not checked there is every possibility of tilting rail outwards. Therefore to prevent this tendency, the gauge of the track on the curve is some times widened. The amount of gauge widening depends upon radius of curve, gauge width and the length of rigid wheel base of the vehicle likely to be used on the track. The rigid wheel base is defined as the distance between two adjoining axles which are held in a rigid frame.

While entering the curved tracks, the rolling stock will strive to retain its original direction because of the action of inertia. Its direction will be changed only when the wheels are acted by the directive force of the outer rail. In order to ensure that the rolling stocks will negotiate the curved tracks smoothly, with minimum lateral force and wear between the wheels and rail, the track gauge should be widened appropriately on curved tracks with very small radius. This is realized by shifting the inner rail inward but still retaining the position of outer rail unchanged.

Nevertheless gauge widening should satisfy certain requirements and confine within certain reasonable limits. Under the concrete conditions of the track and rolling stocks in China, the maximum gauge which can ensure the wheels not to derail on curved tracks is 1,450 mm, or a gauge widening of 15 mm. Gauge widening larger than necessary will cause excessive lateral thrust on the rail, so it should be controlled strictly.

Since the cars occupy a predominate majority in the trains, the requirements of the smooth negotiation of the essential type or cars are used as the basis of calculation while formulating the gauge widening standard. For locomotives and few special type of cars, the gauge required will be checked in case it is necessary.

3.5.1 Geometrical requirements for rolling stocks negotiating (traversing) curved tracks

During curve negotiation, two or tree axles of rolling stocks remain parallel, or nearly parallel. Due to rigid guiding in rolling direction, it occurs additional friction force between wheel and rail. Additional friction is the consequence of: longitudinal creep of wheels on the same axle due to path length difference, lateral slip of wheels on inclined track level, increased slip between wheel flange and rail due to forced guidance of wheel set, and centrifugal force. Force which occurs during curve negotiation is influenced by: condition of wheels and rail head, track curve radius, length of rigid wheelbase, track width and other parameters (impurities of contact surfaces, climate conditions and similar) .

As mentioned before, there are certain definite gap between the rail and wheel flange. The existence of the clearance will cause the frame or bogie of the rolling stocks to occupy different positions in the track while negotiating the curved tracks. That is to say, the cars can negotiate the curved tracks with different geometrical inscribing. Generally speaking, there are four types of inscribing as follows:

(1) Inclined loose inscribing position of bogies negotiating curved track. The outer front wheel flange on the frame or bogie of the rolling stocks is in contact with the gauge line of the outer rail, while the inner rear wheel flange is in contact with the gauge line of the inner rail, as shown in Fig. 3-20(a).

(2) Free inscribing position of bogies negotiating curved track. The outer front wheel flange on the frame or bogie of the rolling stocks is in contact with the gauge line of the outer rail, while the other wheels are free to drive on the track without contact, as shown in Fig. 3-20(b).

(3)Wedged inscribing position of bogies negotiating curved track. All the outer wheels of bogie at the same time is in contact with lateral gauge line, while the middle rim of inner wheels (odd number) or the two wheels closest in contact with the inner track gauge, as shown in Fig. 3-20(c).

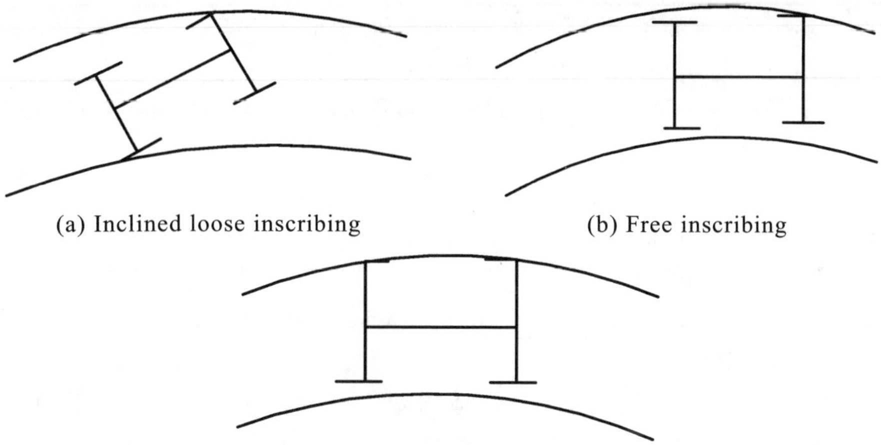

(a) Inclined loose inscribing (b) Free inscribing

(c) Wedged inscribing

Fig. 3-20 Three types of inscribing

(4) Normal forced inscribing position of bogies negotiating curved track. To avoid the vehicles travers the curve track as wedged inscribing position, the gauge needs to increase $\delta_{min}/2$ (minimum clearance) on the gauge of wedged inscribing position. Then the bogie in the position of the curve is called normal forced inscribing.

3.5.2 Gauge widening for vehicle

The running gear of the essential type of cars in China is two axle bogies. When the bogie negotiates the curved track with free inscribing, the outer wheel flange of the bogie is in contact with the gauge line of outer rail and the rear axle occupies the position of the perpendicular radius of the cured as shown in Fig. 3-21. From which, the gauge necessary for the free inscribing S_f will be:

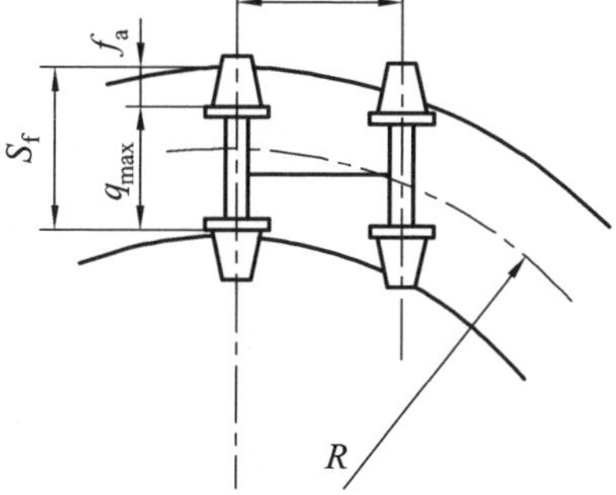

Fig. 3-21 Bogie free inscribing

$$S_f = q_{\max} + f_0 \tag{3-53}$$

Where q_{max}—Maximum wheel set width;

f_0—Versine of outer front and rear wheel flanges on the gauge line of outer rail;

$$f_0 = \frac{L^2}{2R} \tag{3-54}$$

Where L—Rigid wheel base of bogie;

R—Radius of curve.

Designate as the gauge on straight tracks, then the gauge widening on curved tracks will be:

$$e = S_t - S_0 \tag{3-55}$$

Where e —value of gauge widening

S_t—value of gauge for cars to pass over curve in free inscribing.

S_0 —value of normal gauge

The gauge of the curved track should not be less than that of the straight track. That is to say, no gauge widening is necessary for curved tracks with radius larger than 3500 m, and the same gauge for straight tracks 1,435 mm will be used. Tab. 3-3 shows the current standard of gauge widening for curved tracks used in China.

Tab. 3-3 The standard of widening for curved tracks

Radius/m	Gauge widening/mm	Gauge/mm
$R \geqslant 295$	0	1435
$295 > R \geqslant 195$	5	1440
$245 > R \geqslant 195$	10	1445
$R < 195$	15	1450

In China, it is specified that on class I and II railroads, the minimum radius for main lines should not be less than 300 m. This new standard will allow the gauges on most curved tracks to be the same as that on the straight tracks, which will greatly decrease the maintenance works required. It is also very similar to the standards adopted by most countries in the world.

3.5.3 Gauge widening for locomotives

Locomotive's rigid wheel base is very long. If it is allowed to negotiate the curved tracks with free inscribing, the gauge widening required will be very large. In fact, the proportion of locomotive in the train is much smaller than that of the cars, if locomotives are used as the controlling factor thc negotiating of cars along the curved track will be under very unfavorable condition. Weighing the gain and loss, we have to adopt the free inscribing of cars as the controlling factor from which the necessary gauge widening is formulated. After that, using the gauge widening already formulated, check whether the locomotive can negotiate smoothly under normal forced inscribing conditions.

Fig. 3-22 shows a four axle locomotive frame with lateral shift on each axle, negotiating around the curved track with wedged inscribing. If there are no clearance, the minimum gauge required will be

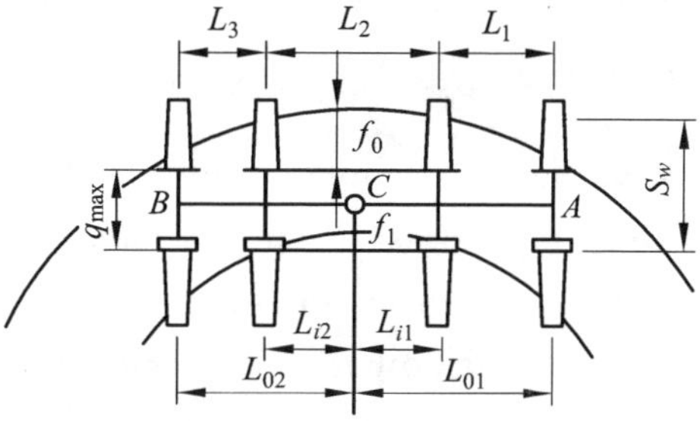

Fig. 3-22 Calculation chart of gauge widening on curve

$$S_w = q_{max} + f_0 - f_c \tag{3-56}$$

Where q_{max}—Maximum wheel set width;

f_0—Versine of outer front and rear wheel flanges on the gauge line of outer rail, equal to

$$f_0 = \frac{L_{01}^2}{2R} \tag{3-57}$$

Where L_{01}—Distance between the first axle and radius perpendicular to the longitudinal axis of the frame;

$$L_{01} = \frac{L_1 + L_2 + L_3}{2} \tag{3-58}$$

L_1—Distance between axle 1 and 2;

L_2—Distance between axle 2 and 3;

L_3—Distance between axle 3 and 4;

f_1—Versine of two wheel flanges nearest to the middle of the frame on the gauge line of inner rail, equal to

$$f_1 = \frac{L_{it}^2}{2R} \tag{3-59}$$

Where L_{it}—Distance between the second axle and radius perpendicular to the longitudinal axis of the frame, equal to:

$$L_{it} = L_{01} - L_1 \tag{3-60}$$

In order to improve the conditions for locomotives negotiating curved tracks with wedge inscribing, the clearance between the wheel and rail must be at least equal to one half of the minimum value on straight tracks. From which, the necessary gauges S'_w will be

$$S'_w = S_w + \frac{1}{2}\delta_{min} = q_{max} + f_0 - f_i + \frac{1}{2}\delta_{min} \tag{3-61}$$

For steam locomotive with very long rigid wheel base, certain measures have to be taken so as to avoid excessive gauge widening on curves, such as, to allow the driving axles with certain lateral shift or to make the driving wheel flanges near the middle thinner than other, even flangeless.

3.5.4 Maximum gauge widening on curves tracks

The maximum gauge on curved tracks should ensure the safe operation of trains, without any danger of derailment. Under the most unfavorable conditions, when one wheel flange of the wheel set is in contract with the rail, the 1 : 10 segment of the other wheel tread should cover entirely the surface of the other rail, as shown in Fig. 3-23.

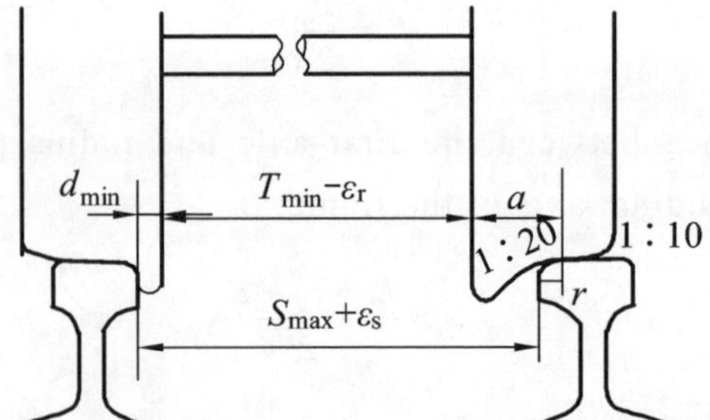

Fig. 3-23 The maximum permissible gauge track

The maximum permissible gauge on curved tracks can therefore be calculated by the following equation:

$$S_{max} = d_{min} + T_{min} - \varepsilon_r + a - r - \varepsilon_s \tag{3-62}$$

Where d_{min}—Minimum flange thickness of car wheel, equal to 22 mm;

T_{min}—Minimum inside diameter between wheel backs of car wheels;

ε_r—Decrease in the inside distance between wheel backs due to the bending of car axles, taken as 2 mm;

a—Distance between the wheel back and point of demarcation between 1 : 10 and 1 : 20 segments on the wheel tread, taken as 100 mm;

ε_s—Elastic squeeze-out of rail, taken as 2 mm;

r—Radius of circular arc at the corner of rail head, taken as 12 mm.

Substituting their appropriate values into the above equation, we have

$$S_{max} = 22 + 1350 - 2 + 100 - 12 - 2 = 1,456 \text{ mm}$$

Since the allowable error of track gauge shou1d not exceed +6 mm, so the maximum gauge and gauge widening allowed on the curved trucks will be 1,450 mm and 15 mm respectively

Professional Words and Expressions

track geometry 轨道几何形位
straight line 直线
horizontal curve 圆曲线
transition curve(or easement line)缓和曲线
vertical curve 竖曲线
gradient 坡度
rail gauge 钢轨规矩
narrow rail gauge 窄轨矩
broad rail gauge 宽轨距
cross level 水平
alignment 轨向
surface (or longitudinal level) 前后高低
super-elevation 超高
free inscribing 自由内接
inclined loose inscribing 斜接
wedged inscribing 楔形内接
normal forced inscribing 正常强制内接
rail cant 轨底坡
coning of wheels 车轮圆锥面
ruling gradient 限制坡度
momentum gradient 动能坡度
pusher gradient 推送坡度
station yard gradient 车场坡度
equilibrium super-elevation 均衡超高
equilibrium speed 均衡速度
super-elevation deficiency 欠超高
super-elevation excess 过超高

gauge widening of curves 曲线加宽

vehicle limited speed on curves 曲线上车辆限速

wheel flange 轮缘

wheel base 轴距

wheel set 轮对

wheel axle 轮轴

gauge widening 轨距加宽

maximum value of unbalanced super-elevation 未被平衡超高最大值

spiral curves (or clothoid) 螺旋型曲线

cubic parabola 立方抛物线

clearance between rail and wheel flange 游间

track twist 三角坑

high order transition spirals 高阶缓和曲线

CHARPTER 4 TURNOUTS

【 Primary Contents 】

(1) Functions and types of turnout

(2) Structure of normal simple turnout

(3) Factors affecting turnout speed

(4) Installation and maintenance of turnout

4.1 Introduction

4.1.1 Concept

In the case of roads the vehicle can be taken along any direction by manipulation of steering by the driver. In the case of a railway train, the driver has no means at his disposal to change the direction of the route from his locomotive. There is a kind of mechanical devices allowing the splitting of the railroad, the cross of two railroads or the circulation-change between different railroads. These devices include various turnouts (also called switch or points),crossing, crossover, etc. Sometimes, workmen refer to turnouts as "switches," but technically a switch is only one part of a turnout. To distinguish between the two terms in this book, the term switch is used only to refer to the pair of movable rails and the necessary connections that are used to divert a train to another track.

These devices consist of specially arranged points and crossings. The coordination between the proper setting of these points and crossings is intimated to the driver of the train by means of interlocking of signals. A signal on position is an indication to the driver that the turnouts are properly laid and the train can proceed ahead to the track indicated by the signal. If no track is free, the signal would be in stop position and the driver in that case stops the train by the application of brakes. The turnouts however are the weakest links in the track as the flanges of the wheels have to jump from one set of rails to the other. The driver has therefore to be cautious in negotiating the train on turnouts. Whenever turnouts are provided to divert train from one track to another, a track junction is formed. The turnout as we know it was patented by Charles Fox in 1832.

4.1.2 Type of turnouts

Turnouts divert trains to other tracks and give entry to body tracks in yards and industries. Turnouts commonly come in various combinations of configurations.

1. Simple turnouts

Various designs of turnouts have been tried, but simple turnouts are in almost universal use today. A single split turnout can make train divert between two tracks. A combination of switch and crossing by manipulation of which train from one track may be diverted to another track(or to branch line or to siding) is known as a turnout. The function of this combination is to ensure safe movement of trains from one track to siding (or branch line) or from branch line (or siding) to the main track.

The simple turnouts are likewise classified according to their shape and geometrical position:

1) Normal simple turnout

Normal simple turnouts are the most simple structure turnout, and have a big proportion in usage, for example, 90% in Chinese railway. Its mainline is straight line and branch line may be a left hand or right hand diversion depending upon the direction to which the train is to be diverted while observing the crossing from the facing direction. As the Fig. 4-1 (a) shows.

2) Symmetrical double turnout

This is also known as equivalent turnout. If two similar turnouts are taken out from a straight track in two different directions such a junction is known as symmetrical turnout. This track junction has the following features.

- The turnout is symmetrical about the centre line.

• The radius of the curve of the main track and the lead curve are equal.

• The junction consists of four curved lead rails, two check rails and one acute angle crossing as shown in Fig. 4-1(b).

• The junction enables the train to be turned either left or right of the main tracks.

3) convergent double turnout

A split is formed when a turnout is taken from a curved track. Its mainline and branch line are all diverted in the same direction, as shown in Fig. 4-1 (c).

4) divergent double turnout

The mainline and branch line are diverted in different directions, but not symmetrical, as shown in Fig. 4-1 (d).

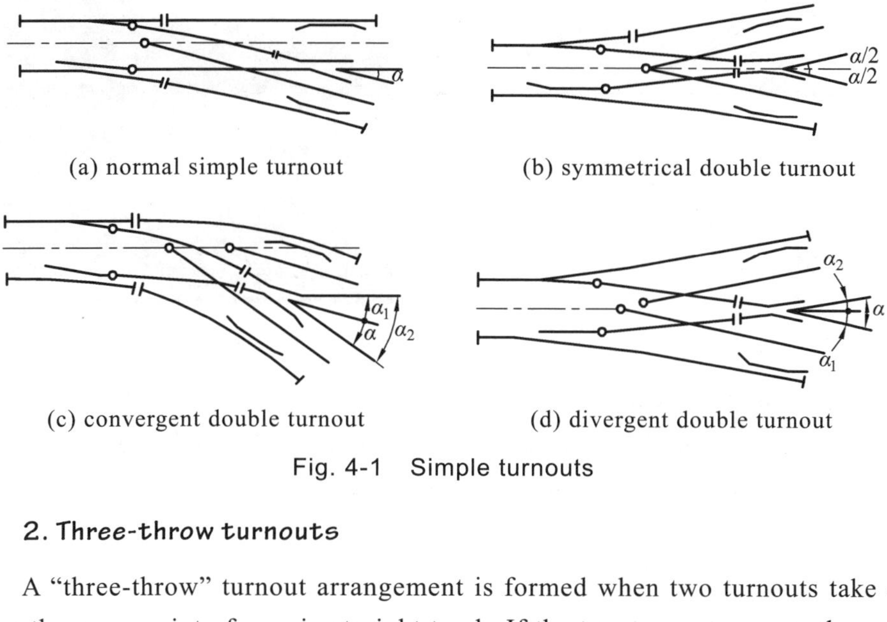

(a) normal simple turnout (b) symmetrical double turnout

(c) convergent double turnout (d) divergent double turnout

Fig. 4-1 Simple turnouts

2. Three-throw turnouts

A "three-throw" turnout arrangement is formed when two turnouts take off from the same point of a main straight track. If the two turnouts are on the same side of the main track they are called three-throw turnout with similar flexure when the two turnouts are on the opposite sides of the main track they are called three-throw turnouts with contrary flexure. Here the switches are separated with the tongue rails bearing against conventional stock rails instead of other switch tongue rails. The angles of crossing a_2 and a_3 may or may not be equal.

The heel block for both the tongue rails of the turnout recombined. It contains two turnouts and each turnout has its own set of tongue rails. There are three crossings and 4 or 6 check rails depending upon whether the junction is of contrary flexure or similar flexure as illustrated in Fig. 4-2. This type of turnout is unsuitable for main lines with heavy traffic, as influencing trains' speed greatly.

3. Crossing

Crossings are installed to carry one track across another at grade. Special provision is made for the passing of wheel flanges through opposing rails. The crossing angle is the angle between centerlines of the two tracks (or tangents to the centerlines if the tracks are curved).

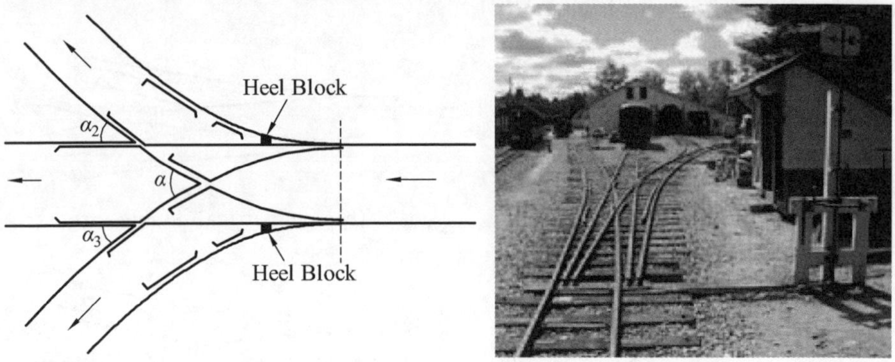

Fig. 4-2 Three-throw turnout (similar flexure)

1) Diamond Crossing

When two unparalleled tracks of the same gauge cross each other at an angle which is less than 90°, the shape of the crossing resembles a diamond and hence the name. It consists of two acute angles α and two obtuse angles β and four check rails illustrated in Fig. 4-3.

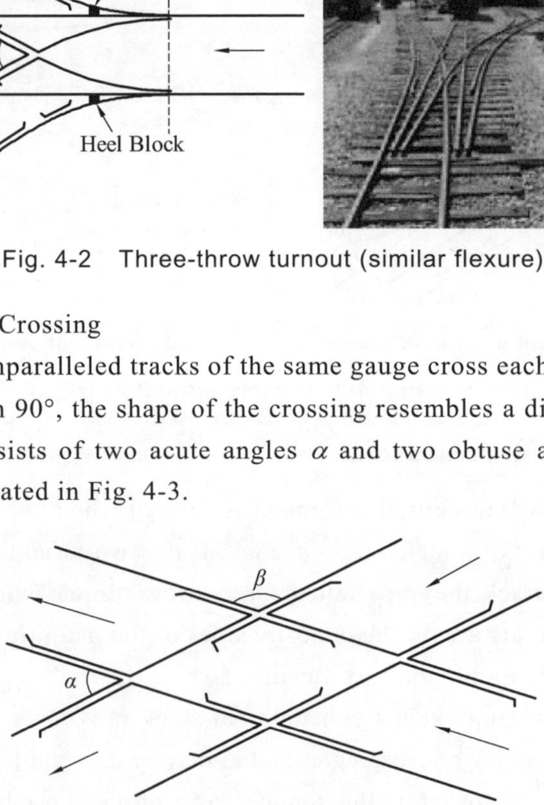

Fig. 4-3 Diamond crossing

2) Rigging-angle crossing or right-angle crossing

When the crossing is at right angles, all crossing angles are equal (90°), and crossings of a standard design can be used. The shape of the crossing is called rigging-angle crossing or right-angle crossing (Fig. 4-4).

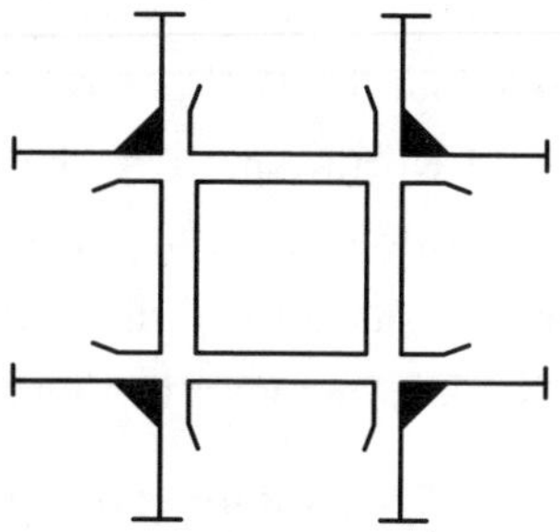

Fig. 4-4 Right-angle crossing

4. Slip turnout

Slip turnout includes single slip turnout and double slip turnout.

Single slip turnout (Fig. 4-5) consists of two point blades and a crossing, so only leading train entering one side track.

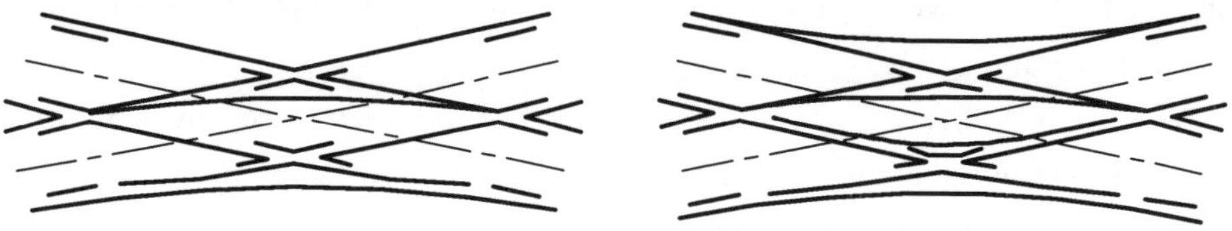

(a) Single ship turnout (b) Double slip turnout

Fig. 4-5 Single slip turnout and double slip turnout

Double slip turnout (Fig 4-6 (b)) is assembled of four simple turnouts and a crossing. The arrangement gives the possibility of setting four routes, but because only one route can be traversed at a time, allowing the pass from one railroad to another in both directions. Four point blades at each turnout are often connected to move in union, so the turnout can be worked by just two levers or

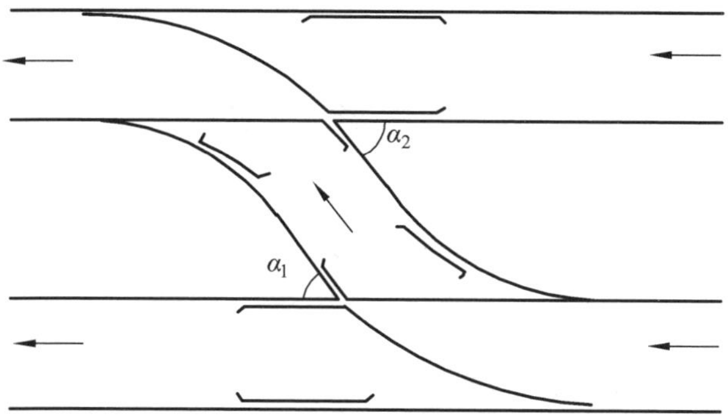

Fig. 4-6 Cross-over track

point motors. These compact and complex turnouts usually are found only locations where space is limited, such as station throats where a few main lines spread out to reach any of numerous platform tracks.

In North America, the arrangement may also be called a double switch, or more colloquially, a puzzle switch. The Great Western Railway in the United Kingdom used the term double compound points, and the switch is also known as a double compound in Victoria (Australia).

5. Cross-over (between parallel and diverging tracks)

Cross-over track junctions are formed when two adjacent track which may be parallel or diverging are connected by two sets of turnouts. These turnovers may or may not have straight length between them. The track consists of two points of turnouts, two acute angle crossings with reverse curves and four check rails as shown in Fig. 4-6.

The use of the reverse curves shortens the length of the crossover but at the same time restricts the speed. The use of this type of track junction is therefore limited to low speed sidings and yards.

6. Scissors cross-over

This is also known as Double Cross-over. This track junction enables trains from opposite direction to change the track. It consists of 4 pairs of points 6 acute angle crossings and two obtuse angle crossings as illustrated in Fig. 4-7 This type of cross-over is especially useful for shunting operation and serves the purpose of two crossovers.

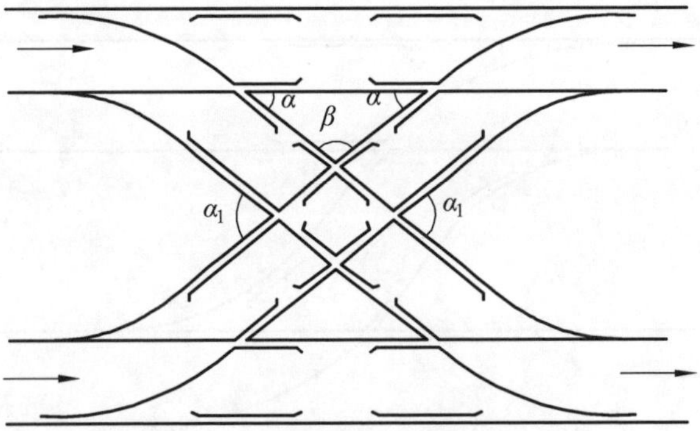

Fig. 4-7 Scissors cross-over

7. Gathering Lines or Ladder Track

This is special type of junction where a number of parallel tracks branch off from one straight track. The track junction is very suitable for railway sidings where wagons for different destinations may be shunted to different loops. Fig. 4-8 illustrates the pattern of the junction.

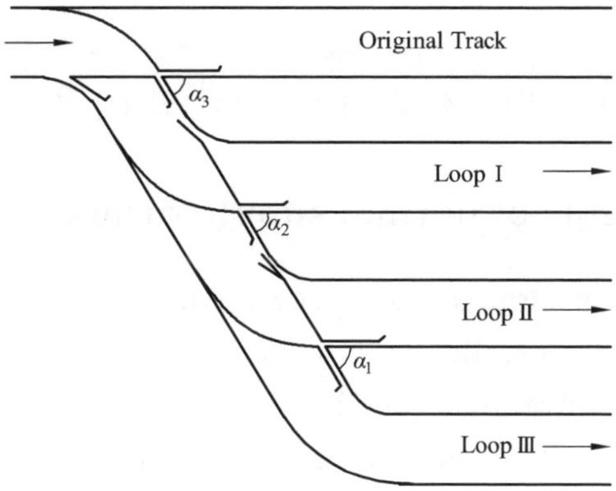

Fig. 4-8 Gathering lines or ladder track

8. Triangle track

The faces of engine are turned either by providing a turntable or by providing triangle junction. In case of an unimportant station and where enough area is available the high cost of installing a turn-table does not justify its construction. The triangle junction as shown in Fig. 4-9 consists of two simple turnouts and one symmetrical split.

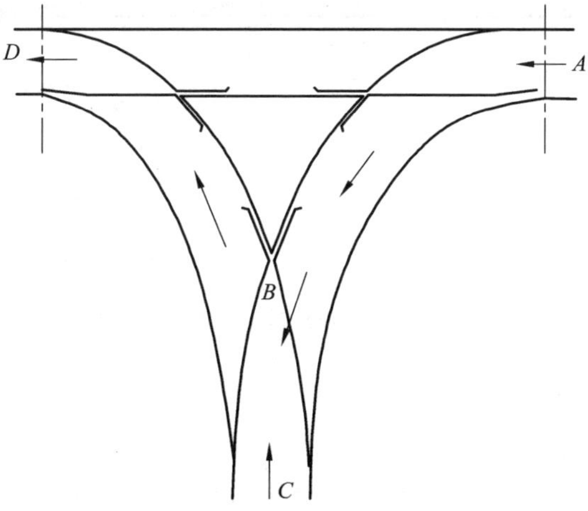

Fig. 4-9 Triangle track junction

The train standing faces the direction AD. In order to change its direction to DA, the train follows the following sequences:

1st stage: moves along *ABC*, from *A* to *B* and *B* to *C*.

2nd stage: moves along *CBD*, from *C* to *B* and *B* to *D*.

At the end of the second stage the train is facing the reverse direction *DA*.

4.2 Structure of normal simple turnout

4.2.1 Components of normal simple turnout

Various designs of turnouts have been tried, but the one in almost universal use today employs the so-called split switch. The normal simple turnout is the main unit of the rest of railroad junction devices, so we are going to study it in depth. A picture of the right-hand turnout is given in Fig. 4-10.

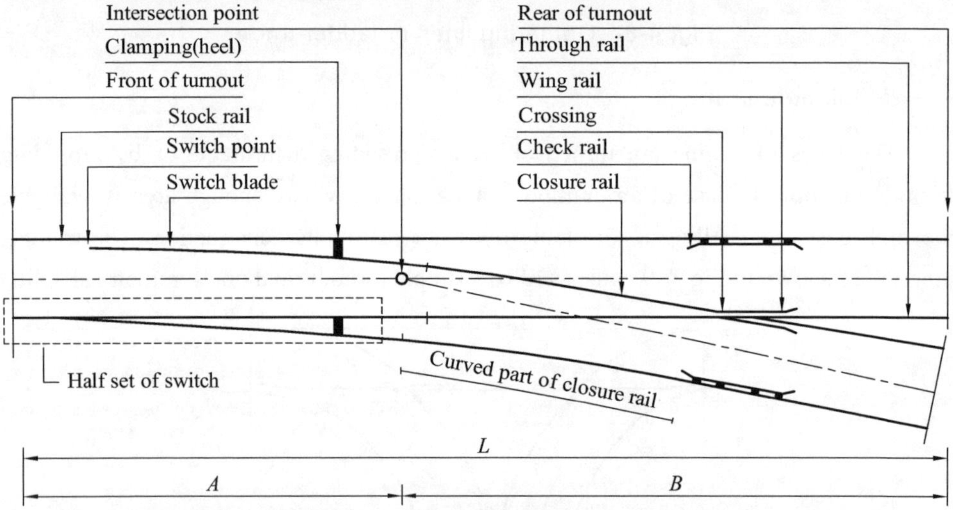

Fig. 4-10 Components of normal simple turnout

The normal simple turnout consists of three main parts:

1. The switches body

Switches is a device to guide wheels into different tracks, including two stock rails and two swithc rails mainly. Stock rails are the main rails of the track to which switch rails fit closely. In Fig. 4-11. AB and PQ are stock rails.

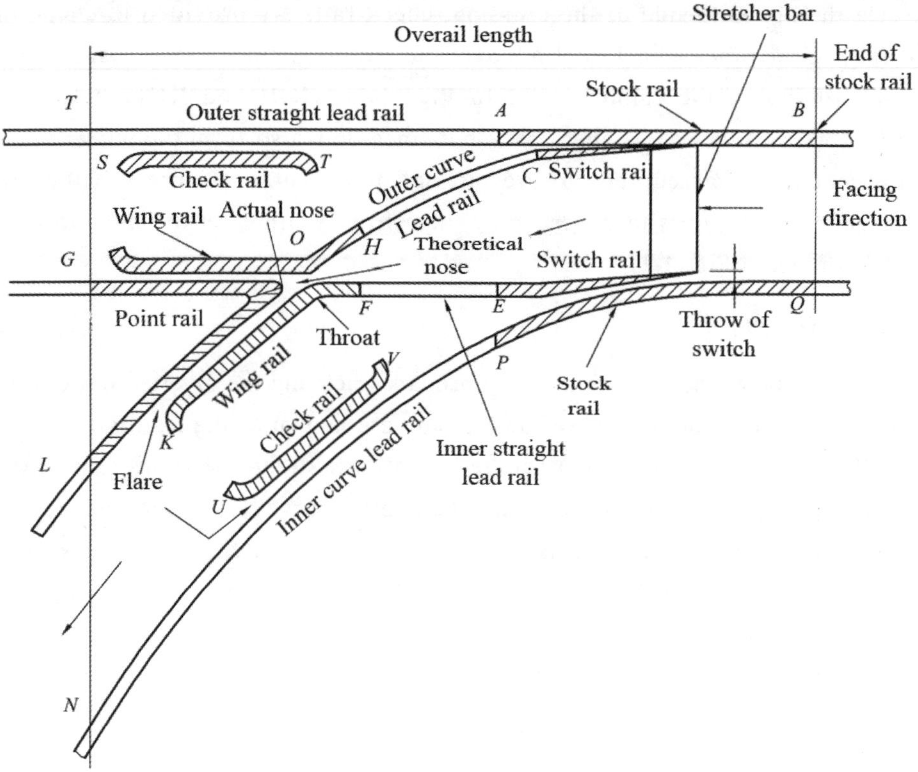

Fig. 4-11 Normal simple turnout

Switch rails (also called as points, tongue rails or point blades) are the movable rails which guide the wheels towards either the straight or the diverging track. They are tapered on most switches, but on stub switches they have square ends. In the UK, the term points refers to the entire mechanism, whereas in North America the term refers only to the movable rails.

2. The crossing and check rails

The crossing, also known as the common frog(or V-Rail in Australian terminology), refers to the crossing point of two rails. This can be assembled out of several appropriately cut and bent pieces of rail or can be a single casting of manganese steel. On lines with heavy use the casting may be treated with explosive shock hardening to increase service life. This term "frog" is taken from the part of a horse's hoof it most closely resembles.

On the opposite side of the crossing, check rails are provided to check the tendency of the other wheel to climb over the crossing, since the crossing causes a discontinuity in the running gap. In Fig. 4-11, GOH and KOFare two rail portions, which function as check rails but since they also form the wings or end sections of the outer curved closure rail and inner curve closure rail they are designated as wing rails to differentiate them from another set of check rails ST and UV shown in Fig. 4-11.

3. Lead rails

The portion of the main rails of the primary track and the diverted track which do not form part of the turnout or the crossing are known as the lead rails. In Fig. 4-11 AT and EF are outer straight lead rails and inner straight lead rail respectively while CH and PN form outer curve lead tail and inner curve lead rail respectively.

A normal simple turnout is composed of the switch proper to initiate diversion of the wheels, a crossing to carry the wheel flanges across opposing rails, lead rails between the crossing and the switch, and check rails to prevent batter and mis-routing at the crossing point. These compositions will be discussed separately below.

Some professional terms:

(1) Main line and branch line of turnout.

The straight route through a turnout is arbitrarily termed the main line (or straight "through" track, main-line), and the curved route the branch line (or diverging side), shown as Fig. 4-12.

(2) The front of turnout and rear of turnout.

The rail gap of stock rail before the point of switch is the front of turnout, and the rail gap on the tail of crossing is the rear of turnout.

(3) Facing-point movement and trailing-point movement.[4]

Facing and trailing-point movements are the terms describing the prevailing moves through a turnout. They are designated in part by the direction from which the train is traveling when it reaches the crossing. A train entering a turnout so that it faces the switch points and passes over them before it comes to the crossing is said to be making a facing-point move. If the prevailing movement is facing point, the switch is called a facing-point switch. A train passing through the turnout so that it gets to the crossing before reaching the switch points is making a trailing-point move. If most of the trains make trailing movements over the switch, it is called a trailing-point switch. The arrows in the diagram of a switch in Fig. 4-12 indicate facing- and trailing-point movements.

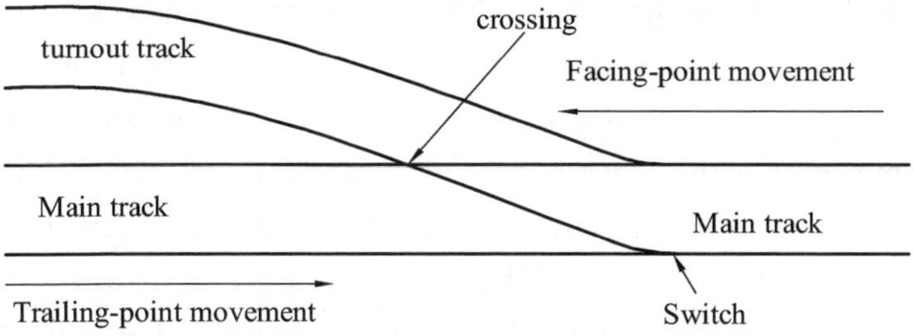

Fig. 4-12 Facing- and trailing-point movements

(4) Right-hand and left-hand simple turnouts.

The direction of a turnout is determined by viewing it from the main track as you face the switch points, that is, the movable rails. If they run to the left, the turnout is left handed; if to the right, right handed.

4.2.2 Switches

1. Stock rails and switch rails

Switches consist of two switch rails and two stock rails. The switch rails can be moved and determine which of the above-mentioned tracks will carry traffic. Switch rails are made of thinner sections at the toe of the switch. The switch rails are carried or supported on sliding plates and each pair of switch blades is connected by a stretcher bar near the toe of the switch. This arrangement keeps a check on the movement of the switch rails, i.e., it keeps the movements of both switch blades equal. A set of switch blades is known as point.

Out of the four rails forming a turnout the two rails of a pair of turnouts are called stock rails. They are fixed together by stretcher bars and are set to give passage for traffic to the track desired.

2. Profiles of the switch rail

The switch rail is provided with a pointed tip by horizontally cutting the railhead and horizontally and vertically cutting the rail base. In this way, the wheel-set can make a transition between stock rails and switch rails easily, and two rails can be properly closed. Additionally, the top of the switch rail will be vertically cut to make the switch rail lower than the stock rail, so as to prevent the actual point of the switch being damaged or bearing excess vertical wheel load.

The hidden tip point structure is applied to prevent collision between the point of the switch rail and wheels traveling from turnout rear. In this structure, the point of the switch rail is about 16-23 mm lower than the stock rail, "hidden" by about 3 mm within the jaw of the stock rail-head. Therefore, the wheel-set will not impact the actual point, even at the maximum vertical wear of the wheel-set and stock rail top, as shown in Fig.4-13. However, the height difference shall not exceed 25 mm, that is, the switch rail shall not be below the wheel-flange; otherwise, the flange may mount the switch rail when the switch rail and stock rail are separated(traveling from the rear of turnout).

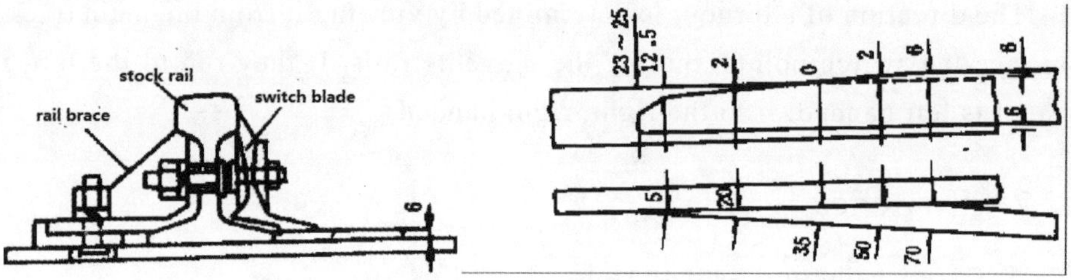

Fig. 4-13 Relative position of stock rails and switch rails

There are two kinds of switch blades according to process. One is ordinary section switch blade cutted from ordinary rail. It has the characteristics of easy to get material, easy to use, and no need for machining at the end of the rail. But its lateral stiffness is small and the stiffness decreases with the increase of the length of the rail. Another is special section switch blade made of special section rail. Its section is strong and rigid, and has better stability than that of ordinary section switch blade. But its heel needs to be processed into a common rail cross section so as to connect with the stock rail. The special section switch blade with the same height as the stock rail is called high-type special section switch blade, and the shorter one is called short-type special section switch blade.

The processes of cutting and bending are combined to make the railhead at the point of cut switch rail be supported by the rail waist, forming the curved surface on a curved switch rail. A curved stock rail may also be bent if required to maintain the gauge, alignment, and closure between straight switch rail and curved stock rail at the switch. The profiles of curved switch rail and straight switch rail may differ slightly due to height difference.

3. Plane geometry of switch blades

The Plane geometry of switch blades may be straight or curved. Switch angle is an important parameter to reflect the design of switch blades.

1) Switch angle

Switch angle is the angle subtended between the gauge face of the stock rail and the switch rail. On the track for fast moving, vehicles turnout angles should be small so that movement of the trains is smooth. In the ease of slow moving trains such as on yards and siding turnout angles should be greater, as shown in Fig. 4-14.

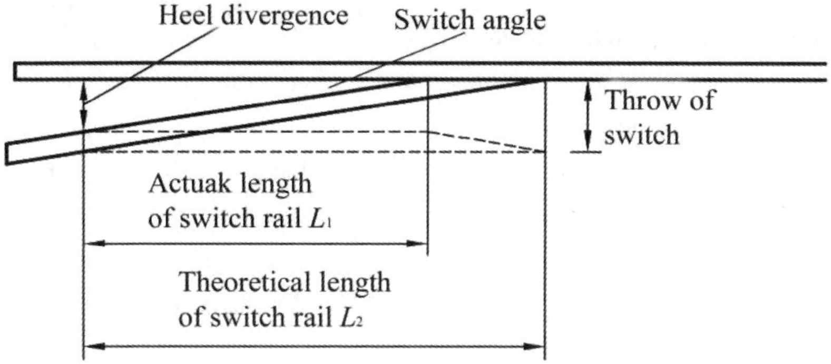

Fig. 4-14 Turnout angle and Heel Divergence

2) Straight switch blade

The switch blade in this case is straight from the tip or toe to the heel of the turnout .The manufacture of this type of switch blade is simple and can be used for right hand as well as for left hand turnouts. In the past, No.12 and below turnouts used in Chinese railway were all of straight switch rails, as shown in Fig. 4-15. The main advantage of straight switch rails are easy manufacture and replacement, less cutting at front tips, large lateral stiffness, small swing and heel flangeway, firm sections, and strong wear resistance, as well as compatibility with both left- and right-hand turnouts. However, this kind of switch rail is in a

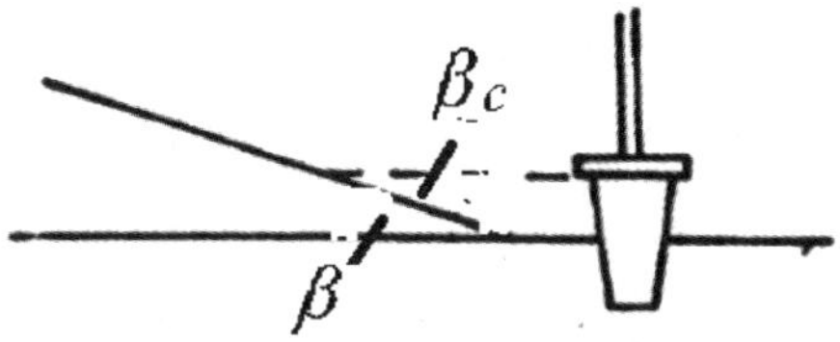

Fig. 4-15 Straight switch blade

straight line, and the angles of the impact β_c and the angles of switch β are equal. Trains may produce a great impact force on switch rail, jeopardizing running quality in the diverging line. Thus, the speed of trains is limited very low on turnouts with straight switch blade.

3) Curved switch blade

Since the speedup of chinese railways in 1996, straight switch rails have been applied to the main line of new No.12 turnouts and above, and curved switch rails to the diverging line. The curved switch rail is conductive to high-speed traffic due to the small angle of impact, large radius of the transition lead curve, and stability of trains when accessing the diverging line, as shown in Fig.4-16. However, the curved switch rails are characterized by a complex manufacturing process, large cutting among at front tips, and non-interchangeability of left- and right- hand turnouts. The line types for curved switch rail are tangent, semi-tangent, secant, semi-secant, and separated semi-tangent types

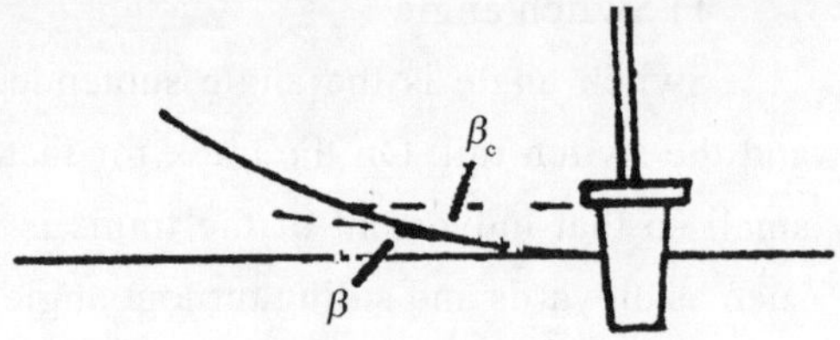

Fig. 4-16 Curved switch blade

A tangent curved switch rail is tangent to the stock rail at the theoretical origin, as shown in Fig. 4-17. In practice, in order to strengthen the actual point and shorten the switch rail, a 100-300 mm long straight section will be installed ahead of the 5 mm wide section of switch rail. Compared with the single turnout adopting a straight switch rail with the same number, the radius of the transition lead curve for a tangent curved switch rail may be significantly increased, and the full length of a turnout can be significantly shortened. For a normal clearance between wheel flange and gauge line, a curved switch rail may have a smaller angle of attack and gauge widening amount at the actual point, providing better riding quality. However, this line type requires a longer weak parts, and the switch rails for the left-and right-hand turnouts cannot be interchanged. The switch rail is prone to severe side wear. This type is less favored now.

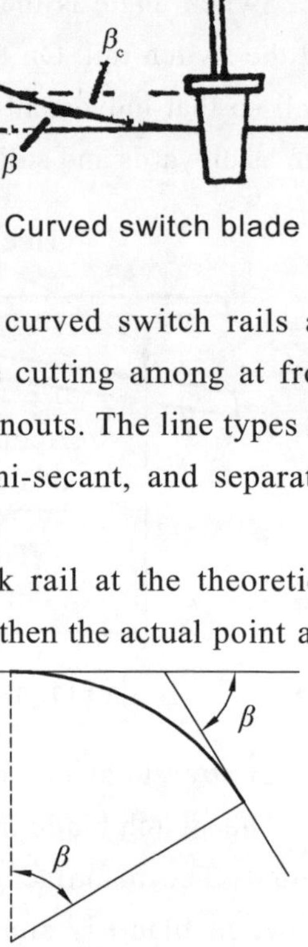

Fig. 4-17 Tangent curved switch blade

The semi-tangent curved switch rail is also tangent to the stock rail at the theoretical origin, as shown in Fig.4-18. However, the tangent is set at a cross section with top width under 40 mm of the switch rail, and the front tip will be straight. Similar to the tangent curved type, the radius of the transition lead curve may be increased, and the full length of a turnout may be shortened. The switch rail and cutting parts of the switch rail are shorter than those of the tangent type, but longer than those of the straight type. The track gauge at the switch rail's actual point is shorter than that at the straight. In normal conditions, the angle of attack of the switch rail is equal to that of the semi-tangent curved part, but larger than that of the tangent curved switch rail. It is widely used in China.

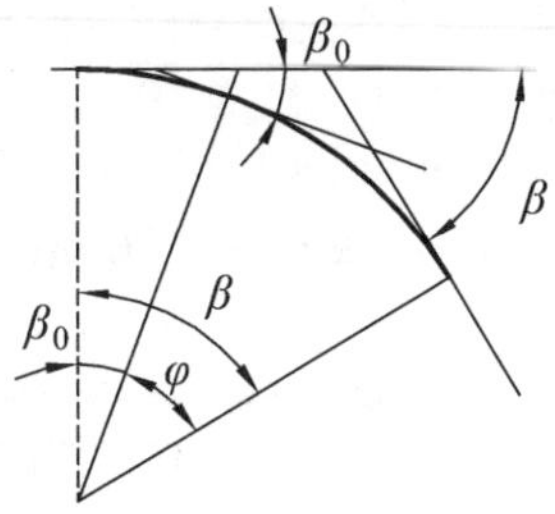

Fig. 4-18 Semi-tangent Curved switch blade

The selection of plane geometry of switch rail is determined by turnout geometry controling, riding quality, wear resistance of the switch rail, simple processing and manufacturing techniques, easy maintenance, repair, and supply of raw materials, etc. If there are no limitations on turnout dimensions and radius of the transition lead curve, and trains travel stability, the separated semi-tangent curved switch rail is more suitable to the running conditions of mixed passenger and freight railways.

4. Switch heels

1) The structure of heels

The heel of switch can broadly be classified into two categories namely: fixed switch heel and loose switch heel.

(1) Fixed heel of switches.

The switch blades are rigidly connected to stock rails by means of heel blocks, bolts and nuts as illustrated in Fig. 4-19. The movement of the switch blades is effected by springing from the first fixed block.

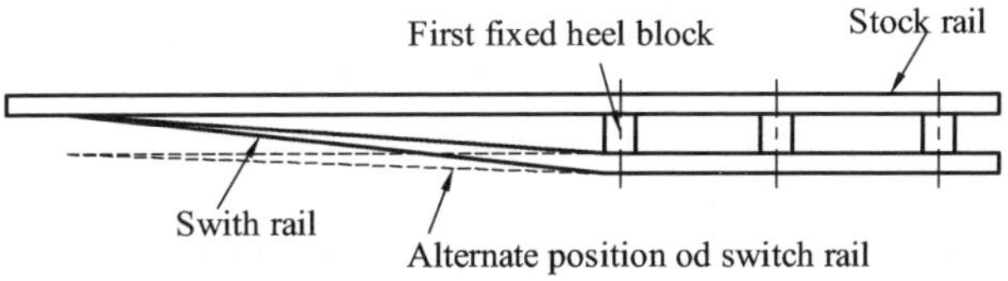

Fig. 4-19 Fixed heel of switches.

(2) Loose heel of switches.

In this type of switch, the rails pivot about heel joints held by blocks and fish plates. The fish plate holding the switch blade is slightly bent. The disadvantage of this type of switch is that due to abrupt change of curvature, the rolling stock is easy to get a knocking, as illustrated in Fig. 4-19.

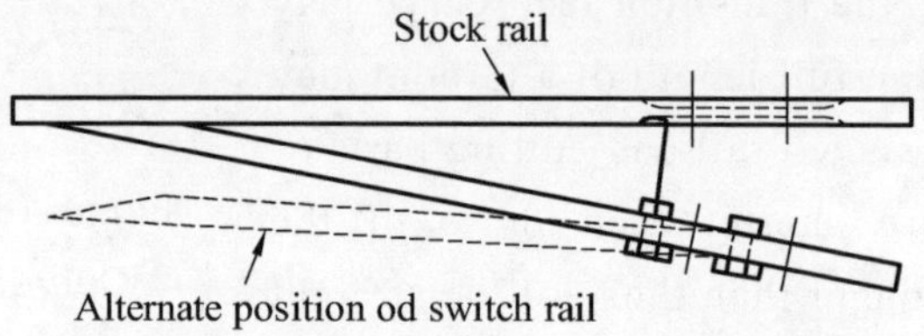

Fig. 4-20 Loose heel of switches

2) Heel clearance and flange-way

Heel clearance or heel divergence is the distance between the running faces of the stock rail and the gauge face of the switch rail measured at heel of the turnout. It is kept equal to flange way clearance plus tolerance for wear plus width of rail.

Flange-way is provided as clearance for the movement of the wheel flanges and for this reason it is known as flange-way clearance. Flange-way depth is the vertical distance between the top of the heel block and top of the head of the stock rail as shown in Fig. 4-20.

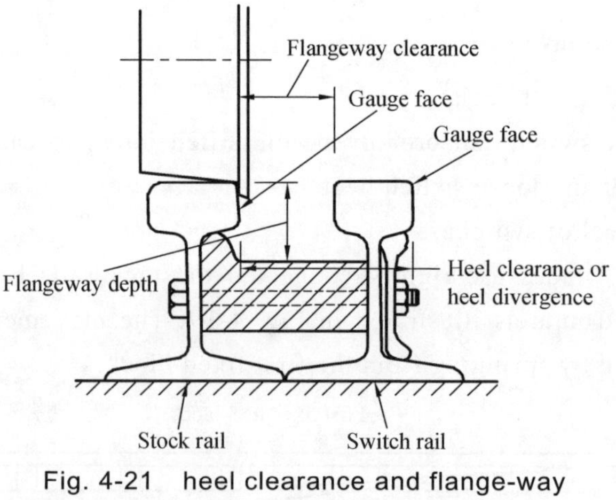

Fig. 4-21 heel clearance and flange-way

The heel clearance, throw and width of the rail head must be balanced so as to give a correct flange-way at the end of the switch planning.

5. Other components of switch body

The various components of single split turnouts also include:

1) Switch rods or stretcher bars

Switch rails are bound together in a unit by the use of switch rods. A head rod is placed vertically at the switch rail ends, and the No.1, 2, 3 and 4 rods(if used) are spaced every two or three sleeper spaces from the end to a distance one-half to two-thirds of the switch blade length. The head rod extends under the stock rails and usually provides connections for the connecting or operating rods from the switch stand or machine. It acts as a hold-down at the front of the switch rail to prevent the switch rail from jumping.

2) Switch plate

The switch blades rest on switch slide plates that are planed to provide a smooth surface on which the bottom of the switch bladescan slide. These plates extend under the stock rails and are graduated in thickness so that the top of the point is kept slightly above the top of the stock rail. Usually, the plates have fixed or adjustable rail braces to support the stock rails, which are subjected to the heavy lateral forces exerted by trains passing through the turnout. Long, narrow tie plates, so-called heel plates, are used to fasten both main-line and turnout rails to the switch sleepers. The heel plates are located beyond the heels of the switch blades, that is, beyond the ends of the switch blades. Switch plates are used until the turnout and main-line rails have diverged far enough to permit use of separate tie plates.

3) Rail braces

Rail braces are secured to the switch plates and gauge plate and bear against the outside base and under the head of the stock rails to resist the side or lateral thrust on the swith blades and stock rails. The braces may be either of a plain, fixed type or of an adjustable variety. Adjustable braces permit occasional tightening to compensate for wear.

4) Studs and stops

These are used to prevent bending of switch bladesin the lateral direction so that when wheels rollover the swith, correct alignment is maintained. They are fixed between stock rail and switch blade.

5) Crank and levers for operating the switches

These are devices by means of which the switch bladeof the turnout is attached to or detached from the main rail depending upon whether diversion is required or not. In the position of turnout shown in Fig. 4-11, the train is shown arriving from the left. The switch of the turnout is attached to the left hand stock rail and detached from the right hand main rail. The track is therefore laid for being diverted to the right diversion. If however, no diversion is required, the switch rail would be detached from the left hand main rail and the other switch rail which acts, in combination with the first one would be attached to the right hand rail. The train in this position would be set for the main track. This operation of attachment and detachment is carried out from the signal cabin by operating the respective levers.

4.2.3 Crossings

It is a device provided at the intersection of two rails to allow the train moving along one of the track to pass across the other.

Depending on the traffic load different types of crossings are used. For normal to medium axle loads and speeds up to 200 km/h, rigid crossings are used. For higher axle loads and higher speeds crossings with movable parts have to be used.

The common crossing and the wing rails are built up geometrically in such a way that the passing wheel remains supported and wheel flange clearance is guaranteed. In a common crossing the intersecting rails form an acute angle.

In the common crossing the unguided part leads to an unquiet behavior of the bogie in the switch and causes an extra dynamic load on the common crossing and on the check rail. To avoid unguided parts in the common crossing movable points should be used.

1. Structure of crossings

Each part of a crossing has a name as shown in Fig. 4-11.

(1)Two point rails. Called point rail and splice rail, machined in such a way so that they form a nose. The point rail ends at the nose while the splice rail joins a little behind the nose

(2) Two wing rail. These rails are known as right and left hand wing rails. They converge to form a throat and diverge again as shown on either side of the nose.

(3) A pair of check-rails. To provide a path for the wheel flanges and guide them, a pair of check-rails is provided. This arrangement prevents side ways movements of

the wheels and saves the hitting of the nose by the wheels during their movement in facing direction.

(4) Other part of crossing. Note that the toe is the opening between the wing rails on the end of the crossing nearer the switch points. The lead rails are attached to the wing rails at the toe. The throat is the narrowest part. The theoretical point is located where the gage lines of the stock and the switch blades would intersect if they were extended past the actual point. If the point were planed to the theoretical point, the impact of the vehicle wheels would soon batter and break it. For that reason, the point is rounded off and is called actual point. The gap between theoretical point and actual point is called hamful space. The end of the crossing away from the switch points is called the heel. That is where the running rails are spliced to the crossing.

2. The features of crossing

The diversion from one track to the other takes place in two stages. In the first stage, the switch rail of the turnout is flush to the right hand stock rail whereas the switch of the left hand rail provides a gap such that there is discontinuity between the main track, and the left hand flanges are automatically diverted to the left hand track. The outer rail of the diverted track then intersects the left hand rail of the main track and the wheels have to jump across this gap. This point of intersection of the diverted track and the original track forms the crossing.

The purpose of all railway crossing is to permit rolling stock moving along one track to pass over one or both rails of the other track with maximum safety and minimum disturbance to the wheels.

The most critical region in the design of the crossing is the section between the throat and some distance behind the nose of crossing. The wheel jumps from the wing rail to the crossing and vice versa. This batters both the wing rails and nose of crossing. The life of the crossing is considerably prolonged by correct positioning and effective maintenance of the check rails. These check rails are positioned opposite all common crossings to contain the wheel flange Passing between the check rail and its parent rail so that flanges of the wheel passing through the crossing is steered clear of the nose.

In order that the functioning of the crossing, characteristics of a good crossing should be given particular attention:

(1) The assembly of the crossing should be rigid to withstand the vibrations which cause loosening of the components. It can be achieved by using a sole plate at turned bolts to connect the point and slice rails and reverting the sole plate with the foot flanges of the wing rail.

(2) The wing rail and nose itself should be protected against damage. For this purpose alloy steel should be used.

(3) The crossing body should be as rigid as possible and long enough. A short body has the tendency to rock at the loaded end and lifting at the other unloaded end. This can be achieved as follows in normal:

By extending the flange of the nose and bolting them to the nose chair.

By using the distance blocks closely touching the waist

By maintaining the correct gauge from toe to heel.

(4) From practical considerations the nose of crossing should be of sufficient thickness.

3. Types of crossings

According to their angle, crossing can be classified as:

(1) Acute angle crossing. It is also known as V crossing. In this crossing, the two gauge faces form acute angel.

(2) Obtuse angle crossing. In this crossing, the two gauge faces meet at an obtuse angel.

According to their manufacture, crossings can be classified as:

1) Rigid crossing

Rigid crossings are divided into three groups: bolted-rigid, hard-centered (manganese insert), and manganese-steel;

(1) Bolted rigid crossings (Fig. 4-22).

Fig. 4-22 Bolted rigid crossings

The bolted-rigid type is manufactured from standard rail sections cut as required and bolted together. It is standard military stock and is issued as a unit. Heel or riser blocks between the point rails reduce wear on these rails form worn car wheels. Rolled-steel filler blocks separate the rails and provide flange ways. This design is inexpensive. It finds use in branch lines, yards, and terminals. The rails used in making the crossings are frequently heat-treated for longer life.

Advantages: their initial cost is low; their repair is easy.

Disadvantages: their rigidity is low; Bolts etc. need frequent checking as they break under heavy and fast traffic.

(2) Cast manganese-steel crossings.

Cast manganese-steel crossings (Fig. 4-24) are as the name implied, cast in one complete unit. Their principal use is in yards and terminals under frequent traffic and heavy tonnages.

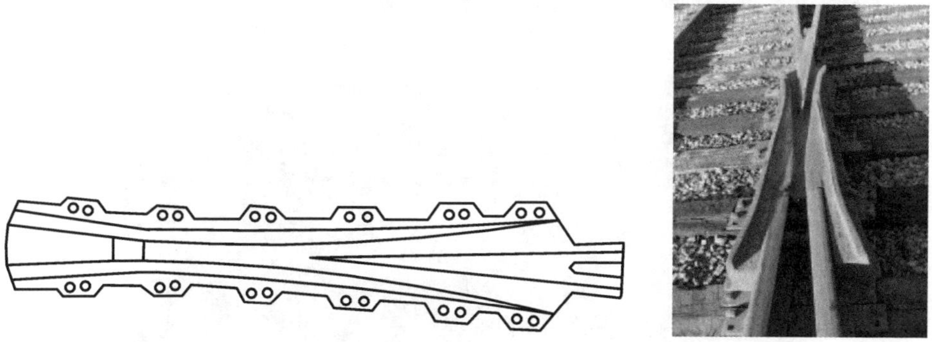

Fig. 4-23 Cast manganese-steel crossings

Advantages: they are one piece cast crossings, having no bolts etc., so they need less maintenance; they are more rigid.

Disadvantages: their initial cost is very high; their repair is cumbersome.

(3) Hard-centered crossings.

Hard-centered crossings have manganese-cast points attached to standard rail sections. Since the point gets the greatest wear, it is made of extremely hard steel and is replaceable. These are the conventional crossings for main line heavy traffic. An explosion-hardened insert and heat-treated wing rails give longer life.

Advantages: This is the combination of the above two types. It has longer life.

Disadvantages: Its repair is very difficult.

2) Spring crossing

(1) Spring wring crossings (or movable wing crossings).

Such structure of cossing has the fixed center rail, and wing rail can move. Spring wring crossings can be divided into two types: single-sided spring wing rail, bilateral spring wing rails. Such crossings can be designed into the same and interchangeable size with the existing fixed crossing, to avoid the station site changed when laying and at the same time to meet the elimination of harmful space requirements. This kind of crossings have some shortcomings: poor lateral stability of the moving wing rail, and the structure of the wing rail fixing device is complicated. Fig.4-25 shows a single-sided spring wing rail.

Fig, 4-24 single-sided spring wing rail

(2) Swing-Nose Crossings (or movable point crossings).

On lines with heavy and/or high-speed traffic, a swing-nose crossing (or moveable point crossing) may be used, as shown in Fig.4-25. A swing-nose crossings is a device used at a railway turnout to eliminate the gap at the common crossing which can cause damage and noise. As the name implies, there is a second mechanism located at the crossing. Swing-nose crossings need to operate at the same time as the main turnout switches to which they belong. This may require excessive effort for manual operation, and require a point motor. The main turnout and the swing-nose crossings will require separate machines, as shown in Fig.4-26.

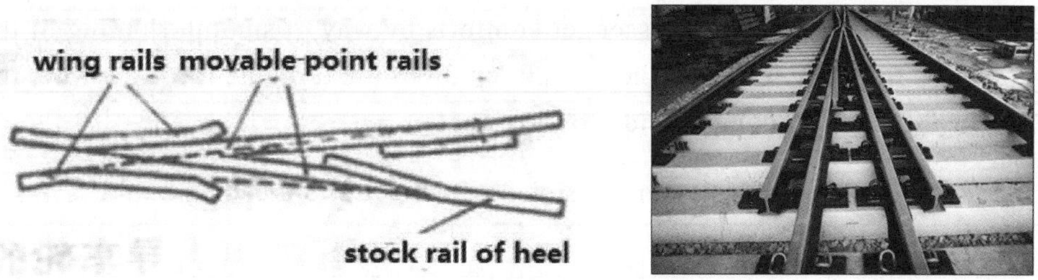

Fig. 4-25 Swing nose crossing

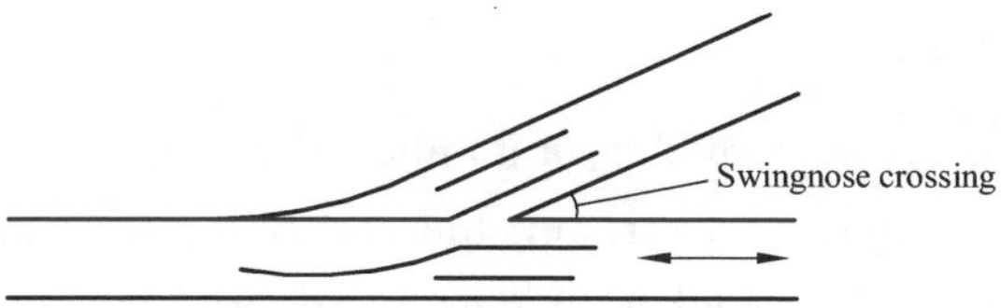

(a) Swing nose crossing in straight traffic position

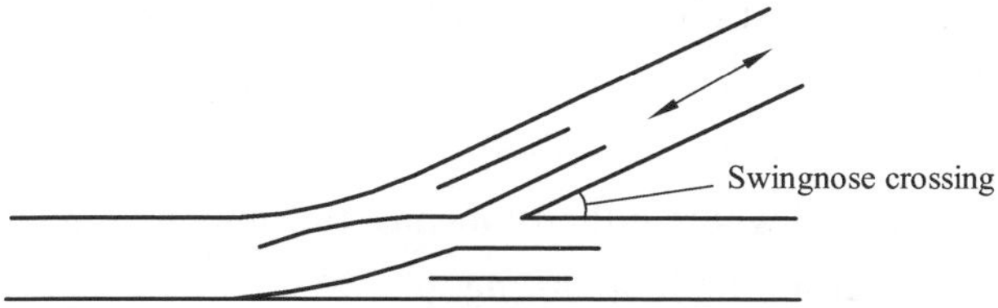

(b) Swing nose crossing in diverging traffic position

Fig. 4-26 Traffic position of swing nose crossing

4. Crossing angle and crossing number

The angle formed between the gauge faces of the *V* is known as crossing angle.

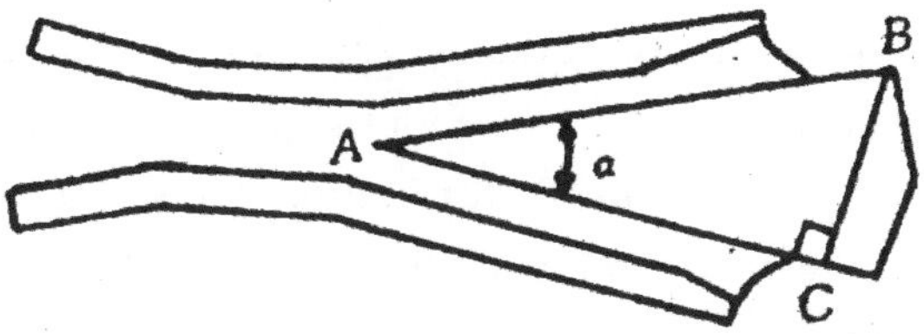

Fig. 4-27 Crossing angle

The number of a crossing is defined as the ratio of the spread at the leg of crossing to the length of crossing measured from it theoretical nose.

Number of crossing= N= cot a.

As has already been explained that as larger the crossing number is better it is from the point of view of passenger comforts by way of smooth running of the train but at the same longer is the overall length of the turnout. Tab.4-1 shows the relations of crossing number and crossing angle.

Tab. 4-1 The relations of crossing number and crossing angle

crossing Number	7	9	12	18	24
crossing angle	8°07′48″	6°20′25″	4°45′49″	3°10′47″	2°23′09″

5. Turnout speed

Turnout speeds are governed by a number of factors. As a general rule, the smaller the crossing angle of a turnout, the higher the turnout speed. In Russia and China switches are marked with tangent of crossing angle. Below is the design speed of some normal turnouts :

#9 ---40 km/h, the most common switch, installed by default.

#11 ---50 km/h, used where passenger trains follow a diverging path. Swing nose crossing may be installed if required.

#18 ---80 km/h, used where either non-interruptible movement is required or the mainline diverges from the branch line.

#22 --- 120 km/h, rarely used, high-speed lines only.

Other considerations include the type of turnout (e.g. normal or swing nose, or slips etc.), wear and tear issues, and the weight and type of the vehicle passing over. Speeds for a trailing movement may be higher than for a facing movement. In many systems, speed limits vary depending on the type of train - for example, a turnout can have a "normal" speed limit for locomotive hauled trains, and a higher speed for multiple unit or high-speed trains. Turnouts with curved or tangential switch blades have higher speed than old style turnouts with straight switch blades.

Following factors are responsible for limiting the speed over turnouts:

(1) Sudden change in direction of the running edges at the entry to the switch from a straight track.

(2) Absence of transition between curved lead and the straight switch.

(3) Absence of super elevation over the turnout curve.

(4) Variation in cross levels caused due to raising of the switch rails.

(5) Gaps in the gauge face and running table of the crossing.

(6) Non transition entry from the curved lead to the straight crossings.

The above shortcomings can be overcome by adopting the following measure:

(1) Long curved switches may be provided to avoid abrupt change in the direction of entry.

(2) Transition curves may be provided between the toe of the switch and the nose of the crossing.

(3) The curvature of switches and crossings should be the same as that of curved lead rails.

(4) Permitting higher super-elevation deficiency.

6. Check-rails(or guard rails)

1) The structure of check-rails

Check-rails are set opposite the crossing point to hold wheels away from the point, thus reducing wear and batter and preventing a possible deflection into the wrong flange way. The midpoint of the check-rails should be set ahead of the crossing point to assure sufficient distance in which to check the wheel position. Distance from the gauge of the crossing point to the face or running rail side of the check-rails (sometimes called the guard-face gauge) must be maintained suitably. If the guard face gauge were too wider, the wheel flange on the crossing side would strike the throat of the crossing and the check-rails. If it were less, the flange could hit the point of the crossing. Excessive wear or derailment would result in either situation. On curves, where track gauge is widened, the width of the flange way will be widened accordingly, since guard-rail face gauge cannot be changed.

Check-rails may be made from ordinary rail sections, with the base and head partially sheared to permit close proximity to the running rail. The ends are undercut and bent down to avoid dragging equipment. The ends are also bent away from the running rail, or a chamfered flare is planned to guide the wheels into the flange way between the check-rails and running rails. To facilitate smooth entry and exit for the flange of the wheels the check rail or wing rail is splayed at the end. This gradual widening of the flange-way is known as flare as illustrated in Fig. 4-28. Check-rails are secured in place by track spikes, rail braces, clamps, and bolts. Filler blocks near the ends are secured with bolts through both the block and the two rails and act as foots guards as well as fastening. Modern check-rails are made in one piece, usually of cast manganese-steel, and with plates and rail braces integrally cast or attached to form a complete unit.

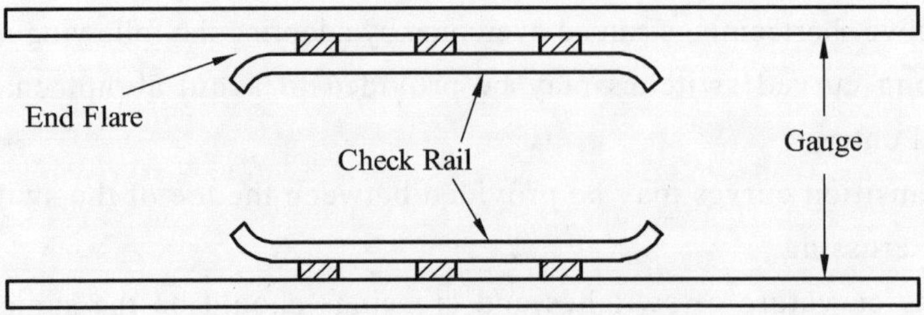

Fig. 4-28 check-rails Flare

2) Check-rails for high-speed turnouts

In the early speed-up turnouts in china, an H-shaped check rail was used. Check rail is made of common rails, with a groove reserved beneath the bedplate of the rail plate. Spring sheet steel will be inserted from the inside. The inside of stock rail will be clamped by an elastic clip through pinning. The two side of the stock rail are fastened by elastic fastenings of different types. The gauge at the inside of the stock rail cannot be adjusted easily because of the existence of the bedplate. Check rail plates are welded to the rail, featuring poor integrity and easy breakage and fracture.

For better integrity and channel quality of plate, rolled channel check rail with solid plate was developed in China. The rolled check rail is of stable quality. The cast plate has improved integrity. Clamped by elastic clips, the two sides of stock rails are exposed to even elasticity. However, casting greatly affects the use life of plates and causes maintenance inconvenience to elastic fastenings under the check rail. Channel check rails, with the basic features of H-shaped check rail, lower height, and leave greater space beneath for elastic fastenings. Therefore, they are widely used in China.

4.2.4 Lead rail[14]

The connection part between the switch and the crossing is generally equipped with 8 rails, called lead rails, including 4 straight lead rails and 4 curved lead rails.

The location of the insulation joint of track circuit and the requirement of square joint should be considered when the rail is allocated, and the standard rail with a length of 12.5 m or 25 m should be used as far as possible. The short rail used in connection part is usually not shorter than 6.25 m; in difficult cases, it is not less than 4.5 m The dimension of lead rail for No. 9, No. 12 and No. 18 turnouts in China is shown in table 4-1.

Tab. 4-1 The relations of crossing number and lead rails

N	9	12	18	N	9	12	18
l_1	5 324	11 791	10 226	l_5	6 836	12 500	16 574
l_2	11 000	12 500	18 750	l_6	9 500	9 385	12 500
l_3	6 894	12 500	16 903	l_7	5 216	11 708	10 173
l_4	9 500	9 426	12 500	l_8	11 000	12 500	18 750

The structure of the straight lead rail is the same as that of the straight rail in the section, but the curved lead rail differs from the curved rail in the section in geometry type and structure.

The plane geometry of curved lead rail include: a circular curve, an easement curve, and a compound curve.

(1) Circular curve lead rail:

The circular curve type may be used with straight switch rails and curved switch rails. It is commonly used as it easy to design, manufacture, lay, and maintain. When it is used with straight switch rail, the tangent point of the transition lead curve may be appropriately set at or in the rear of switch rail heel. This curve type is generally used in small number turnouts with low speed in the diverging rail line, typically for a straight crossing. When it is used with curved switch rail, the radius of the transition lead curve and curved switch rail may be equal or unequal. This curve type is used mainly in turnouts for high-speed in the diverging rail line, such as No.12 and 18 turnouts. The curved lead rail of the turnouts with curved switch rail and curved crossing may have relatively large radius.

(2) Easement curve lead rail

The easement curve may be quadratic and cubic parabola, spiral, or sinusoid. Considering the design, manufacture, laying, and maintenance difficulties, it is applicable to larger number turnouts where high-speed trains will travel in the diverging line. This curve type is advantageous in the gradual change of centrifugal acceleration and its incremental improvement of passengers' comfort. The cubic parabola is the simplest and most common form of easement curve.

(3) Compound curve lead rail

The compound curve type is composed of curves with different curvatures, generally including compound circular curve, double-easement curve type, "circular +easement" curve type, and "easement +circular+curve" type. In order to avoid vibration superposition on curves, the length of each component of compound curve should be larger than the distance that a train may travel in 1s. Thus, the line types for a compound curve shall match with the length of turnouts and speeds in the diverging line.

In order to prevent the leaning and expanding of rail distance under the action of dynamic load, a certain number of rail braces or gauge rods can be set up, and a certain number of anti-creep anchors and anti-creep braces can be set up to reduce the crawl of rail.

4.3 Turnouts Sleepers

Because of the divergence of tracks, ordinary sleepers are not suitable under turnouts. Special lengths of switch sleepers are necessary. These begin with standard-length sleepers and increase in different lengths as the size and spread of turnout requires. For increased stability the sleepers are usually continued under both tracks for several sleeper spaces beyond the heel of crossing. In laying out the gradient for a diverging route, both tracks must be no the same gradient throughout the distance of the switch sleepers. Immediately under the switch points the first two sleeper space are occupied by long timbers called head blocks. They give stability at that point and act as a base on which to set the ground throw are not available, temporary or emergency installations of turnouts may be made by interlacing standard sleepers alternately under one track and then the other. This system is structurally weak. Switch sleepers are specified in sets for the designated number of the turnout and individually by length.

1. length

The length of sleepers varies as impacted by layout type and other factors of the turnout, but generally taken as 2.6-4.8 m (increment: 01. or 0.15 m). The entire turnout is supported on switch sleepers. Look now at Fig. 4-29. Notice at point A that the two

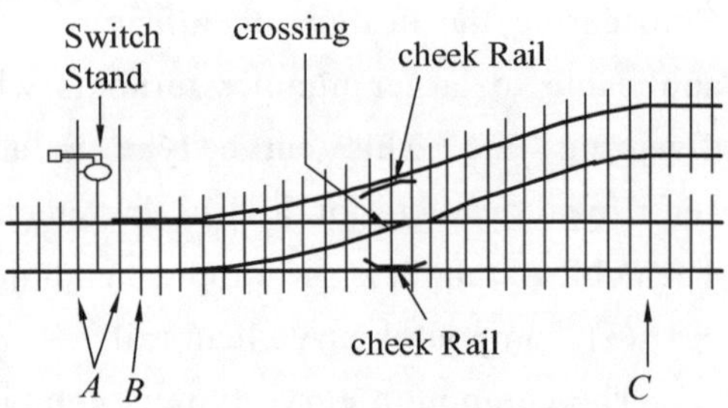

Fig. 4-29 Arrangement and Location of Switch Sleepers

sleepers supporting the switch points also support the switch-throwing mechanism, 2.6 m long. They are referred to as headblock timbers. The succeeding sleepers, the actual switch sleepers, gradually become longer toward the frog end of the turnout, as shown in Fig. 4-29 between points B and C.

The distance between the center of outer rail in curved track and the end of sleeper is not constant; however, it must at least satisfy the requirement of anchorage length of prestressed reinforcement. To minimize the number of long sleepers at turnout rear and ease laying and maintenance, short sleepers may be used in the transition between turnout rear and adjacent section. For sleepers at traction points, which must accommodate conversion equipment, three installation holes will be arranged, and the sleeper will be lengthened by 120-280 mm as compared with nearby sleepers.

The distance from sleeper end to the first bolt hole is essential for preventing longitudinal cracks on the concrete surface around the bolt hole. In china, high-speed and speed-up turnout adopt the same design value, 364 mm.

The sleeper spacing is 600 mm for Chinese high-speed turnouts. All sleeper will be perpendicular to the main direction of the turnout. The sleeper is applicable to turnouts in crossover and receiving-departure lines with track distance of 4.6 m and above.

2. Profile

The sleeper may have a shoulder or not. Compared with shouldered concrete sleepers, the non-shoulder type has features such as less longitudinal cracking, greater carrying capacity, easy manufacture, simple profile, and good appearance; moreover, it enhances the carrying capacity of the intermediate section of sleepers without necessary increasing the reinforcement quantity or impairing the carrying capacity of the rail substructure. Non-shoulder sleepers of uniform height are used in high-speed turnouts in China. The rail-supporting surface is not canted at the base.

3. Section

The bottom width of a sleeper is designed as 300 mm to achieve the same effective bearing area as type III concrete sleepers in china. The design top width is 260 mm, wider than that of its type III concrete counterpart, so as to facilitate the installation of special sleeper plates and avoid demolding difficulty. The design height of sleeper section is 220 mm to meet the requirement of carrying capacity.

4. Bolt hole for fastening

Sleepers are coupled with plates by a row of bolts. As sleepers are perpendicular to the rails in the main line, pre-embedded plastic sleeves will be located on the longitudinal axis of symmetry of the sleeper. The bolt holes on the plates under rails in curved track will be provided with graded deflections, enabling the perpendicularity of the assembled plate and sleeper to the rail. In either left-hand or right-hand turnouts, the plates under rails in curved track are in symmetry.

4.4 Installation and maintenance of turnouts

It is important that the foundation under a turnout be especially stable and well drained. Good surface, an absolute necessity, cannot be obtained from a weak subgrade, insufficient high-grade ballast, and excess moisture. The use of insufficient high-grade ballasts such as crushed basalt or slag, especially under the hump and retarder leads, and ladders in yards (where inferior ballast is often found) has proved advantageous.

When installing a turnout piecemeal under traffic, the crossing, main track lead rail, and switch point are usually put in as a unit. The turnout side stock rail and main track check-rails must be applied at the same time. Other portions may then be installed as convenient. A more desirable procedure, when time permits, is to clear everything away from the site and build from the ground up, as in building new track. Switch sleepers may be installed in existing track before the turnout is placed. This requires the withdrawal of the spikes and the plugging of spike holes, an operation likely to deteriorate the timbers. Preferably switch sleepers are placed after the crossing and main track portion of the switch have been installed on the old track sleepers.

Turnouts in whole or, more conveniently, the switch and the crossing and check-rails assemblies may be separately fabricated in advance as panel units and set in place with a crane. Two cranes and a stiffening member would be required to install a complete turnout, or the assembled turnout may be pulled or jacked laterally into place.

Maintenance begins with frequent, careful inspection. A regular, on-the-ground inspection should be carried for main line tracks. All bolts should be kept tight, and switch plates clean and well lubricated. The throw rod must be kept in adjustment so that the switch points fit tightly against the stock rails. Flowed metal must be ground from the stock rail to insure proper fit and prevent switch-point chipping. suitch rails can be ground to a suitable contour, but excessive chipping is a cause for replacement.

Professional Words and Expressions

turnout 道岔
normal simple turnout 单开道岔
symmetrical double turnout 对称双开道岔
convergent double turnout 同侧单开道岔
divergent double turnout 异侧单开道岔
three-throw turnouts 三开道岔
diamond crossing 菱形交叉
rigging-angle crossing or right-angle crossing 正交叉
single slip turnout 单式交分道岔
double slip turnout 复式交分道岔
cross-over track 渡线
scissors cross-over 交叉渡线
gathering lines or ladder track 梯线
triangle track 三角线
switch body 转辙器
switch Blades 尖轨
stock rail 基本轨
fFrog or crossing 辙叉
check rail 护轨
fixed heel of switches转辙器的固定跟端
loose heel of switches. 转辙器的弹性跟端
switch angle 转辙角
angle of impact 冲击角
heel clearance 跟端间隔
flange-way 轮缘槽
switch rods or stretcher bars 尖轨连杆
switch plate 尖轨垫板
rail braces 轨撑
studs and stops 顶铁
crank and levers 道岔拉杆
point rails 心轨
wing rail 翼轨
theoretical point 理论尖端
actual point 实际尖端
bolted rigid crossings 钢轨组合式辙岔
cast manganese-steel crossings 锰钢整铸式辙岔
hard-centered crossings 铸造叉心组合式辙叉

closure rail or lead rail 导轨
main line of turnout 道岔正线
branch line of turnout 道岔侧线
the front of turnout 岔头
the rear of turnout 岔尾
facing-point movement 逆向通过道岔
trailing-point movement 顺向通过道岔
right-Hand Turnouts 右开道岔
left-Hand Turnouts 左开道岔
straight switch blade 直线型尖轨
spring wring crossings (movable wing crossings) 可动翼轨辙岔
swing-nose crossings (or movable point crossings) 可动心轨辙岔
throat 咽喉
curved switch blade 曲线型尖轨
semi-tangent curved switch blade 半切线型尖轨
harmful space of crossing 有害空间
crossing angle and crossing number 道岔号码
turnout speed 过岔速度

CHARPTER 5 CONTINUOUS WELDED RAIL (CWR)

【 Primary Contents 】

(1) Significance of laying CWR

(2) Theories of temperature force, temperature stress

(3) Construction methods of CWR

(4) Stability of CWR

5.1 Overview

The joint is the weakest section of the rail and is an unavoidable evil. Because of rolling difficulties, rails were earlier rolled in short lengths.The length of the rails can be considerably increased by welding the rail joint. It has been noticed that the earlier conception of having gaps on joints proportional to the length of the rails is not realistic. The fear that longer rails would necessarily have longer gaps at joints was not justified by results on the ground and this has cleared the way for going in for welded rails. This explains the reason why against provision of expansion gap after every rail length in the conventional track continuously welded rail of a kilometer or more requires none. Continuous welded rail(CWR), sometimes referred to ribbon rails. Because there are few joints, this form of track is very strong, gives a smooth ride, and needs less maintenance; trains can travel on it at higher speeds and with less friction. Welded rails are more expensive to lay than jointed tracks, but have much lower maintenance costs. The first welded track was used in Germany in 1924 and US in 1930 and has become common on main lines since the 1950s.

Connecting each 12.5 m or 25 m long rail link into orbit, it is clear that every 12.5 m or 25 m will have a connector. There is a gap between the rail joints, which is about 6 mm. The truth left rail joint gap is very simple, is to prevent the rails when the temperature generated in the thermal expansion and contraction force. Do not underestimate the power of this temperature, changes in rail temperature every 1 °C, each rail will withstand the 1.645 tons of pressure or tension. Rail temperature variation amplitude is 50 °C, a rail will have to withstand up to 82.25 tons of pressure or tension. Such a huge power enough to be worth a crooked twisted rails, causing irregularity, affect the safe operation of the train quickly. If not restrained, rails would lengthen in hot weather and shrink in cold weather. To provide this restraint, the rail is prevented from moving in relation to the sleeper by use of clips or anchors.

There is no theoretical limit to how long a welded rail can be. However, if longitudinal and lateral restraint are insufficient, the track could become distorted in hot weather and cause a derailment. Distortion due to heat expansion is known as sun kink, and elsewhere as buckling(the tendency of the track to suddenly snap into a large lateral displacement profile). A rail broken due to cold-related contraction is known as a pull-apart or breakage(breaks typically occurring at a weld where the rail is weakest). The movement of a long rail due to temperature changes continues until the sum of the individual restraints provided by the fastenings and sleepers equals the expanding or contracting force.Attention needs to be paid to compacting the ballast effectively, including under, between, and at the ends of the sleepers, to prevent the sleepers from moving. In extreme hot weather special inspections are required to monitor sections of track known to be problematic. Fig.5-1 shows the compression and tension failures in rail.

Fig. 5-1 Compression and tension failures in rail

CWR is laid (including fastening) at a temperature roughly midway between the extremes experienced at that location (this is known as the "rail neutral temperaturc(NT)"). It is a related critical paramcter at which there is no longitudinal tensile or compressive stresses. To ensure safety of operation in CWR, reliable information on the level of stress in the rail is critical. This installation procedure, along with normal track structure strength, is intended to prevent tracks from buckling in summer heat or pulling apart in winter cold. Flash butt welding is the preferred process which involves an automated track-laying machine running a strong electrical current through the touching ends of two un-joined pieces of rail. The ends become white hot due to electrical resistance and are then pressed together forming a strong weld. Thermite welding is a manual process requiring a reaction crucible and form to contain the molten iron. Thermite-bonded joints are also seen as less reliable and more prone to fracture or break.

CWR has two types of ceremony :temperature stress and relief temperature stress. Currently the vast majority of countries in the world are made of temperature stress seamless lines. CWR is an important part of modern railway track, significant economic benefits. According to relevant statistics, in comparison with the normal line, CWR can save at least 15% of the recurrent maintenance costs, extend the life of the rail 25%. In addition, CWR also has reduced driving resistance, reduce vibrations and road noise, etc.

1. Purpose of welding of Rails

(1) To reduce the number of joints and joint fitting thereby effecting a saving in construction as well as maintenance cost.

(2) To restore the worn out or damaged rail section.

(3) To repair damaged or worn out points and rails along the curves.

(4) To restore the burnt sections of head of the rail or to repair any other defect.

2. Advantages of Welding of Rails

(1) Reduction in the number of joints resulting in saving in construction and maintenance cost.

(2) Increase in the life of the rail due to reduction in wear at the end.

(3) Increased traveling comfort due to reduction of joints.

(4) Reduction in creep.

(5) Increase in carrying capacity of the track.

(6) Saving in fuel due to reduction in tractive effort.

(7) Reduction in theft and sabotage.

(8) Increase in the stability and stiffness of the track.

5.2 Fundamentals Theory of CWR

5.2.1 Rail temperature force and temperature stress

The fundamental difference between CWR rail line and traditional rail line lies in a huge rail temperature force. Therefore, to study the strength and stability of CWR, we must understand the variation of temperature stress and its variation.

When rail temperature changes, rail will stretch freely. And it is phenomenon of thermal expansion and contraction. If both side of the rails are fixed up in order not to let it stretch freely, when the track temperature changes, the rail inside is affected by a force which is caused by the rail temperature changes. So, it is called temperature force.

If the rail can stretch freely without any constraint and its length is l, when the rail temperature changes Δt°C, its retractable volume Δl is:

$$\Delta l = \alpha \cdot l \cdot \Delta t \tag{5-1}$$

Where α—coefficient of linear expansion, usually $\alpha = 11.8\times10^{-6}$ m/(m · °C);

l—length of rail;

Δt—range of rail temperature change.

Normally a free rail would have experienced the longitudinal movement corresponding to the variation in rail temperature, but as the rails are fastened to sleepers which are embedded in ballast, their expansion and contraction due to temperature variations is restricted due to the restraint offered by fixtures and ballast etc. Due to the restraint in the longitudinal movement of the rail, internal stresses in the rail material are produced. These stresses may put the track out of alignment due to bukling and may result in derailment of the trains. According to Hooke's law, temperature stress inside the rail:

$$\begin{aligned} \sigma_{\mathrm{t}} &= E\times\frac{\Delta l}{l} = E\times\alpha\times\Delta t \\ &= 2.1\times10^{5}\times11.8\times10^{-6}\Delta t \\ &= 2.48\Delta t \end{aligned} \tag{5-2}$$

Where E—modulus of elasticity of steel, E=2.1 × 10^5 MPa.

α —coefficient of linear expansion, $\alpha = 11.8\times10^{-6}\ m/(m{\cdot}°C)$

Δt —— change range of rail temperature (°C)。

The resulting force in rail metal is known as thermal force and is given by the relation

$$P = \sigma_{\rm t} \times A = 2.48 \times \Delta t \times A\ (\rm N) \tag{5-3}$$

So, the value of thermal force depends upon the sectional weight of the rail and the temperature variations.

If P is the force in a rail due to temperature change, A is the cross-sectional area say 66.15 cm^2 for 52 kg/m rail, then the force exerted per degree of change of temperature =EaΔt =1.55 tones /°C. The value of the force exerted is therefore not governed by the length of the rail. If the variation of temperature with reference to the temperature of laying is taken as 35°C, the force generated in the rail would be 54.6 tones.

However, if this contraction or expansion is constrained, as is the case when the rail is properly anchored and fastened, a net state of longitudinal tension or compression will exist (Fig. 5-2) and result in longitudinal force proportional to the deviation from neutral temperature.[17]

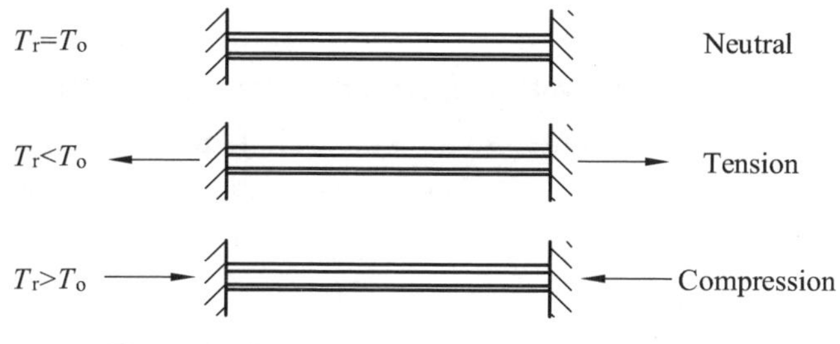

Fig. 5-2 States of longitudinal force in CWR

5.2.2 Rail temperature

1. Neutral temperature

The key environmental variables used in installing CWR were the absolute expected maximum and minimum air temperatures over the lifespan of the rail installation. These temperature variables were selected because they are used to calculate the appropriate "neutral temperature" for laying rail. Neutral temperature is the temperature at which zero thermal stress would occur. The desired neutral temperature is determined by the temperature of the rail (not the ambient temperature) at the time of its installation and fixing to the sleepers.

2. Range of rail temperature change and lock rail temperature

There is an optimal range at which to set the neutral temperature that is based on the expected temperature patterns at the installation site. Installing a rail at too high temperature might result in a higher risk of pull-aparts in cold temperatures and installing it at a temperature too low may result in greater risk of sun kinks during warm temperatures.

The rail temperature at the time of installation is influenced by the ambient temperature but can be adjusted in the field as needed using specialized equipment so that the desired neutral temperature can be achieved regardless of weather conditions at the time of installation.

Range of rail temperature change is range from locking rail temperature to calculating temperature.

$$\Delta t = t_j - t_s \tag{5-4}$$

Where t_j—calculating temperature;

t_s—lock rail temperature.

As the size of the force CWR temperature has a direct relationship with the range of rail temperature change, so locking rail temperature has became the important information about designing, laying and maintaining CWR.

In order to reduce temperature force inside the long rail, we need to choose a suitable locking rail temperature. Lock rail temperature is instantaneous rail temperature, when CWR is completely fixed up. Lock rail temperature is determined as the basis of temperature stress level. If the highest and lowest laying CWR rail temperature is known in some region, we choose middle value as lock rail temperature . Considering stability of the track, in order to prevent expansion in track, usually, we need maximum temperature allowed is slightly smaller. So, lock rail temperature is often higher than the middle value.

$$T_s > \frac{T_{max} + T_{min}}{2} \tag{5-5}$$

Considering CWR's construction need lots of time, rail temperature of change may be lifting during this time. Ensuring the strength and stability, it allows change in the actual lock rail temperature between the design lock rail temperature of ± 5 °C.

3. Rail stress measurement[17]

Track stress is responsible or contributes to the occurrence of rail breaks, track buckling, block joint failures, certain track geometry deviations and component failures in turnouts. It is important that track engineers know the stress and stress free temperature in the rail so that appropriate action can be taken where necessary. CWR measurements are usually carried out by using one of the following methods:

1) Strain gauge based measurements(Fig. 5-4)

The use of strain gauges to measure strain in structural members is a common measurement technique. The strain gauge measures the strain, or change in length per unit length, of the member either mechanically or by means of electrical resistance. The mechanical strain gauge uses two indentations spaced a fixed distance apart that are punched along the rail's neutral axis when it is unloaded. This procedure is done on both the rail and on a standard, usually a short segment of similar rail that is left in the field near the rail being measured. The standard is measured for thermally induced strain and the net strain in the standard (strain in the standard minus the strain in the rail) corresponds to the longitudinal stress experienced by the rail constrained in the track. The electrical resistance strain gauge simplifies rail longitudinal strain measurement. The electrical resistance strain gauge can either be bonded or spot-welded to the neutral axis of the rail. More commonly spot-welded gauges are used on rail because they are better suited for severe environments.

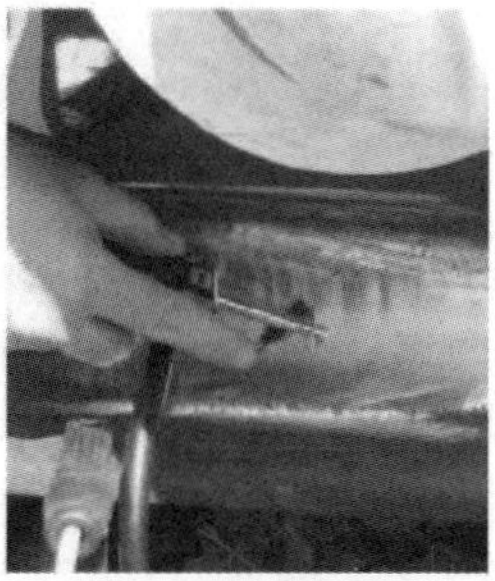

Fig. 5-3 Spot-welded strain gauge installation

An advantage of the strain gauge technique is that temperature and rail lateral bending are compensated for. Its use, however, requires cutting and destressing of the rail or the use or another technology to calibrate the gauges.

This is probably the most commonly used technique to monitor stress free temperature.

2) Lifting frame method

This method determines the longitudinal force characteristic of a rail (or indeed any beam or string) in tension or compression by measuring the load applied versus the resulting deflection. The main advantages of load deflection systems are that they measure the total force and use technology that a semiskilled operator can use. Potential issues with these systems when applied to measuring the SFT of rails are:

- They require a reasonable length of rail to be unclipped
- End effects can influence the measurements
- Horizontal curvature can influence the measurements
- They can only be used when the rail temperature is lower than the SFT(Stress Free Temperature) as they rely on measuring tension in the rail.

3) Ultrasound method(Fig.5-5)

Ultrasound techniques are commonly used in the analysis and characterization of mechanical stress states because wave velocities depend on physical properties of the propagation medium. It is well known that ultrasound velocity is changed by the stresses in a metal. This technology uses the known relationship between the speed at which sound travels through steel and the stress within the steel. The main advantage of this approach is the potential simplicity and flexibility of measurement, and the potential. The acoustic brief ringence technique involves probing the rail head and pulsing waves downward from the rail head to the rail base. The difference in flight times of pulses polarized along and perpendicular to the rail axis is proportional to the longitudinal force in the rail and the average value of residual stresses. The main issues to be accounted for when applying the technique are:

- The effect of residual stresses at the point of measurement or along the path of measurement.
- The temperature directly affects the speed of the sound significantly more than the stress affects the speed.
- The metallurgy of the rail has a significant effect on the measurement.

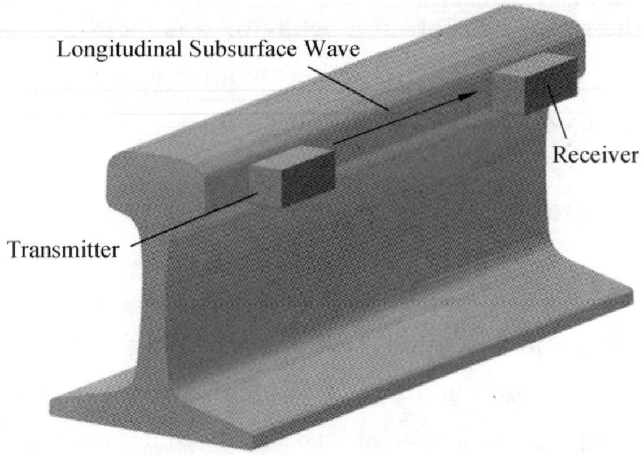

Fig. 5-4 longitudinal wave propagation method in rail

4) Magnetic properties

There are various relationships between stress and the magnetic properties in ferro-magnetic materials, which a range of technologies can measure. These approaches offer the potential for portability and flexibility of measurement and potentially, some form of vehicle mounting. The main issues for this approach are:

- It tends to be a very localized measure of the stress, which inevitably includes residual stress. This is difficult to separate from the applied stress.
- Material metallurgy affects the magnetic properties.

5) Vibration(Fig.5-6)

The rail vibration behavior in terms of frequency and amplitude depends on

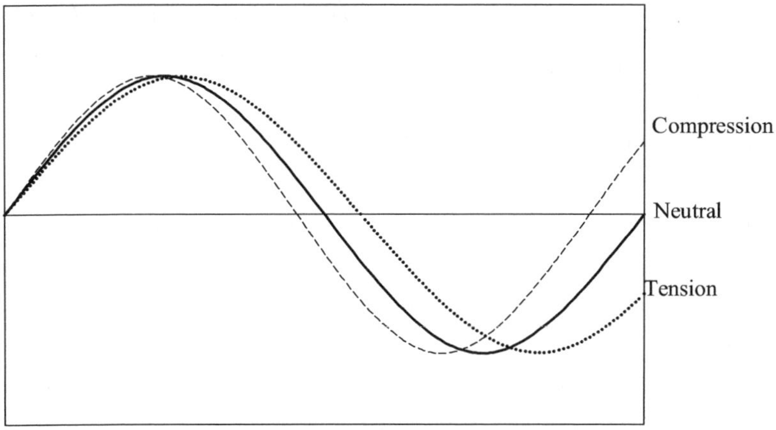

Fig. 5-5 effects of longitudinal force on wavelength

the axial load in the rail. The vibration behavior was measured using a calibrated hammer, where the acceleration from the hammer and the rail were compared using a spectrum analyzer.

5.2.3 Longitudinal resistance and diagram of rail temperature

1. The Process of expansion

If a rail is free to move without restraint, it changes 0.011,8 m of its length per centigrade. A restraining force is found in angle bars, rail anchors, double-shoulder sleepers, and special fastenings that prevent movement of the rail through the sleepers except at the rail ends.

For any temperature change Δt, the free change in rail length is Δl. If external compression or tensile restraining forces are applied parallel to its length, the new change in rail length $\Delta l'$ per unit length results from the stress-strain relation of mechanics, where stress divided by strain equals the modulus of elasticity:

If the possible changes in rail length due to temperature changes are to be entirely overcome by track restraint, the unrestrained changes in length (Δl) must be opposite change in length $\Delta l'$. To restrain completely a rail with a cross-section area A and with a maximum temperature change t, one would require a total restraining force $F=2.48 \times \Delta t \times A$ (N).

Available restraining force is found in the joint bars at each end of the continuous rail and in adjacent sleepers, until a sufficient number at each end are exerting a combined restraining force to balance the forces, and intermediate sleepers would not be required to exert any restraining force unless a rail failure or sun kink occurred.

Rail anchors transmit the rail thermal forces to the sleepers. The sleepers are restrained, in turn, by the ballast. Joint restraint is usually omitted from calculations, serving only as a factor of safety.(When rail is expanding, the ends of adjoining rails obviously provide an additional mutual restraint.) Joint restraint is shown here in equations and diagrams, even though its value will be taken as zero.

The amount of restraint exerted by one sleeper per rail has been given a wide rage from 454kg-907kg per sleeper per rail for alternate sleeper anchorage. The restraint values become approximately twice as great when the ballast is frozen.

Experience has indicated that considerable restraint is also obtained between the rail and the sleepers. Such restraint, ignored in the foregoing discussion, serves as a further safety factor.

2. Diagram of Rail Temperature

Temperature force diagram is a very important issue of CWR. We can systematically analyze distribution and variation of temperature force of inside CWR rail under different conditions with temperature force diagram.

The longitudinal distribution of temperature force along long rail is represented by temperature force distribution diagram (referred to temperature force diagram).The horizontal axis represents the length of long rail L; the vertical axis represents the value of the force temperature, with one end of the long rail as the coordinate origin. Further, temperature pulling force is predetermined positive, plotted on the abscissa axis above, and temperature pressure force is negative, plotted on the abscissa axis downward.

The longitudinal distribution of temperature force along long rail is uneven; it is not only related with the factors such as track temperature magnitude track longitudinal resistance, but also with the change process of track temperature. Therefore, there are two kinds of temperature force diagram: one is the one-way change of rail temperature, the other is the reciprocating change of rail temperature change. When a long rail is locked on a same track temperature, even if rail temperature increases or decreases, the rail cannot expand immediately. The temperature force is firstly balanced with the joint resistance. Temperature force diagram is rectangular when temperature force is less than or equal to the joint resistance,as rectangular $ABB'A'$.

When temperature force exceeds joint resistance, long rail terminal generates expansion and contraction, and rail displacement generates track longitudinal resistance. To balance the increasing temperature force, long rail terminal generates longitudinal resistance of sleepers. The more temperature force exceeds over the joint resistance, the more longitudinal track ballast of resistance sleeper is needed to balance. At this time, the longitudinal track ballast resistance and the joint resistance work together to balance temperature force, until the temperature reaches its maximum value (max P_{tp} represents the maximum temperature pressure force, max P_{tl} represents the maximum temperature pulling force) (shown as $ABCC'B'A'$ in Fig. 5-8).

As shown in Fig. 5-7, temperature force enclosed the middle of the long rail *CC'* is fully balanced by joints resistance and longitudinal track ballast resistance, that is when temperature force reaches its maximum value, rail cannot telescopic, and this section is called fixed area. In the both ends of long rail, *BC* and *B'C* segment, when the temperature force is greater than the joint resistance, longitudinal track ballastresistance balance a part of the increasing temperature force. But, temperature force that hasn't been balanced has released, expressing as telescopic and deformation. So, section at both ends of long rail that generate stretching and deformation is called telescopic area.

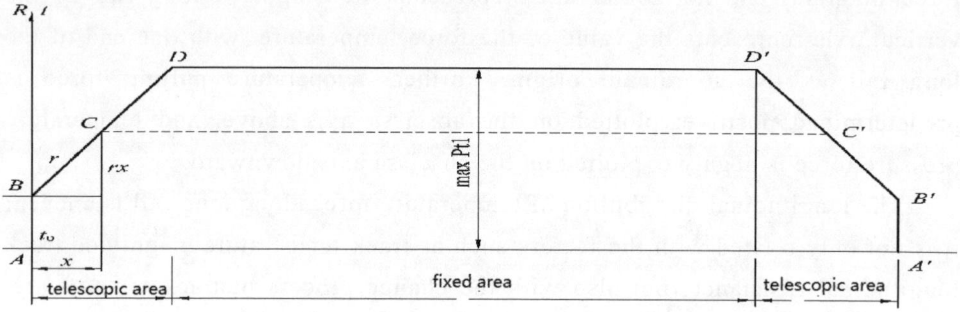

Fig. 5-6 Temperature force diagram with one-way change rail temperature of

According to Fig. 5-7, an equation showing when the force balance can be obtained:

maximum temperature pulling force of rail when at lowest rail temperature: $\max P_{\mathrm{tl}} = P_{\mathrm{j}} + ls \cdot r$.

Telescopic area length:

$$l's = \frac{\max P_{\mathrm{tl}} - P_{\mathrm{j}}}{r} \tag{5-6}$$

Where P_{j}—joint resistance (N);

R—unit length longitudinal track ballast resistance (N/mm);

ls—stretching area length (cm) caused by the rail temperature pulling force

3. Tension release[16]

Readjustment of the longitudinal state of stress in the rail to set the rail neutral temperature is a maintenance procedure known as stressing, including destressing and restressing. Destressing the rail involves subtracting steel from the rail. Restressing the rail involves pulling the rail back together to increase lost tension.

Destressing the rail (Fig. 5-8) involves cutting the rail, freeing the rail of anchors and fastenings for a specified length, adjusting the gap length to achieve the desired neutral temperature, welding the rail, and refastening it. Destressing the rail is the maintenance action performed when the rail neutral temperature is low or the rail is under large compressive forces. During the procedure steel is substracted from the rail and neutral temperature is increased.

Fig. 5-7 Rail destressing

Restressing the rail involves the use of hydraulically powered rail clamps to pull the two rail sections together and then welding or bolting them to increase the rail tension (Fig. 5-8). Restressing is the practice commonly used in cold weather where it would be difficult to provide the heat-energy required to set the desired neutral temperature.

5.3 Methods of Welding of Continuous Welded Rail

Welding is the process of uniting two pieces of similar metals or of adding extra metal to build up on existing piece of metal. Four methods of welding have been successfully used.

5.3.1 Chemical or thermit welding

The oldest and simplest of methods is the thermit process, which has for many years been the standard method for interurban rail welding. It makes use of the chemical reaction between iron oxide and metallic aluminum oxide, $FeO+Al_2 \longrightarrow AlO+2Fe$.

The older pressure-fusion method combined a pressure butt weld of the head areas with a fusion weld of the waist and foot of rail. The waist and foot were undercut to produce a gap, the heads were drawn together with clamps, and the molten thermit metal flowed in from the sides. Several commercial processes have been developed based on the thermit reactions.

Detailed procedure:

(1) Cleaning rail ends. The thermit process makes a full fusion weld. The rail ends are thoroughly cleaned of rust and dirt by soaking them in kerosene oil and brushing vigorously with wire brushes.

(2) Placement of ends. The rail ends to be welded are then placed on the proper place and a gap of 10 mm to 12 mm is kept between them.

(3) Alignment. The prepared ends as above should be aligned both in vertical as well in horizontal plane. The alignment in horizontal plane should be correct up to 0.5 mm when checked with a one metre straight edge. It is provided due to the fact that due to differential cooling, the joint tends to sag down after welding.

(4) Placing of mould around the ends. To prevent the flow of the mixture, moulds made of special sand are placed around the rail ends. This sand should have about 6% moisture content. The moulds are prepared in two halves to the profile of the rail ends.

(5) Heating of rail ends. Before welding, the rail ends to be welded are preheated for about 20-25 minute to attain a temperature of about 950 °C. At this temperature the ends will become yellow red, which can be checked by seeing through colored glass.

(6) Placing of crucible around the joint, after the above operations, a special type crucible lined with magnetite is fixed near the rail joint in such a way that when required, it can be brought exactly over the joint. The hole in the bottom of the crucible is plugged with a pin and to protect the bottom from liquid thermit steel , asbestos wool is sprinkle over it.

(7) Now thermit mixture is placed in the crucible.

(8) Actual welding. As soon as the heating is completed, the thermit mixture is ignited by special igniters made of Barium peroxide and aluminum. The thermit mixture turns into the liquid state with the evolution of heat. This

reaction is very violent and takes about 10-15 seconds to attain the temperature of 2,450 °C required for the process.

(9) The crucible is then swung round and the pin is removed molten iron flows down and fills the spherical area around the mould. The crucible is then swung round and the slag flows away.

(10) The molten thermit steel fuses around the pre-heated surfaces of the rails ends and a homogeneous weld is made.

(11) The moulds are removed after about 5 minutes. The excess metal is chipped off from sides and top while it is still red hot.

Advantages:

(12) Thermit welding is mobile in nature and welding can be done at site.

(13) No extra power is required for fusing the mixture as enough heat is generated during the chemical reaction

(14) It takes only about 35 minutes to weld a joint by this process

(15) Removal of rails from site is not required.

Disadvantages

(1) The cost of welding is very high.

(2) The welded joint is found weak in fatigue strength in comparison to flash butt welded joint.

5.3.2 Flash butt welding

This method of welding for the first time was introduced in 1928. In this method the heat required for fusing the metal is generated by electric resistance method. The two ends of the two rails to be welded are firmly clamped onto the jaws of a welding machine. One of the jaws of the machines is stationary while the other one is movable. By moving this rail end the gap between the two rail ends can be adjusted. If necessary the rail ends can be preheated up to a temperature of 950 °C, however it is not necessary to specially prepare the rail ends.

The rail ends to be welded are brought together such that they almost touch each other and a powerful electric current of the order of 5 V and 35,000 A is passed between inter faces of the two rails. By the passage of this current, considerable heat and flashing is generated. The rail ends are moved to fused by the machine till the temperature rises to the fusion limit in the range of 1,000 °C to 1,500 °C. At this stage the rail ends are pressed together under a pressure ranging from 20 tons to 37 tons. The final flashing takes place joining the two rail ends together.

The welding time varies from 150 seconds to 200 second and the loss in rail length is about 20 mm for each weld.

Detailed procedure:

(1) Pre-straightening of rail. In order to get a good alignment of the welded rail, their pre-straightening is done. Pre-straightening can be done either manually or by machines.

(2) Cleaning of rail ends. In order to ensure better conduction of electric current in the rail ends, they are cleaned for a length of 15 cm to 23 cm by electric or pneumatic grinders.

(3) Adjustment of rail ends. The rail ends then brought together in the flash butt welding machine and the longitudinal and vertical alignment of the rail is corrected.

(4) Welding. The rail ends are welded in the flash butt welding machine.

(5) Stripping. Just after welding the rails they are passed through a stripping machine, where all extral metal called up set metal is chipped off.

(6) Hot chipping. In case stripping machine is not available, then extra metal is removed by chipping off this material from the head of the rail either manually or by pneumatic chisels when the metal is still hot.

(7) Spray cooling. After chipping off the material, the rails are cooled by spray cooling by a sprayer at a distance of 60-70 m from the welding machine.

(8) Profiling. The rails are finally ground to correct profile.

(9) Post straightening. In order to give perfect alignment in both vertical as well as in horizontal direction, the rails are straightened and their vertical and horizontal kinks are removed if any.

(10) Examination and inspection. The rail ends are finally examined and inspected with regard to specified tolerances.

Advantages:

(1) The quality of weld obtained by flash butt welding is of very high order.

(2) Control over welding is possible with the help of a welding recorder.

(3) Welding cost is less in comparison to other welding methods

(4) Flash butt welding has been found very satisfactory.

Disadvantages: this methods of welding can be used in work shops only involving heavy welding plants and buildings etc. The initial capital expenditure is more.

5.3.3 Gas butt welding

In this method of welding, the heat is produced by means of oxy-acetylene flame. The apparatus required in this method is very simple and handy, which can be taken from one place to the other easily. Hence welding at site is possible.

Procedure: The rail ends to be welded are brought together and temperature of about 3,300 °C is achieved by burning oxygen and acetylene gas through regulating tubes. This temperature produces sufficient heat to melt the metal at the ends of rails. At this temperature fusion takes place, welding the rail ends together.

Advantages: This method of welding is handy. This can be used for cutting of steel. The welding can be done at site also.

Disadvantages: The cost of welding is high. The quality of weld is not of high order. Hence it is not a popular method for welding.

5.3.4 Electric arc welding

In this method, the heat is generated by the passage of an electric current across a gap between two conductors. A metal electrode is energized by an electric voltage and brought close to the other metal object, which produces an arc of electric current. This electric arc generates lot of heat, causing the two rail ends to weld

Advantages:

(1) Mobile electric arc welding plants are easy to handle.

(2) This method of welding is used for building up worn up ends or rails, turnouts and other small welding operations.

Disadvantages: Normally welding by this method is done in work shops. Hence it is not a popular way to welding.

5.3.5 Welding failure

A properly made weld is a dependable rail connection, but weld failures do occur, principally through production errors. Rail ends improperly aligned during the welding process can produce weakened or overstressed welds. All welds require grinding to proper contour. Thermal cracks can arise from heavy grinding on a cold weld, while excessive depth of grind can weaken the cross section.

Thermit welds can suffer slag and mill scale inclusions, misalignment of rail ends, and improper heat treatment after the weld is formed. With the gas butt and electric processes, mill scale or other foreign matter can get into the weld process. Partial fusion of the metal, and to unmatched rail-end surfaces, a result of improper sawing.

With electric welding improperly cleaned contact areas can cause electrode burns. Current variation from external sources or through contact pad slippage result in uneven welding—in addition to insufficient welding pressure from the slippage. With all systems heavy grinding can contribute to failure.

Metallurgical rails offer some welding problems. Heat-treated rails may be softer at the weld or more batter or surface depression forming, while alloy rails may lose toughness and/or experience fracture because of increased brittleness, with batter occurring on each side of the weld zone.

5.4 Regional CWR and Seamless Turnout

5.4.1 Regional CWR

According to the principle of CWR laying, theoretically, the length of the CWR line can be infinite. However, due to various reasons such as production technology, transportation and so on. the current average CWR rail length is about 1,500 m, concluding buffer zones, and there are still a considerable number of joints on the line, and the superiority of the CWR is not fully utilized. Take a CWR line of 160,00km length as an example, if each buffer zone is set by four buffer rails---100 meters rails totally. In this 16,000km CWR track, there are nearly 1,000 km of jointed lines, and the annual maintenance and care work is very large. Therefore, it is necessary to develop an regional CWR line. With the development of high-speed railway, it is required to improve the smoothness and integrity of the line. Therefore, it is necessary to develope regional CWR, eliminate the buffer zone, weld the switch together, and eliminate the rail joints as possible.

Regional CWR structure is an important symbol of technological progress, is the best choice of the modernization of track structure, the superiority of it to justifiably are recognized by the national railway. It has the high strength of track structure, have good driving conditions and working condition of CWR line, less maintenance and repair materials and labor cost advantages. Regional CWR line has the consistent basic principle with ordinary CWR line.Therefore, ordinary CWR line theory and its method of design calculation, construction maintenance, also can be applied to regional CWR line. Regional CWR line, however, has its new characteristics in such aspects as structural conditions, stress features, and the construction maintenance. Among all the factors, strengthening regional CWR maintenance and repair work is the key.

1. regional CWR length design

The length design of long rail of the regional CWR line is different from that of the ordinary CWR line. The reasonable quantification of the length of the long rail is the main content of the unit laying length design. The length deign of the long rail is conditioned by maintanence time windows, railroad plane conditions, rail laid methods, welding technology, temperature change state of rail, construction organization, personnel quality and many other factors. The problems existing in the railway administrations and pavement site should also be considered. According to the existing technical ability, the base of unit rail should be 2~ 2.5km, and strive for 2.5~ 3.0km.

2. Glue insulated joint

Except for the initiating terminal of long rail string, regional CWR line basically eliminates the buffer zone of 2~4 standard short rails for every 1,000~1500 m setting in the ordinary CWR line. The insulation joint of the interval signal is replaced by the glue insulated joint, and the integrity of the line is greatly enhanced. The success research of glue insulated joint is the important guarantee for the development of regional CWR line, with good features such as good integrity, high strength, large rigidity, good insulation, long life and less maintenance. The service life of this kind of glue joint is required to meet the service life of the basic rail. It should be noted that the glue joint and the welded joint are not the same in nature. Welded joint can not bear the tear force, and lack the elasticity, can not bear the excessive bending and impact. According to laboratory tests, fatigue strength of glue joint is lower than that of welded joint. Therefore, in the process of transportation and laying, the glue joint should avoid violent impact or bending.

3. Welding and construction of regional CWR line on site.

Restricted by the technical conditions and operating conditions of the regional CWR line, it is impossible to lay the regional CWR in one maintanence window time (only 1~3 km can be laid at one time), and can only divide the regional CWR line into a number of unit rails. Usually the length of rail laid on one time is called a unit rail. The turnout area and its front and back area about 200 m lines is an unit. The welding should be carried out on online way between the two units, and the locked rail temperature of each long rail string should be same. This needs to be equipped with a large tensile capacity of welding equipment or a good strencher machine. Because the long and CWR line is not completed in one time, it is necessary to keep the whole rail temperature uniform, namely consistent lock rail temperature. In laying construction, how to organize the construction team, arrange construction procedures, make all the work(pavement, sealing, stress dispersion, locking) in an orderly manner and guarantee the rail locking temperature meet the requirements have become the key problems in the construction.

4. The selection of the welding temperature and the locked rail temperature

The design of lock rail temperature of regional CWR is the same with the design method and principle of common CWR. The whole line should maintain the same design intermediate rail temperature. As the regional CWR line is welded together by the various unit rails that are laid at different times, how to ensure that the temperature force is uniform in the whole line is a key problem. The ordinary CWR line takes the actual situation into account, the lock rail temperature allowing for a range of 5 degrees Celsius generally. If the intensity and stability are guaranteed, the special case may be relaxed to 8 degrees Celsius, but this does not mean that the lock rail temperature of one rail is subject to this range. Therefore, when welding each unit of regional CWR, the locked rail temperature difference between two adjacent units should less than 5 degrees Celsius and the stress of rail is adjusted uniformly before and after welding. The final welding temperature must be carried out near the middle rail temperature, and the local stresses dissipate measures should be well done.5. maintenance and repair of regional CWR

Maintenance and repair work should be strictly controlled in the lock on the rail temperature change, CWR maintenance repair operations, must be measured and grasp the rail temperature, observed displacement of rail, rail temperature according to the actual locking arrangement work, and strictly comply with temperature conditions and maintenance operations. On a regular basis to do a good job of CWR line, CWR line often keep in a stable state; Maintenance and repair work should be paid attention to strengthen the track structure, improve the rail resistance to deformation ability; Maintenance and repair work should keep track of ride comfort, should notice to control harden pumping, sleeper, ballast track to bad and geometric dimension overrun aspects.

5.4.2 Seamless turnout

With high-speed railway and track traffic expanding rapidly, increasing numbers of seamless turnout are being employed on bridges to offer an efficient use of land resources and the effective control of settlement. When temperatures rise within the seamless turnout, the inner rail tends to stretch, thereby transferring force to the outer rail through fastenings, turnout sleepers, and the ballast bed, unlike the force path between a welded rail and its bridge. Welded turnout is a key part for continuous welded rails. Longitudinal force and displacement of rails should be considered in the design of welded turnout.

Seamless turnout has these features:

(1) Allowed speed is improved

With the removal of rail turnouts between various units within the rail joints, increasing the overall turnout within the rail ride, turnout allows can greatly improve the speed, especially speed in straight.

(2) Destroy the joint gap

In order to realize seamless turnout, in addition to fixed crossing and the frozen joint, the rest of the unit rail are connected through seamless turnout, destroy the joint gap, prevent the occurrence of the inner joint disease.

(3) Partly design of turnouts is improved

There is a strong interval iron or limiter between the stock rail and switch rail, the point rail and wing rail. Turnout elements are connected together by high strength bolts, or at the same time by cementing so as to transfer the temperature force from straight line. Limit the creeping of all the rails of turnout,especially switch rail and point rail.

Must make the pledge to keep the turnout performance, the overall structure to strengthen inspection, maintenance, guarantee the ministries accessories are complete, effective and are often in normal working condition.

Professional Words and Expressions

continuous welded rail(CWR)无缝轨道
buckling 弯曲,臌曲
rail neutral temperature(NT) 中间轨温
temperature stress CWR 温度应力式无缝线路
relief temperature stress CWR 放散温度应力式无缝线路
temperature force 温度力
temperature stress 温度应力
longitudinal force 纵向力
lock rail temperature 锁定轨温
strain Gauge 应变仪
rail Uplift 钢轨拉伸
ultrasound 超声波
magnetic 磁性能
vibration 振动
diagram of rail temperature 温度力图
longitudinal resistance 纵向阻力
3xpansion 膨胀
contract 收缩
telescopic area 伸缩区
tension release 张力释放
rail distressing 钢轨应力放散
chemical or thermit welding 化工或铝热焊
flash butt welding 闪光对接焊
gas butt welding 气体焊接
3lectric arc welding 电弧焊接
compressive forces 压缩力
typical track response curve 典型轨道响应曲线
lateral ballast resistance 横向道床阻力
gauge irregularity 轨距不平顺
regional CWR 跨区域无缝线路
seamless turnout 无缝道岔
buckling zone 臌曲变形区
adjoining zone 相邻区

CHARPTER 6　TRACK MAINTENANCE

【**Primary Contents**】

(1) Significance, features and types of track maintenance

(2) Contents and activities of track maintenance

(3) Track maintenance management of Chinese railway

(4) Features of high-speed rail line maintenance

6.1　Introduction

6.1.1　Outline

Once a structure is completed and subjected to its normal use, it is essential to maintain it in proper working condition. In case of the highway, immediately after its construction and opening to traffic only a nominal maintenance is required, and even in the absence of such a maintenance the road would give effective service to the users. The railway track requires proper watch and ward for security reasons and satisfactory maintenance for effective functioning of numerous fixtures, fittings and fastenings. These fittings may have been properly laid but on being subjected to the heavy dynamic stresses due to the high-speeds of heavy trains, they may get loosened and if regular inspection is not carried out and defects are rectified, the safe running of the trains may be adversely affected.

One solution for optimal maintenance is to do the right measure at the right time to fulfill the requirements of safety, comfort and availability. This task is virtually impossible, since it requires complete knowledge about the current condition of the track and what effect different kinds of maintenance, or no maintenance, will have on the track. Instead, the goal of condition based maintenance is to come as close to this optimum as possible. This is done with the help of measurements of important parameters which are analyzed to give knowledge about the condition of the track. After that, regulations, budget constraints and knowledge about the deterioration (from models and/or skilled engineers) are used to make decisions about maintenance.

Of course, the track could be maintained in different ways. Good/optimal maintenance can add life to the track, saving lots of money. Since such a large part of a railway authority's budget is spent on maintenance, it is of vital importance to have a clear maintenance strategy. Otherwise sub-optimal maintenance will be likely with a high degree of maintenance and run to failure. Proactive maintenance will in most cases be a better solution than reactive maintenance, provided it is done with correct timing. A maintenance strategy can also include scheduled activities such as tamping, component replacement, grinding etc. This is quite common, but is also sub-optimal if not a large part of the track in question is in need of the maintenance operation. One strong argument for scheduled maintenance is safety. Fig. 6-1 shows the high-capacity ballast cleaning machine.

Fig. 6-1 The high-capacity ballast cleaning machine

6.1.2 Good maintenance features

Railway lines are investments with very long life. Today some tracks are over 100 years old. Of course components have been exchanged during the years, but parts of the track might remain the same–especially the substructure. Typical lifetimes of for example rails are 30-60 years and turnouts 20-30 years. However, to ensure this long life a large amount of maintenance is necessary.

There are several, quite obvious reasons for maintenance, for example:

- Safety—Probability for accidents needs to be low.
- Comfort—Comfort is important, both for passengers and freight as well as for the environment in terms of noise and vibration.
- Availability—With lots of failures and speed restrictions due to safety etc. the availability of the track will be low.
- Economy—A track with low quality is cost driving, since the deterioration of both track and trains will be higher. At the same time maintenance is expensive.

Since many railway tracks are old, the demands put on the tracks today are different from the ones when the tracks were built. There is a clear trend towards higher speeds and higher capacity (more trains on the tracks and heavier trains). To face the new circumstances, more effort has to be put on track maintenance to ensure the issues of safety, comfort, availability and economy.

Maintenance will also have the following advantages[1]:

(1) Saving in the operation and maintenance cost. A "stitch in time saves nine" fits very well in the maintenance of railway track. For example loosened bolts if tightened in time would cost practically nothing but if the defect is ignored it may lead to derailment.

(2)A defect free track would ensure safe travel to the passengers and safety of goods. This would create confidence in the railway users and would act as publicity for the railways.

(3) A well maintained track provides a smooth ride of the vehicles and comfortable journey for the passengers.

(4) A proper maintenance increases life of the track as well as that of the rolling stock.

Fig. 6-2 shows the maintenance work of railway track.

Fig. 6-2 Maintenance of railway track

6.2 Type of Maintenance

6.2.1 Period of Maintenance

A good maintenance of a track consists of daily maintenance and periodic maintenance.

(1) Daily maintenance

The railway track is divided into segments of 5 to 8 km lengths. If a segment is not inspected for a long time, its risk of having track defects increases and accidents may occur. Therefore, a railroad company usually has a fleet of inspection vehicles (teams) that travel through the railroad network and inspect the track continuously.In chinese railway, each segment is looked after by the repair crews who is responsible for carrying out daily repairs consisting of the following:

- General inspection of the beat.
- Checking up of all fastenings and fixtures.
- Tightening of bolts, wherever required.
- Reporting any unusual occurrence.

The crews are supplied one set of working tools and each member of the gang is allocated a specific job or duty. The cess is used by track repair crews to walk to a work site, and as a safe place to stand when a train is passing. This helps when doing minor work, while needing to keep trains running, by not needing transport vehicle blocking the line to transport crew to get to the site.

(2) Periodical maintenance

After being maintained for a period of two to three years, a detailed inspection of the track is necessary, so that certain defects which may not have been noticed by the daily maintenance gang are detected and rectified.

6.2.2 Level of Maintenance[12]

When the track state falls below the acceptable limit value, an appropriate action should be conducted to fix the defect and to ensure that the railway track meets the required safety and quality standards. Intervention has to be done in a systematic way, i.e., avoiding any potential conflict that can disrupt the operation of train services.

Several levels of maintenance actions have therefore been identified according to the application timing. Such interventions are classified as:

(1) Corrective maintenance

This type of maintenance can be considered as the oldest intervention activity in the railway systems. It is carried out based on the occurrence of failure or worn out of the structural elements and is, therefore, performed at unpredictable intervals. The corrective maintenance may be two fold: replacement of fault components and repair action. Preferences between these alternatives are based on the cost and benefits resulting from each option.

(2) Preventive maintenance

Preventive maintenance is contradictory to the previous type of intervention. The activity is performed according to a regular scheduled time which aims to prevent the breakdown and failure of the railway system. When proposing this intervention work, one should consider the economical aspect as the main criteria.

(3) Predictive maintenance

The predictive maintenance attempts to forecast the "future" condition of the equipment. By implementing this strategy, maintenance can be performed at a scheduled point in time when the maintenance activity is the most cost-effective or before the performance of the system drops to a threshold limit. In order to determine the intervention time, statistical processes, such as regression analysis and probability methods, are used.

In order to determine the intervention time, statistical processes, such as regression analysis and probability methods, are used.

6.3 Contents of Maintenance

According to its purpose, track maintenance can be divided into two distinct categories. The first category refers to the repair of defects which occurred in the railway geometry caused by the deformation of supporting materials such as ballast and sleepers. To remove this defect, a particular track intervention known as tamping is applied by using either manual or automatic tamper machine. In the second category, the maintenance is carried out to repair the mechanical parameters which in most cases could not be restored without parts replacement.

6.3.1 Maintenance of track geometry

Even the best aligned track gets disturbed due to the cumulative effect of the following factors:

(1) Jumping of wheels over the joints. The hammer action of the jumping of wheel pushes the rail ahead of the joint forward. This hammer blow may be concentric or eccentric. The eccentric blow causes lateral shifting of the track.

(2) If the track is not properly drained it may cause mud pumping or heaving of the track.

(3) If the quantity of ballast used is inadequate or it gets loosened under the sleeper, it may cause lateral and vertical shift in the rail.

(4) On curves, the centrifugal force tends to push the track aside.

(5) Due to rise in temperature, the temperature stresses along with creep stresses may result in horizontal displacement of the rails.

Once the track gets distorted and the defect is not timely detected and rectified it might lead to serious consequences in reduction in the safety of the track and increased cost of repairs. The realignment of the track is done in the following ways:

(1) By “slewing”. The operation consists of lateral displacement of the rails by means of crow bars. A working party of gang is required for the operation. The ballast under the rail is loosened, the rail shifted to the desired position and ballast replaced thoroughly.

(2) By Track liners. When the shifting of the track from the original alignment is large, the use of track liner is resorted to. The rail can be realigned by two or three workmen only. The track liner works in one direction only and hence the shift can be gradually increased.

In the case of curved section of the track, the curve is rechecked by means of theodolite or by the string line method and pegs indicating the corrected level and position are fixed at every rail length. The track is then realigned in respect of super-elevation and horizontal position of the rail by the gangmen.

6.3.2 Maintenance of track components

The track components consist of the following: rails, sleepers, track fittings.

1. Rails

The maintenance of rails consists of the following:

(1) Oiling of fish plates and fish bolts. This ensures free movement of rails due to temperature variation.

(2) Oiling and cleaning of sliding turnouts at points and crossings.

(3) If a rail is found to have cracked or broken, a sleeper is placed immediately below the rail and spiked till the damaged rail is replaced. It is not advisable to replace the damaged rail by new rail. The tables of the new rail would be higher than that of the adjoining rails. This would result in damage to the rail ends. Such damaged rails should therefore be replaced by used but serviceable rails.

(4) If excessive wear is detected on a curve in the inner rail or on the check rail, the inner check rail should be replaced.

(5) If the rails are subjected to corrosion, especially in the rail yards, lubrication of rails should be carried out by applying waste oil to the foot and waist of the rails.

2. Sleepers

The maintenance of sleepers consists of the following:

(1) Replacement of decayed wooden sleepers.

(2) Replacement of damaged concrete sleepers.

The renewal of sleepers may be done on individual sleeper basis or over a portion of the track depending upon whether only one sleeper is defective due to some local defect in the sleeper or the sleepers have lived their useful life and need replacement. In case only one sleeper is to be changed, the operation is known as "SPOT RENEWAL". In this only the spikes and fittings of the sleeper to be replaced are removed and the sleeper is taken out from the rails by removing form the ballast. New sleeper is set in position. The old fittings may or may not be used depending upon their condition. In case a number of sleepers for a section are to be renewed as a part of renewal program, the complete rails along with sleepers and the top ballast are removed from the track and new sleepers are placed in position. The rails are then placed in position, fixed to sleepers and joined by foot plates. This method of renewal of sleepers is known as "THROUGH RENEWAL".

To prevent corrosion of fish plates they are lubricated with a lubricant containing graphite and grease compound. This is normally done before the beginning of the hot season. In addition to prevention of corrosion, graphite increases the life of fish plates and fish bolts free expansion and contraction of rails are provided.

3. Wear

Abrasive wear occurs when there is contact between the side of the flange of a wheel and the gauge face of the rail. This contact usually takes place between the leading outer wheel of a vehicle bogy and the outer rail of a curve.

On curves careful periodic check must be carried out of the outer rail to ensure that side wear is kept within prescribed limits. Failure to do this could result in a derailment. Where curves are tighter than 200 m radius, continuous check rails should be provided inside the inner rail. This check rail is to be set at a distance that will ensure that the inside face of the flange of the inner wheels will bear on the check rail thus sharing the centrifugal force between the check rail and the outer rail through flange bearing.

Abrasive wear of rails can be reduced by the use of rail lubricators placed at strategic positions. Great care needs to be exercised in the use of lubricators to ensure that only flanges are lubricated. Lubricant deposited on the top of rail heads can cause problems with braking, acceleration and wheel-spin. This is particularly important where trains are automatically driven or where stopping positions are critical such as rolling stock doors lining up with platform doors.

Where rails become side worn near to limit on curves, extra life can be obtained by either turning the heavy rail on jointed track or transposing the two rails on continuously welded rail. Close inspection of the existing inner rail outer edge must be carried out before transposing to ensure that there are no other defects present such as roll-over, “lipping” or plastic flow that would make the ride rough and precipitate failure of the new running edge.

Wear on turnouts needs to be carefully watched on a regular basis. Some repair of bad wear can be done by welding but in most cases components need to be changed.

In jointed track excessive wear often takes place at rail joints or fish-bolt holes and is the main reason for re-railing. Joints also increase wear on rolling stock. This is one of the main reasons why main line railways are progressively changing to continuously welded rails.

When a derailment occurs on any railway at any location, rail wear must be fully investigated as this can often prove to be the root cause. All rails should be closely inspected including any tell-tale signs of where wheels ran at the time of and just prior to the derailment.

6.3.3 Maintenance of turnouts

The strength of a chain is known by the strength of the weakest link. If therefore, the minimum strength of the chain is to be retained, every attention should be given to the strength of this weakest link. In a railway track the weakest links are the turnouts. Most of the derailments take place due to faults in the turnouts only and occurs due to the following causes:

- Excessive gaps in switch points.
- Lifting of toe of switch due to inadequate fittings.
- Excessive wears of the switches.
- Tight gauge.
- Defective check clearances at the nose of crossing.
- Improper assembly of the crossing.
- Loose crossing bolts or wing rails etc.

The following details should be looked into in connection with the maintenance of turnouts.

(1) Wear of top sides of the stock rails and the point rail. Worn out, damaged or broken stock rails and switch rails should be replaced as complete set. Bent switch rails should be straightened.

(2) Anti-creep devices such as creep anchors should be provided behind the heel of the turnout and the wing rail of crossing. If creep is detected it should be removed.

(3) Clearance between check rail, wing rail and switch rails should be checked with respect to the specified clearances and readjusted if so required.

(4) Fixtures to the sleepers should be checked thoroughly.

(5) Tightening of bolts should be carried out daily, if the Heel-block is loose type, the lead rail bolts are kept tight and switch rail bolts arc kept loose. If the Heel-block is fixed type, all bolts are kept tight.

(6) Interlocking connection should be clean of ballast.

(7) The leads and radius of turnouts should be inspected for the given rail

section and the crossing angle.

(8) Gauge should be checked and in case of variation from the specified gauge, it should be rectified.

6.3.4 Maintenance of level crossings

The special feature of the level crossing is that the head of the rail is flush to the road surface, so that when the road traffic is open, the rails do not obstruct the smooth passage of the vehicles. To allow the movement of train wheels over the rails, grooves are left on the inner site of the rails for the wheel flanges. These grooves are provided with the help of check rails, which are spiked to the sleeper. The following points therefore have to be taken into consideration for proper maintenance of the level crossing.

(1) As far as possible the road surface should be flexible type so that removal and replacement are easy.

(2) The level crossing should be opened out once a year and rails and fittings should be repaired.

(3) Sinking of approaches hamper the smooth riding qualities of the track and hence approaches should also be examined.

6.3.5 Maintenance of drainage

Too much water content in the substructure can cause series of different problems, therefore drainage is of vital importance. As for most of the substructure issues, drainage should be made properly when building the track. The first requirement to achieve substructure drainage is to keep the ballast clean enough to be able to drain the water as fast as it enters. The second requirement is to have the surface of the sub-ballast and subsoil sloped towards the sides of the track. The third requirement is to provide a means of carrying away the water that comes out of the substructure. Control of ballast fouling followed by ballast cleaning fulfills the first requirement. Reshaping of surfaces to get correct slopes is important for the second requirement. The solution for the third requirement has to be done with consideration of the surrounding water drainage situation. Maintaining a properly built drainage can be easy. Simple actions like flushing culverts can improve the drainage function considerably.

If the drainage provided does not function properly it will result water getting into the subgrade formation. This in turn would result in reduction in the bearing power of the subgrade formation, mud-pumping and formation of water pockets. The formation may get eroded. The following points should be attended to in respect of the maintenance of the drainage.

(1) Weeds or grass should be removed from the track or on the subgrade formation as they tend to accumulate water.

(2) Side drainage should be cleaned from time to time so that silting does not take place. If section of the drain is not adequate for the discharge of water coming into the drain, capacity of the drains should be increased.

(3) If the track section is in cutting or there is appreciable cross slope, catch water drains should be provided on either side or on the higher side as the case may be.

(4) The banking slopes should be pitched to prevent erosion.

(5) In case of heavy rainfall and cohesive soil of the subgrade formation, underground cross drainage pipe should be provided as part of maintenance if not provided originally.

(6) The ballast should be cleared to ensure that the dust formed due to pounding of wheel loads does not give rise to growth of weeds. The weeds if formed should be uprooted.

6.4 Track maintenance activities

Track maintenance was at one time hard manual labour, requiring teams of laborers, or trackmen, who used lining bars to correct irregularities in horizontal alignment of the track, and tamping and jacks to correct vertical irregularities (surface). Currently, maintenance is facilitated by a variety of specialized machines.

The surface of the head of each of the two rails can be maintained by using a rail-grinder.

Common maintenance jobs include changing sleepers, lubricating and adjusting switches, tightening loose track components, and surfacing and lining track to keep straight sections straight and curves within maintenance limits. The process of sleeper and rail replacement can be automated by using a track renewal train.

Spraying ballast with herbicide to prevent weeds growing through and redistributing the ballast is typically done with a special weed killing train.

Over time, ballast is crushed or moved by the weight of trains passing over it, periodically requiring relevelling ("tamping") and eventually to be cleaned or replaced. If this is not done, the tracks may become uneven causing swaying, rough riding and possibly derailments. An alternative to tamping is to lift the rails and sleepers and reinsert the ballast beneath. For this, specialist "stone blower" trains are used.

Rail inspections utilize nondestructive testing methods to detect internal flaws in the rails. This is done by using specially equipped trucks, inspection cars, or in some cases handheld inspection devices.

Rails must be replaced before the railhead profile wears to a degree that may trigger a derailment. Worn mainline rails usually have sufficient life remaining to be used on a branch line, siding afterwards and are "cascaded" to those applications. Various methods of intervention, repair and replacement applied to the track maintenance are shown below briefly . The description includes the procedure and technology used in the current management technique.

6.4.1 Tamping(Fig. 6-3)

Tamping is the most common railroad maintenance activity. It is operated by the tamping machine which aims to correct the geometry faults and to compact the ballast beneath the sleepers. The most sophisticated machine, currently available, is capable of adjusting the ballast position simultaneously at a speed of up to 1.6 km/pr, providing the efficiency of 50 manual workers.

At present, the line maintenance operates tamping machine. In addition, there is a especially dedicated tamping machine for tamping turnouts. There is a tamping and lining machine with tamping and lining the two functions, and assembled into dedicated vehicles line the road job. Tamping pickaxe is increased by 16 to 64, using laser lining, and provided with a mechanical device for measuring the degree of ballast tamping and track position.

Fig. 6-3 The principle of operation of such tamping machine comprises several procedures

a. The tamping machine takes the position, as shown in Figure 6.4 (a).

b. The lifting rollers elevate the sleeper and rails to the adjusted level, leaving a void beneath the sleeper over the sleeper to be tamped, as shown in Fi. 6-4 (b).

c. The machine arms bars are pushed down vertically into the ballast in either side of the sleepers, as shown in Fig. 6-4 (c).

d. By squeezing and vibrating the arms, the ballast fills the void beneath the sleeper and its packing is improved. , as shown in Fig. 6-4 (d).

e. The arms are withdrawn from the ballast and the machine is moved forward to the next sleeper to repeat the cycle operation, as shown in Fig. 6-4 (e).

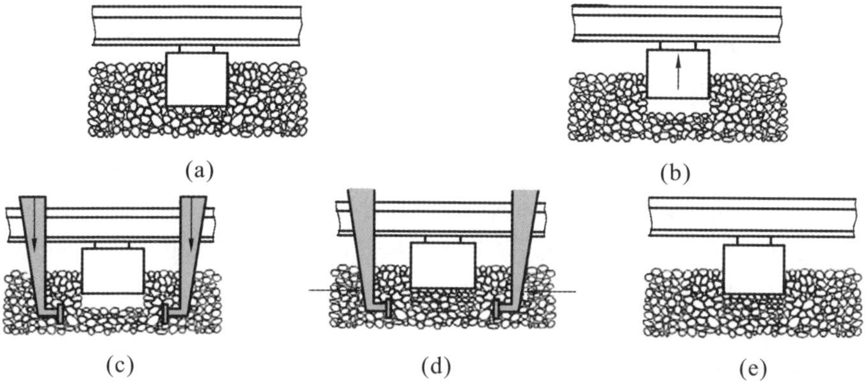

Fig. 6-4 Tamping

Some undesired effects may occur during the tamping procedure. The vibration generated by tamping may, for instance, result in completely disturbed and loosened ballast. The disturbed ballast thus leads to lateral track instability, putting the track at risk of safety. In order to reduce this drawback, the infrastructure manager usually performs the activities of re-compaction of the ballast after tamping, using mechanical stabilization.

6.4.2 Dynamic track stabilization

The lateral track instability commonly occurs due to the loss of compaction of the ballast as a side effect of the vibration induced during the tamping operation. To mitigate this problem, the dynamic track stabilizer (Fig. 6-5) is used to consolidate ballast more densely and to provide an optimum homogenous settlement of the track.

Fig. 6-5 Dynamic track stabilizer

The dynamic track stabilizer consists of 4 axle wagon fitted with a diesel engine and pressurized cylinders on the stabilizing unit. When the stabilizing action is carried out, the machine generates a vertical force beneath the track with an approximate load of 356 kN. The vibration that is transmitted to the ballast, lies in the natural frequency range and caused the stones to settle closer together within the cavities. This method allows the track to settle more uniformly and systematically, resulting in a 30% extension in the maintenance cycle.

6.4.3 Ballast cleaning

Ballast becomes degraded due to the repeated passage of trains and to very intense compression during wheel-track interactions. Such ballast crushes into small particles of stones known as fines. When the fines combine with water, the ballast loses its primary function of support to the track bed, as well as its drainage capability.

In order to remove the fines, ballast cleaning can be performed using an automated machine with adjustable excavating chain. Variety of ballast cleaning machines (Fig. 6-6) are used instead of manpower. The ballast is transferred upwards to the machine frame to be vibrated in order to eliminate the dirt and any other particles smaller than 35 mm. Afterwards, the conveyor arrangement distributes the clean coarse materials back to the ballast bed.

Fig. 6-6 Ballast cleaning machine

6.4.4 Rail grinding

Irregularities in the geometry of the rails can cause a very high dynamic load. These irregularities partly occur due to faults in the manufacturing process or as a result of the train operation activities. This special type of track imperfection is the so called rail corrugation, which is a periodic vertical irregularity on the railhead. Although rail corrugations do not pose a risk of immediate derailment, some undesirable problems can occur, such as increase in noise and in the vibrations experienced by passengers, ballast deterioration and higher maintenance cycles.

At present, grinding can be considered the most effective maintenance practice to remove the irregularities and to restore the original rail profile. There are two types of rail grinding strategies. The first one is preventive grinding, which serves to prevent the development of defects growing from the surface or into the subsurface of the rail. In this method, the maintenance operation relies on the application of one pass of a large production grinder or multiple passes of a lighter grinder. The second strategy is the implementation of corrective grinding with the purpose of removing the defects.

Typically, the grinding machine (Fig. 6-7) consists of a series of vehicles equipped with grinding wheels. As it moves along the track, the equipment performs a grinding operation on the rail surface while it re-profiles the rail. When it is used for grinding operation, several grinding units are blocked in one angle plane while performing the re-profiling operation; the grinding wheels are set at different angles so that a polygonal profile is achieved.

Fig. 6-7 Rail grinding machine

6.4.5 Rail lubrication

Rail lubrication is a technique to reduce the friction and wear that occurs between the flange part of the wheel and the gauge side of curved tracks. Using lubrication, the wear rate can be reduced about 10 to 15 times in the 300-400 m curve radius and 2 to 5 times in 600 m curve radius. Fig. 6-8 shows a machine dedicated to perform lubrication.

Lubrication may also be made by automatic applicators which are installed in the track or mounted on the motive stock. The selection of the application method will depend on the combination of economic factors, the nature of the railway network and the traffic levels.

Fig. 6-8 Rail lubrication equipment

6.4.6 Replacement

Traditionally, replacement simply consists of replacing the worn-out track components by new ones. As technology steps forwards, the estimate of the service life of a track structure or of a particular component can be easily determined. The replacement Strategy is then conducted based on the prediction of the economic life span of the track materials. In this section, some replacement methods commonly used in the track maintenance will be briefly described.

1. Rail replacement

Prior to rails replacement, new welded rails are transported to the site using a train vehicle. When these arrive, the rails are brought down and placed beside the defected track for installation. A rail exchanger is then used to take out the old rails from turnout and insert the new rails to the sequence.

2. Ballast replacement

A ballast replacement machine and its technique are quite similar to ballast cleaning. However, when the ballast replacement is carried out, a number of hopper wagons are normally attached in the sequence of the machine as storage and supplier of the new ballast. When the wagon arrives at the excavated site, the bottom of a bucket is then opened and the ballast falls down to the track.

6.5 Maintenance management of Chinese railway

Currently, Chinese railway carries out a three-level agency to manage railroad maintenance:

(1) Track Maintenance Department of the Chinese Railway Corporation. Make out the principle, technical measures and regulations of railway maintenance. Give the guidance to the railway maintenance work within the whole railway network.

(2) Track Maintenance Office of Railway Bureau. Under the leadership of the Track Maintenance Department of Chinese Railway Corporation and the directors of Railway Bureau, make out the maintenance plan and supervise the work of railway maintenance within its Bureau.

(3) Track Maintenance Depots of Railway Bureau. The Track Maintenance Depots are the executive branches belong to every Railway Bureau, with the mileage scope of about 500-700 km single rail line or 800-1,000 km double rail line. If the scope of any track maintenance depot includes mountain railway, marshaling stations or first-class stations, the management mileage can be reduced properly. The Track Maintenance Depots of Railway Bureau are responsible for the maintenance and repair of rail-line, bridge and tunnel within their mileage scope, also responsible for rail-line check, level-crossing guard and so on. Track Maintenance Depots set up lot of track maintenance workshops (routine maintenance of track and related equipment, level-crossing guard and so on), bridge maintenance workshops(routine maintenance of bridges, tunnels, culverts, etc.), emphasis maintenance workshops(medium-scale and large-scale maintenance work, etc.), comprehensive machine repair workshops (machines maintenance, fittings repair, auxiliary processing, etc.) and so on. Each workshop has several operation teams. The Types of workers are: track maintenance worker, bridge maintenance worker, track watchman, level crossing guarder, rail inspection worker.

The type of maintenance includes overhauls maintenance and daily maintenance:

(1) The overhaul maintenance includes replacing rails and sleepers, updating the ballast, etc., during which relevant rail line must be blocked, and the work time are fixed according to the train timetable.

(2) The daily maintenance has emergency repairing and routine maintenance. The cycle of routine maintenance is carried on at any time, including the small

amount of damaged equipment replacement and track realignment, the maintenance of subgrade, bridge and tunnel every year. Emergency repairing means adjusting track deformation to required standard caused by train operation timely, and keep the rail line in good condition always.

Maintenance management modernization of Chinese Railway shows three changes:

(1) From qualitative and traditional experience management to a quantitative scientific management transition.

(2) Track status and quality of detection from static detection to dynamic testing, integrated testing changes.

(3) Track management system to cover the whole path integration, networking, and intelligent systems into a separate system from the scattered.

6.6 High-speed rail line maintenance (Fig. 6-9)

The modern railway track has to carry heavier train loads at high-speeds of 120 km/h. Efforts are being made to increase the speed to 200 km/h or above. For the same load the energy of the moving vehicles increases as the square of the velocity and hence the track has to be specially designed for higher stresses, which means use of rails of higher section, stronger sleepers, higher bearing capacity of the subgrade formation and special measures for track maintenance. Some of these special measures in respect of maintenance are given below:

(1) The surface should be perfect in respect of horizontal and vertical alignment.

(2) Proper gauge should be maintained all along the track.

(3) Geometric design standards to be improved to cater for higher weights and increased speeds. These involve easing of curves, gradients and super elevation.

(4) Soft formation should be strengthened by stabilization or other methods.

(5) Larger section of the rail should be used with reduced number of joints by using welded joints instead of conventional fish plates and fish bolts.

(6) Damaged rails should be replaced forthwith.

(7) Wooden sleepers should have bearing plates to avoid heavy concentrated loads on the sleepers.

Fig. 6-9 High-speed railway maintenance

With the continuous development of high-speed railway, high-speed railway maintenance mode will certainly be improved to avoid the blindness in the maintenance and repair, and ensure the equipment always in reliable and controlled. Among them, high-speed rail inspection vehicle can be used usually.

High-speed rail inspection vehicle (Fig. 6-10) can run at high-speed more than 200 km/h to check automatically the state of track geometry under dynamic load, and can deal with data at same time. Track inspection vehicle can measure gauge, level, direction, super-elevator, vehicle vibration acceleration, axle load, vertical and horizontal deformation and other projects.

Fig. 6-10 High-speed rail inspection vehicle

For the deformation of the measured track, high-speed rail inspection vehicle has provided with plenty of converters, and the measured value is converted into a voltage, then transfer to electrical signal to calculation and display. What's more, the important feature of modern inspection vehicle is to use a computer and a variety of analytical instruments to detect, and timely handling testing data, completely abolishing the time-consuming and the errors of human judgment.

Professional Words and Expressions

track maintenance 轨道维护

daily maintenance 日常维护

periodical maintenance 周期性维护

corrective Maintenance 修复性维护

preventive Maintenance 预防性维护

predictive Maintenance 预测性维护

rail-grinder 钢轨研磨

gangmen 巡守人

tamping 夯实;捣固

dynamic track stabilization 动态轨道稳定性

ballast cleaning 清筛道砟

rail lubrication 钢轨涂油

replacement 更换

maintenance management 维修管理

Track Maintenance Department of the Chinese Railway Corporation 中国铁路总公司工务部

Track Maintenance Office of Railway Bureau 铁路局工务处

Track Maintenance Depots of Railway Bureau 铁路局工务段

overhaul maintenance 大修

high-speed rail inspection vehicle 高速铁路检修车

CHARPTER 7 RAILROAD SUBGRADE

【Primary Contents】

(1) Cross section and geometric design of subgrade

(2) Stability of subgrade

(3) Drainage of subgrade

The subgrade(also called roadbed) is a very important constituent of the track as the ultimate burden to bear the load falls on the formation. It may be prepared either by excavating the ground surface or by filling additional soil over the existing ground. The depth of cutting or the height of embankment depends upon the ground contours and the gradients adopted. The side slopes are based on the shearing strength of the soil and its angle of repose. In practice however only the angle of repose forms the basis of side slopes. The width of the formation depends upon the number of tracks, center line distance between the track and so on.

Whatever the wheel-axle load and however it is distributed, final support rests with the subgrade. Subgrades perform a three function:

(1) Bear and distribute the load of locomotives and rolling stock.

(2) Facilitate drainage.

(3) Provide a smooth platform at established grade on which to place the track and ballast.

Fig. 7-1 shows the spreading train weight to subgrade.

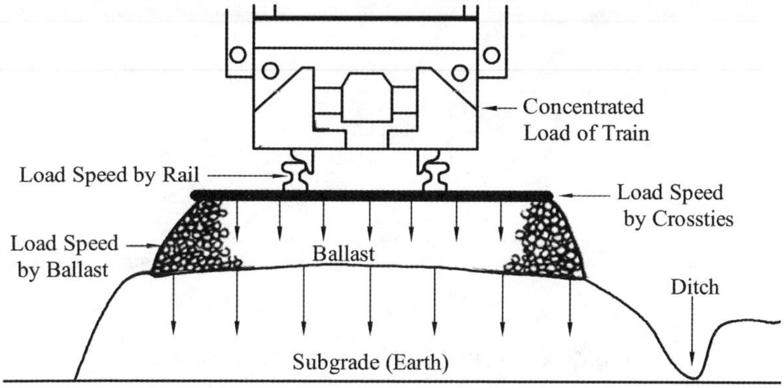

Fig. 7-1 Spreading train weight to subgrade

7.1 Subgrade Design and Construction

7.1.1 Typical cross sections

Most railroad subgrades of embankments (or filling) are trapezoidal in form (Fig. 7-2 (a)). When cuttings (or excavation) are made, the trapezoid is inverted (Fig. 7-2 (c)). Sidehill cuttings may be completely in natural ground (Fig. 7.2 (b) or a composite cutting and embankment (Fig. 7-2 (e)). The latter is the least stable, as the embankment portion may have a tendency to settle or slide. Typical cross-sections for single and double I-class railway line in embankment and cutting have been illustrated in Fig. 7-3, 7-4, 7-5 and 7-6.

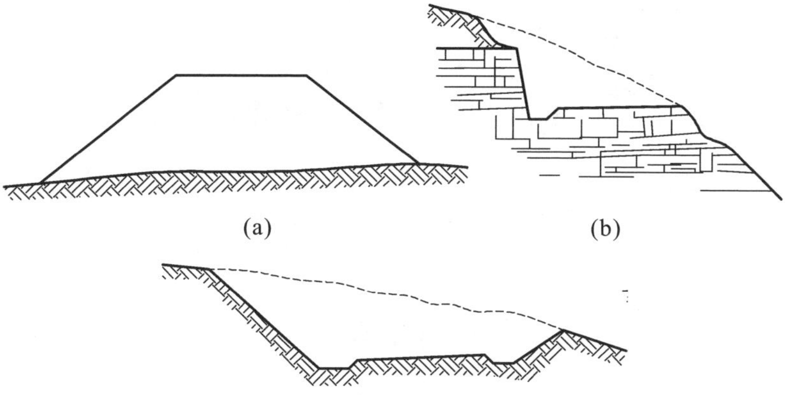

(a) (b)

(c)

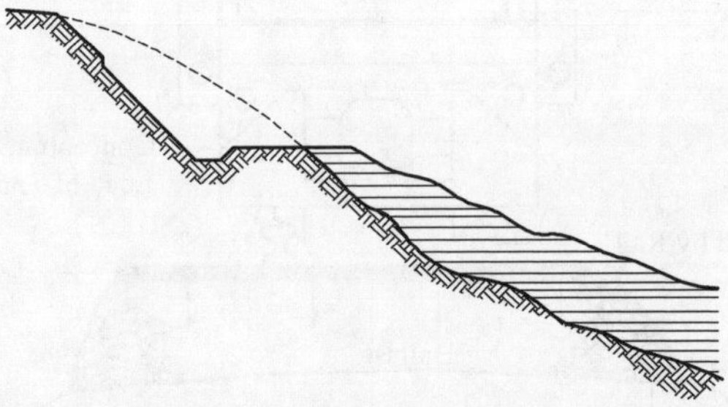

(d)

Fig. 7-2 Typical subgrade cross sections

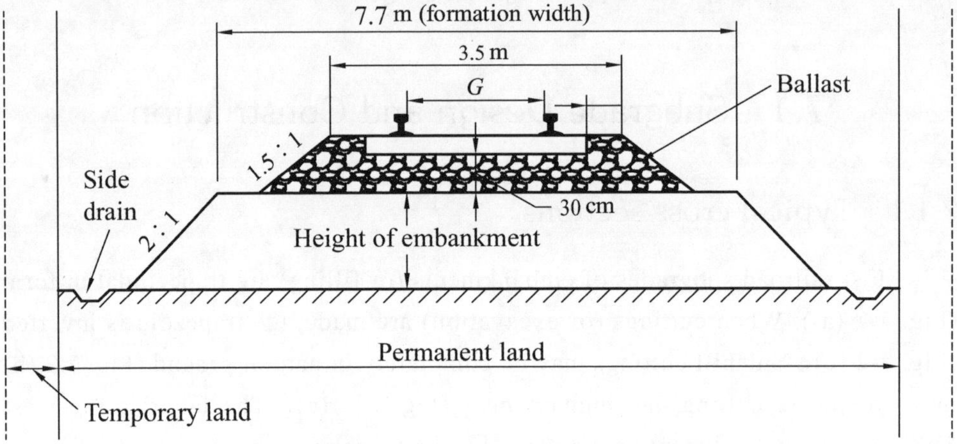

Fig. 7-3 Sing line track of embankment I-class railway

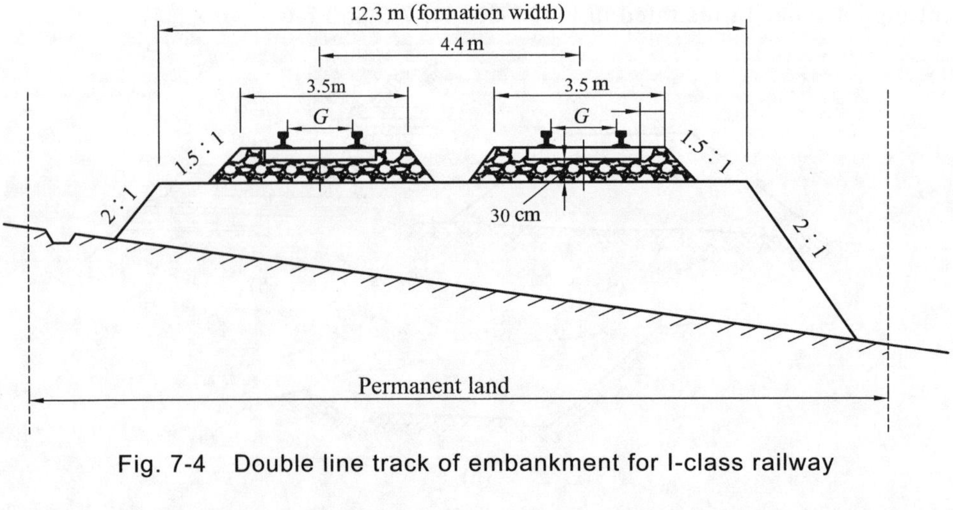

Fig. 7-4 Double line track of embankment for I-class railway

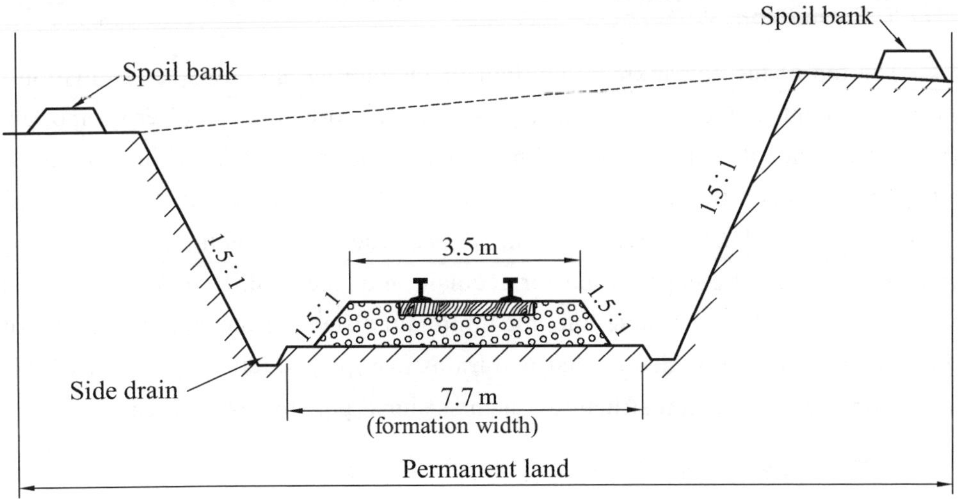

Fig. 7-5 Single line track of cutting for I-class railway

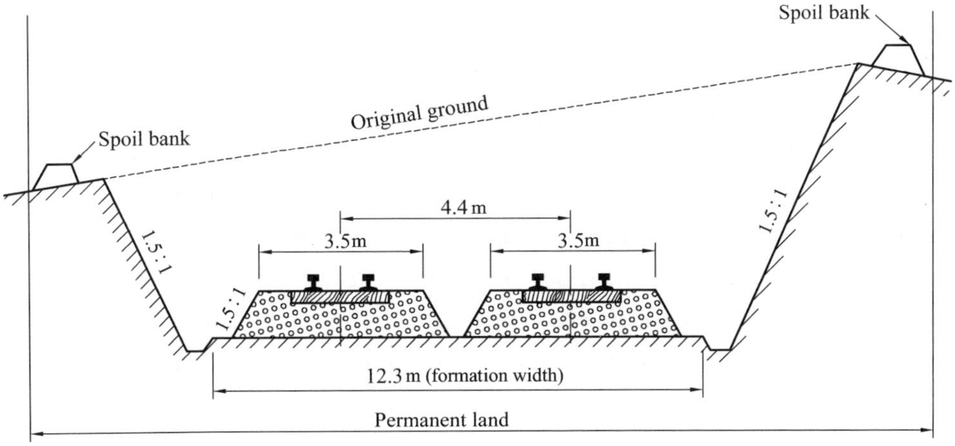

Fig. 7-6 Double line track of cutting for I-class railway

The various elements of the subgrade cross-section are as given below[1]:

(1) Permanent land.

(2) Temporary land.

(3) Formation.

(4) Slopes of cutting or embankment.

(5) Drainage.

These elements are briefly described below:

1. Formation

The top of the embankment or floor of the cutting is known as "formation". From the point of view of the track, the width of formation is a very important parameter. Since the track is laid with formation as its base. The width should be adequate to meet the track requirements. Width in excess of the minimum requirement would mean the increase in the permanent land and the width resulting in increased cost of compensation for acquisition of the land. In order to arrive at the formation width for double line, the minimum distance from centre to centre of the track has to be provided so that two trains may pass safely leaving reasonable space for intermediate rail structures, such as signal post to be provided.

2. Permanent land

Before any railway project is initiated, a tentative decision in respect of the proposed construction is arrived at on the individual merit of the project. A certain strip of land on either side of the center line of the proposed track is acquired by the railway concerned either by transfer of land from other state or central development of the government or by acquiring private property from the owners of the land. The strip of land thus transferred to or acquired by the railway is termed as permanent land. The width of permanent land depends on the gauge of the track, whether single line track or double line track, formation width, side slopes of the formation, side drains and the side slopes of cutting or embankment as the case may be. While considering single line or double line track the possibility of future expansion namely addition of another line to meet the increased demand is also to be borne in mind.

3. Temporary land

In every rail project the preparation of the formation is the first stage of execution of the work. The formation is prepared either by earth filling over the existing ground surface or by excavating the ground to the designed depth. In the former case, the earth has to be arranged for banking while in the latter case, the earth has to be disposed off. An ideal condition would exist when the cutting from the adjoining stretches is used for filling the strips in embankment. When however, cutting and embankment do not balance, it is better to temporarily acquire a strip of land adjoining the permanent land from which earth may be "borrowed" for making up the embankment. It may also be utilized as spoil bank for the excavated earth which can not be economically utilized for the project work. Thc strip of land thus acquired temporarily for the duration of the project is known as temporary land.

4. Drainage and Slope Protection

Adequate drainage is essential. The cross-sectional design must provide for track ditches, intercepting or berm ditches, terrace ditches, and culverts.

Where special slope protection features such as rip-rap, retaining and toe walls, or other slope blankets are involved, drains to reduce hydro-static pressures behind these covers must be included in the design.

7.1.2 Geometric design

Here are at least four basic geometric features in designing a railroad subgrade. Each of these must be developed in terms of the class of line and of the soil and rock materials being used. The advice of a soils engineer should always be available. The four basic geometric features are:

- Width of top of subgrade or bottom of cuttings.
- Height of embankment or depth of cutting.
- Side slopes of embankment or cutting.
- Provision for drainage.

1. Width of subgrade surface (or formation width)

The minimum possible width of the top of the subgrade is determined by the width of ballast section. Its width depends primarily on the depth of ballast beneath the sleeper. A minimum subgrade width is desirable to give stability and permit adequate ballast depth, although low-density branch section and subgrade are based properly on the expected traffic at least 10-15 years in the future. The cost of extra width at the time of construction should be balanced against the estimated future cost of subgrade widening. Usually different standards of ballast and subgrade section are established by a railroad for its main line, for secondary lines, and for light-traffic branch lines and spurs.

The subgrade shoulders should extend a enough width, beyond the toe of the ballast slope to support the ballast section. A ballast section at the base would require a minimum subgrade width plus two times subgrade shoulders width. The shoulder width of embankment should not be less than 0.8m. The shoulder width of cutting should not be less than 0.6m. Table 7-1, table 7-2 shows the surface width standard of high-speed and normal-speed nonelectrify railway subgracle subgrade.

Table 7-1 Surface width standard of high-speed railway subgrade

Track type	Design maximum speed(km/h)	Distance of two railroads(m)	Width of subgrade surface	
			Single line(m)	Double line(m)
Ballasted track	250	4.6	8.6	13.2
	300	4.8		13.4
	350	5.0		13.6
Ballastless track	250	4.6	8.8	13.4
	300	4.8		13.6
	350	5.0		13.8

Table 7-2 Surface width standard of normal-speed non-electrify railway subgrade

Items		Unit	I-class railway								II-class railway	
Design speed		km/h	200		160			120			≤120	
Ballast thickness		cm	35	30	50	35	30	50	35	30	45	30
subgrade Surface width	Single line	m	7.7	7.5	7.8	7.2	7.0	7.8	7.2	7.0	7.5	7.0
	Double line	m	12.3	12.1	12.2	11.6	11.4	12.0	11.4	11.2	11.7	11.2

Some additional width at the time of construction protects against the sloughing of shoulders due to erosion, settlement and wind, rain, frost, and soil action. The amount of widening for these purposes is more than the widths for a seasoned roadbed. Where soils are particularly susceptible to wind or water erosion, the required amount of widening is greater. With modern compaction less allowance need be made for these reasons. An extra foot of width on each shoulder has been found satisfactory for gravelly materials or for those of greater stability. Additional width as determined by soils engineering principles is required for soils low in shearing strength or cohesion. Some engineers widen embankments as the height increases, but there is little uniformity in the practice. Width must be added for anticipated settlement, otherwise, with successive ballast applications during maintenance, the top of the embankment becomes too narrow to support the ballast width.

In cuttings, the question of settlement does not arise, but side ditches through the cuttings may cause erosion. It is desirable to use the same width of subgrade in cuttings as in embankments. The most important factor affecting the width of cutting (at the base of the cutting and differentiated from width of the subgrade) is side ditches. Standard plans usually show minimum dimensions only and local conditions of length of cut, gradient, depth, rainfall, and runoff. And natural groundwater must be studied for increased width of ditch requirements. In longer cuttings wider ditches are needed to handle the increased accumulation of water. If the gradient is steep. The subgrade shoulder must be protected against erosion widening the side ditches, and/or paving or rip-rapping the ditch slopes may serve to prevent the erosion. Increased width of cutting is required where danger exists from falling rocks and slides and from heavy rains and snows space is also available to dispose of debris or snow cleared from the track and ditches.

2. Depth of subgrade

Depth is the difference between the ground line and profile elevations. In embankments some shrinkage or settlement may occur, depending on the soil and subsoil types and construction methods. The practice of adding height compensate for settlement is obsolete. An exception is surcharge placed on the fill to hasten settlement. The excess is later bladed to proper elevation.

At bridge abutments, the proposed grade must be maintained because of the fixed elevations of these structures. Settlement can be minimized by a careful selection of materials and the use of compaction methods. Rebuilding sloughed-off embankments at bridge ends is a maintenance expense. The embankment at bridge ends should be flared out like a fan to provide support for ballast. Too often swinging cross sleepers are found at bridge ends on the embankment.

Where permafrost conditions are encountered, it may be desirable to provide a maximum depth of embankment to lessen the severity of frost action and to facilitate drainage. High water levels in flood stages may also prompt the raising of the grade line and height of embankment above those normally required.

3. Slopes

The third critical dimension, the rate of side slope, depends primarily upon the shearing strength and the angle of repose of the materials forming the slope. The ratio of the slope height to the slope width is expressed in the form of H:b, and H=1 is taken as the form of 1:m (embankment) or 1:n (cutting) to represent the slope ratio. A slope of 1.5 : 1 and 1.75 : 1 is commonly used in railroad design for both cuttings and embankments and gives reasonable stability for most materials. The slope of subgrade generally should be determined by design calculation, and it can also be used according to the engineering practice experience and the recommended values of design specifications.

Sands or clays may require a 2 : 1 or even 3 : 1 slope; solid rock cuttings stand on a 0.5 : 1 or 0.25 : 1 slope. Flatter slopes, through having a larger area, receive a greater fall of rain and are subject, therefore, to move erosive action. A slope of 2 : 1 is approximately one-third longer than a 1.5 : 1 slope and receives, consequently, one-third more rainfall. Fresh cuttings stand on a steeper slope but are more susceptible to wash action. The amount of erosive action from wind, rain, stream flow, or wave action is a factor in determining slope. A final decision on the rate of slope must depend on the type of soil being used rather than on the application of any rule of thumb.

A question sometimes arises as to whether cuttings should be widened or slopes flattened. This question may occur when the improvement of an existing line is contemplated or when additional material is being removed from a cutting in lieu of opening a borrow pit. No increased stability is achieved by flattening unless the existing slope is steeper than the angle of repose of the material that comprises it. More right of way will probably be required for flattening than for widening. The increased erosion of flat slopes has already been noted. In shallow cuttings some advantage may be got by going to a slope of 4 : 1 in preventing snow drifts. One western railroad has used as flat a slope as 6 : 1 in snow cuttings. Slopes flatter than 2 : 1 permit the use of a tractor-mounted mower for cutting weeds, brush, and grass. The comparative effects of cutting widening and slope flattening can be seen in Fig. 7-7. The same amount of material must be removed in reducing from a 1.5 : 1 to a 2 : 1 slope as in widening a distance equal to half the amount of top cutback for the 2 : 1 slope. As just noted, the effects of widening are likely to be more beneficial.

For high cuttings increased stability of slope can be obtained by terracing or providing setbacks. Terracing has been performed both on embankments and in cuttings. It can be beneficial in either situation. There is no uniformity in the practice. In terracing a paved gutter at the toe of the upper slope is helpful in preventing erosion and channeling runoff from the bean of the cutting. If the gutter is not carefully built to grade, it is likely to overflow and add to the danger of erosion and slides.

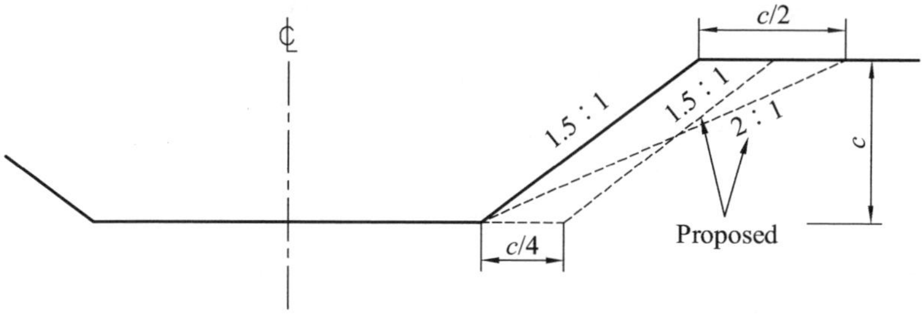

Fig. 7-7 cut widening versus slope reduction

4. Drainage [22]

The purposes of drainage works are to prevent mud pumping, ensure the strength and prevent deterioration of the subgrade, and to prevent erosion of the surface layer of slopes and slope failure. On both sides of the embankment or cutting sufficiently wide drains are provided to carry away the rain water both from the track as well as from the upper reaches of the drains. In the case of the natural slopes of the ground exists at right angles to the track alignment, no drain need be provided on the lower side. In the case of the section running in excavation, or in the absence or adequate cross slope, drains have to be provided on both the side of the track.

The strength and durability of an embankment is greatly influenced by how well or how poorly it handles water. Failure of an embankment during torrential rainfall is caused by a rise in pore water pressure inside the embankment due to mainly concentrated runoff of rainwater or seepage of groundwater or rainwater.

Therefore, drainage works must correctly handle the water that causes these problems. But in special sections with a cutting-banking boundary or with both cutting and embankment, additional measures must be taken depending on the situation.

Failure of cutting slopes during torrential rainfall is caused mainly by concentrated runoff of the rainwater and the increase of the ground pore water pressure caused by seepage of groundwater or rainwater. Therefore drainage works must be planned to appropriately handle water that is the cause of these problems. Fig. 7-8 shows standard embankment drainage plan. Fig. 7-9 shows a standard cutting drainage plan.

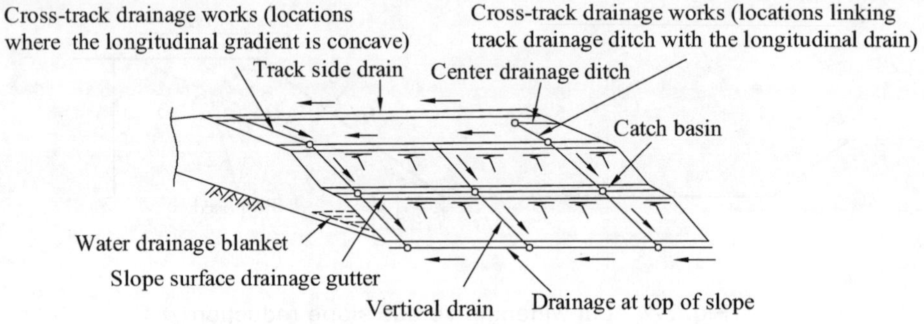

Fig. 7-8 example of an embankment drainage plan

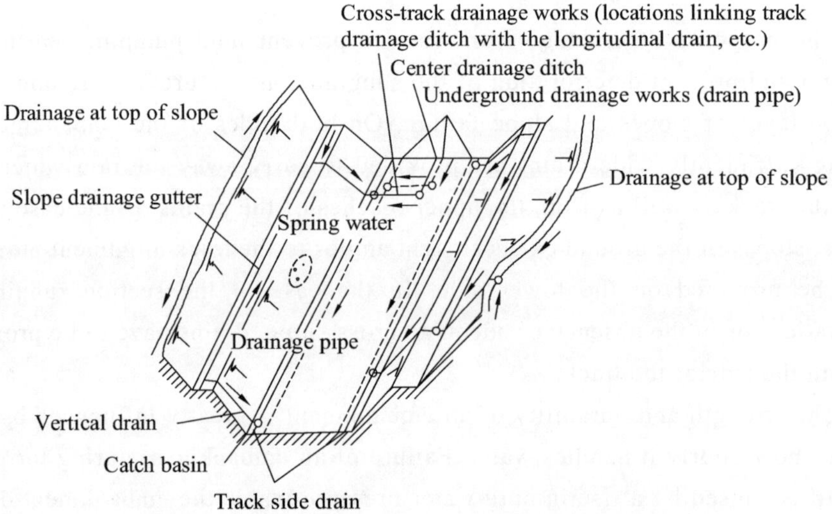

Fig. 7-9 example of a drainage system for cutting

7.2 Stability of Subgrade

Many sections of subgrades today offer serious maintenance problems in the form of "sinks," "soft spots," water pockets, slides, subsidence, and occasionally complete failure, these unstable conditions are not necessarily limited to older structures. Instabilities and failures have occurred in recently built structures. Unstable subgrades lead to increased maintenance, slow orders, loss of train speeds, reductions in track capacity, and sometimes outright disaster. The problem becomes one of improving and stabilizing the existing structures.

Because some instability can be anticipated and corrected during construction, one might divide stabilization procedures into pre-construction and post-construction categories. A third group of problems, slope stability, for example, may be present either during or after construction. The application of geotextiles may occur during construction or become a part of maintenance after construction.

The initial step in stabilization is to determine the characteristics of the soils involved and how these relate to unstable conditions and to the methods available to gain stability。Instabilities can arise from combination of causes. The services of a geo-technical engineer should always be available.

Stabilizing efforts are directed toward increasing the shear strength and cohesion of the soils. Primarily, this means removing excess moisture and lowering plasticity, but it also involves compacting the particles, tightly together to enhance internal friction and reduce inter-granular voids that hold excess moisture. Additives can be introduced to lessen moisture, reduce plasticity, increase internal friction, and, sometimes change the chemical nature of the soil. Mechanical restraint has been effective in certain circumstances. Any procedure that reduces the intermingling of subgrade and ballast particles will be helpful. Excavation and backfill with select materials, and relocation are possible solutions when other measures fail. Some of the more common situations will be considered in this chapter.

Ground water is a vital factor in slope stability. Both in cuttings and embankments surface water must be channeled to storm water drains or natural water courses. Where drains are blocked, progressive softening of the subgrade structure will take place probably resulting in slipping.

7.2.1 Instability performance of subgrade

1. Subsidence

A not uncommon cause of track instability is the weakness of the supporting subsoil or natural ground and of the slopes adjacent to the subgrade. Subsidence is the overall vertical settlement or side flow (sometimes both) of the subgrade due to inability of soil materials under the filling to support the imposed load. Almost any soil, except rock, compacts and settles a small amount under the fill. A series of exploratory trenches and borings on one railroad indicated an average settlement in firm ground.

The initial soil exploration combined with a study of local geology should indicate the presence of unstable ground of whatever type. The depth of unstable material and the nature of the underlying strata as well as the exact extent of the deposit along the route must be determined by means of drill holes and core samples plus a series of soundings between the holes. If a very soft clay stratum is involved, its position must be determined as above, and the characteristics of the clay learned from laboratory tests.

Subsidence and/or sides are likely to occur when the load imposed by a filling exceeds the bearing capacity of the natural ground. The unconfined compressive stress should be established to determine the allowable height of filling.

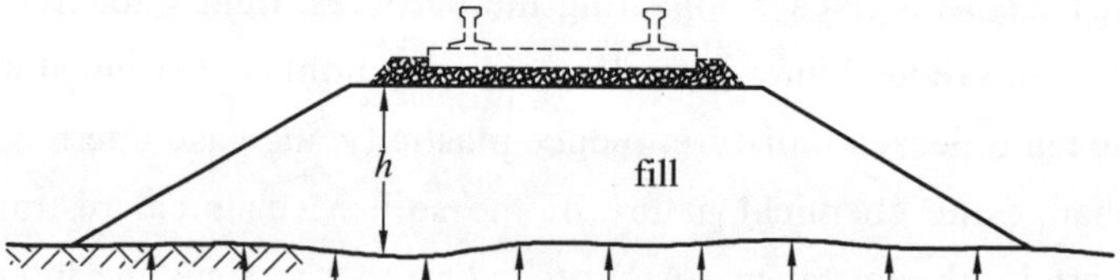

Fig. 7-10 Subsidence of embankment

2. Subgrade slope failures

Property damage has been incurred, maintenance costs accumulated, trains delayed and derailed, and tracks and pole lines lost because of the sliding and falling of earth and rock masses. The slid or rock fall need not be large to cause disaster for a swiftly moving train. Landslides, rapid or slow moving, are superficial movement of earth masses having essential a horizontal component. Slope failure may occur either in the slopes of cuttings or embankment. Rock falls may be either rock masses or individual boulders falling from the face of rock slopes.

Three types of slide failures in railroad subgrade embankments have been recognized: slides resulting from a failure of the soil in shear, sliding failures along lubricated surfaces, and foundation failures. Slides are an especially dangerous type of instability, since failure may occur suddenly and without warning, possibly during the passage of a train. Investigation of slides should include an effort to determine the plane of sliding so that strength and friction may be restored. Deep borings and soil tests may be necessary to determine the source of sliding. Variable characteristics of soils make it impossible for embankment materials to behave as perfectly uniform plastic soils. The classification of a slide into any one type is thus rendered difficult. Characteristics of the several slide types will assist in analyzing slides.

Slides in homogeneous soft clays (Fig. 7-11 (a)) arise from failure in hear when given too steep a slope. Movement may be rapid and along in approximately semicircular path, usually accompanied by a heaving at the lower end of the slide (adjacent to the toe of the slope) and presenting a typical S formation. When a slide of known magnitude has already occurred in the same type of soil or situation, moments may be taken by the laws of mechanics through the centers of mass from the center of the arc of sliding and the shearing strength determined as indicated in Fig. 7-11 (b).

A second type of overstressed foundation failure occurs with lateral displacement of the underlying materials. This failure may take place either in the basically weak swampy soils or in soft clays. Both types may be accompanied by sliding of long duration. The rate of sliding will then be a function of slope and depth and the character of the subsoil materials. These must be determined as a part of any program of stabilization. Fig. 7-11 (c) indicates how displaced material is forced outward and upward at the toe of the embankment. Heavy and frequent replenishing of embankment materials required to replace the shifted soil. Again there may be sudden and complete failure.

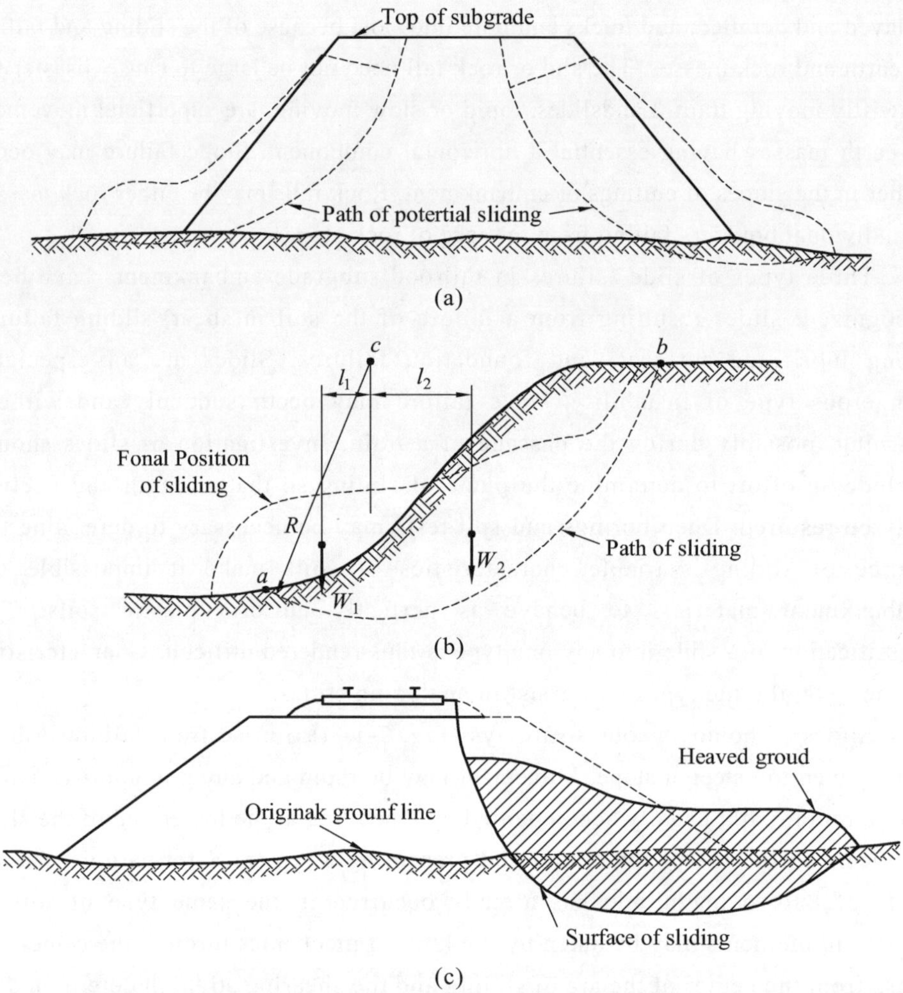

Fig. 7-11 Slides due to failure in shear

Sidehill fills or composite cut and fill sections may slide on the plane between the fill and natural ground material (Fig. 7-12). Groundwater seepage through the roadbed, surface runoff, of other moisture may serve to lubricate the boundary surface and cause sliding. The plane of sliding may also occur between two soils in the fill itself.

Slide in stiff clays may occur when weakened by hair cracks or slicken-slides, which serve as small waterways and permit saturation in the immediate area. A soft mass with a hard core is formed that slide along a circular path tangent to the toe. The slide may occur long after the original cut was made. Drainage of the upper edge of the cut aids in preventing this type of sliding.

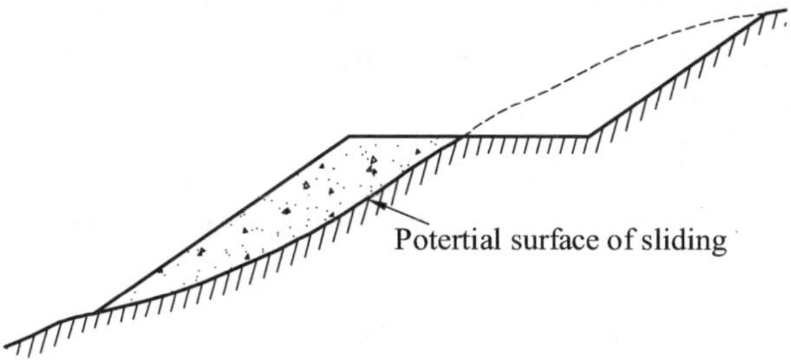

Fig. 7-12 sliding of embankment

3. Other types performance of instability

Within the subgrade itself several types of instability occur with unpleasant frequency. The causes of individual types may be related, and two or more problem types may combine in contributing to overall instability and in blurring the distinctive features of each.

(1) Weak Ballast Restraint. The resistance of a ballast material to permanent deformation depends in part on the confining restraint to which it is subjected. A principal source of restraint is the subgrade. A strong, stable subgrade offers considerable vertical restraint to the ballast. A weak and plastic subgrade permits ballast settlement and deformation, with concurring adverse effects on track surface and line.

(2) Frost Heaving. Earlier mention has been made of track displacement caused by the formation of pockets or lenses of ice within the upper reaches of the subgrade or within the ballast section. Frozen water expands by 9%-10% in volume. Pockets of fine-grained soils (3% or more less than 0.02 mm in grain size), saturated through capillary action with a free supply of water, combined with subfreezing soil temperatures will expand and distort track surface and line. The ice expansion and distortion will continue, fed from below by capillary action, until a state of temperature equilibrium has been reached. Shimming and slow orders are immediate remedies. Ballast cleaning, excavation and backfill, and improved drainage offer more lasting relief.

(3) Water Pockets. Uncompacted or frozen soil lumps or the arching of embankment materials against rocks, stumps, or timbers left in the embankment from old filled-in trestles leave voids in which moisture collects to form water

pockets; timber decay also forms voids in which moisture readily collects. Water pockets are causes of uneven track settlement and, if permitted to grow unrestrained, can cause complete failure of the embankment.

(4) Ballast Pockets. By patting a sample of fine-grained soil held in the hand, an iridescent sheen will appear on the surface from moisture drawn from within the sample. Passing wheel loads contribute the same patting action to subgrades. When a small quantity of moisture exists at the interface between the ballast and fine-grained subgrade materials. The repetitive load and release of passing wheels can form a slurry. The natural water content of the soil may be sufficient to form the slurry, but additional moisture, as with water pockets, comes from rain, snow melt, and capillary rise. Moisture may also seep in from adjacent wet cuts. The slurry will work upward through the ballast, fouling it, reducing the draining properties, and causing “pumping” track. At the same time ballast particles are forced downward into the plastic slurry, the action is repeated at lower levels of contact, and eventually ballast pockets similar to those indicated in Fig. 7-13 are formed. The pocket may shift in the direction of greatest weakness or plasticity in the embankment, pushing other materials out and upward at the toe of the embankment. The more material thus pushed out at the toe, the greater the probable depth of the pocket. The pocket may contain water sufficient to flow several hours or days if tapped. There is a weakened track structure, sink, or soft spot, requiring excess maintenance-additional ballasting and resurfacing-and causing an accelerated wear of rails, sleepers, and fastenings. Slow orders may be necessary. Complete failure of the embankment sometimes occurs.

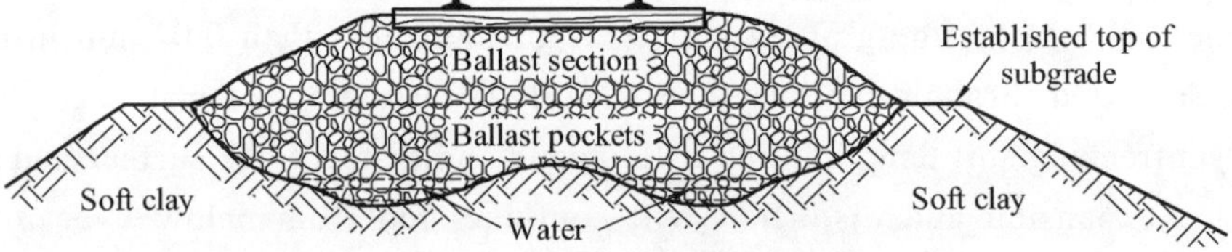

Fig. 7-13 Typical ballast pocket

Water pocket explorations are made with earth augers, hand or power driven, or by digging trenches across the embankment. The extent and depth of the pocket, the types of soils involved, and the amount and sources of water present in the pocket must be determined.

7.2.2 Stabilization methods

A wide variety of stabilization procedures are in use, all of which offer a certain amount of immediate relief, but with varying degrees of permanence and economy. All methods cannot be applied to all situations. The procedure used must be related to the type of soil involved and the particular situation. Some methods are best applied during construction.

1. Systems of drainage

Surface drainage is basic and absolutely necessary. Rain and groundwater must be diverted away from embankments and into proper channels and culverts. Where fills cross depressions, water must not be sub wed to accumulate and stand against the toe of the fill. Borrow pits must be drained. Most instability is probably a result of surface water rather than ground flow.

Sub-drainage is intimately connected with roadbed stabilization. Sub-drainage systems, used both in cuttings and in embankment, consist of longitudinal drains laid between tracks or under the side ditches, or deeper, depending on the depth of water pockets encountered, with laterals extending at right angles under the track from the main drain. (Fig. 7-14)

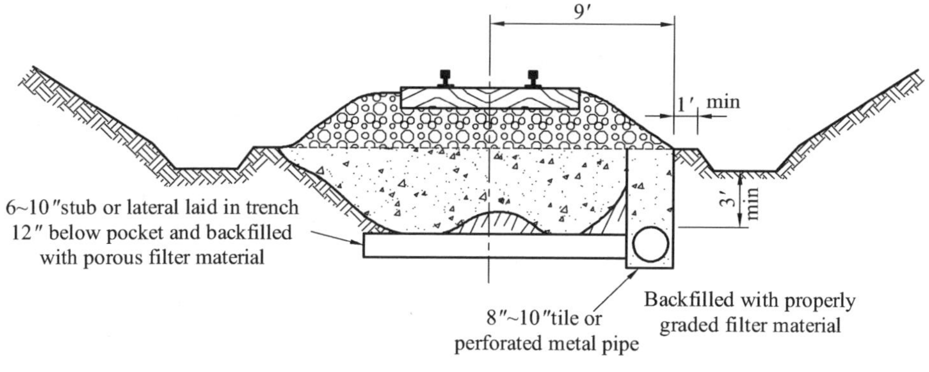

Fig. 7-14 Sub-drainage system

Laterals of a sub-drainage system have been laid at regular intervals, for instance, one to a rail length. A better method is to investigate sub-surface conditions beneath the ballast, locating the low points of ballast pockets and placing the pipe below the pocket bottom. Such pockets, when first tapped, may flow steadily for several hours or days. It should be borne in mind that water may be channeled to a water pocket area through permeable roadbed materials from a point some distance removed from the pocket in question (Fig. 7-15).

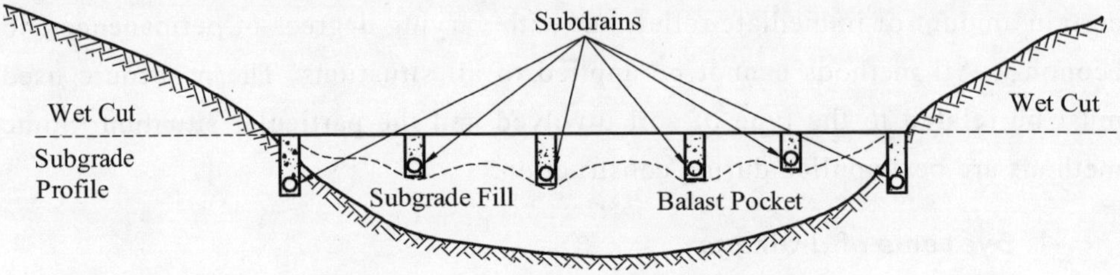

Fig. 7-15 sub-drainage system

2. Retaining wall

In order to prevent deformation or instability of filling or soil, retaining walls are used to support subgrade fill or hillside soil. The common types of retaining walls are:

(1) Gravity retaining wall (Fig 7-16)

The stability of gravity retaining wall under earth pressure is maintained by gravity of retaining wall. Gravity retaining wall is a kind of retaining wall commonly used in China. Gravity retaining walls can be built of stone or concrete, usually made of simple trapezium.

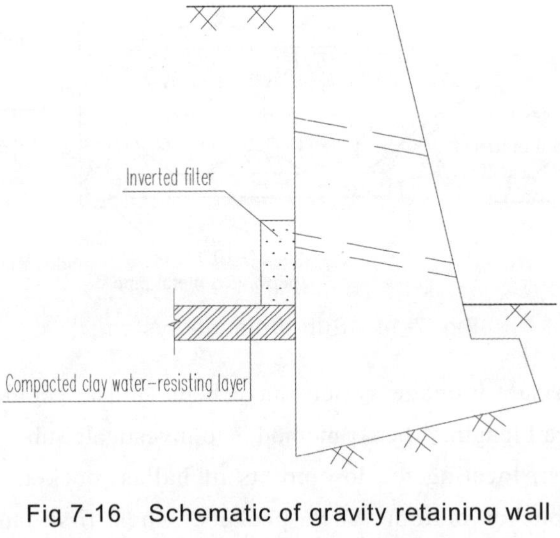

Fig 7-16 Schematic of gravity retaining wall

(2) Tied retaining wall (Fig 7-17)

Tied retaining wall belongs to light retaining wall, usually including two kinds of anchor and anchor plate.

The anchor retaining wall is mainly composed of wall and anchor bolts, and the wall is made up of precast reinforced concrete columns and retaining plates, the steel bolts are buried horizontally or horizontally in rock or soil. It mainly depends on the anchoring force of anchor bolts embedded in the rock to pull the column to ensure the stability of the soil. For anchored plate retaining wall, the anchor bar is changed into a pull rod, and an anchor plate is connected to the end of the pull rod. Such retaining walls are used for shoulder walls or embankment walls in areas lacking stones.

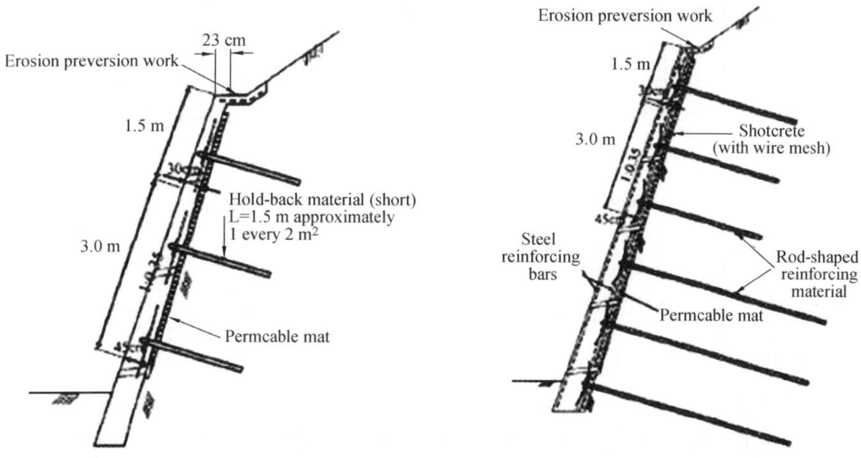

Anchored retaining wall　　Reinforced soil retaining wall for natual ground

Fig 7-17　anchor reinforced walls for cuttings

(3) Thin wall retaining wall (Fig 7-18)

The thin-walled retaining wall is reinforced concrete structure, including cantilever and buttress type two main types. The structural stability of cantilevered and buttressed retaining walls is guaranteed by the gravity of the wall body and the gravity of the fill above the heel. Their main features are simple construction, convenient construction, smaller wall section and light self quality. It can give full play to the strength of the material and can adapt to the lower bearing capacity of the foundation. However, the consumption of a certain quantity of steel and cement, especially when the height of the wall is large, increases sharply and affects its economic performance. Usually, cantilever is used when wall height below 6 meter, and buttress is adopted for 6 meter above. They are suitable for lack of stone and earthquake areas.

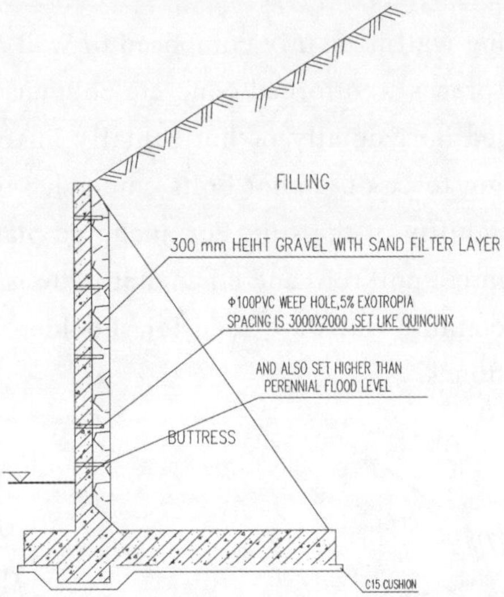

Fig. 7-18 Schematic of buttressed retaining wall

(4) Reinforced earth retaining wall

Reinforced earth retaining wall composed of earth fill, tension belt and masonry block, which supports the lateral pressure of the soil. In order to achieve the purpose of stabilizing the soil, tendons are added to the soil, and the friction between the reinforcement and the soil is used to improve the deformation conditions of the soil and improve the engineering properties of the soil. Reinforced earth retaining walls are generally applied to fill roads with fairly flat and broad terrain.

(5) other retaining walls

Column plate retaining wall, pile plate retaining wall, frame retaining wall, etc.

3. Sand piles and blast holes

Sand may be introduced into the subgrade to increase internal friction and shearing strength. Simplest in concept is the sand-filled spud hole.

A series of holes are driven into the subgrade inside and outside the rails, using a steel or timber spud. The pattern of holes should cover about 20% of the subgrade surface. After the spud is withdrawn, the holes are filled with sharp engine sand. The method is limited to easy driving and withdrawal of the spud.

Driving is done by a light on-track or off-track driver. Water pockets should be pierced by the spud. Some vertical drainage and compaction from the driving are obtained. The procedure has had success with clays of high plasticity.

4. Soil additives

Various substances such as lime, cement, silica, gypsum, and salt have been added to clay-silt soils to reinforce and promote stability, especially in the top of the subgrade. Improved cohesion between the soil particles and some mechanical support are obtained. The additions are introduced into the soil either by injection or by blending. The trending process is best performed during construction.

5. Cement grouting

Injecting cement grout into a subgrade is the oldest of the injection processes. A cement and sand slurry is injected into the roadbed through injection points driven into the subgrade and connected by flexible hose to grout-mixing machine. Grout is forced through the injection points by pneumatic or hydraulic pressure. A "rich mix," are part of cement to one to six parts of sand, is used for relatively part stretches and for pockets where a rich grout mass with some mechanical strength is required. The high sand/cement ratio saves cement while introducing friction-creating sand into the soil. Pneumatic injectionis usually associated with rich-mix spot grouting. The equipment is more readily transported from one spot to another. Hydraulic injection uses a hydraulic pump to force grout into the subgrade for dimness up to half a mile and is generally used on out-of-face work and in heavy fills where total acceptance is high.

6. Geotextiles

Several "fabrics" of polyester fibers are claimed to perform functions similar to a filter-to prevent the intermigration of soil and ballast particles yet provide drainage. The geotextiles are of a nonwoven polyester or polypropylene fiber. The fibers may be heat bonded or mechanically interlocked by needle punching.

Stabilizing effects come from establishing a physical barrier between the ballast or sub ballast materials and the subgrade (or between clean and uncleaned portions of the ballast section). The fabric permits drainage to occur through the fabric to eventual evaporation from the ballast section without intermingling of ballast and subgrade soil. Certain types serve as wicks, carrying moisture from the interface to the edge of the ballast section. Successful use has been reported in the use of geotextiles over soft, cohesive soils and firm, medium soils.

7. Rods

Tensile core materials used as ground reinforcing material are, based on past experience in railway work, basically deformed steel rods and vinyl on FRP rods. Generally, small diameter and medium diameter rod shaped reinforcing materials that are used include fully threaded steel rods of SD295 and D22, while large diameter reinforcing materials are fully threaded steel rods of SD295, D32, and D35. FRP rods are adopted in cases where reinforced ground may be excavated in the future or to take advantage of the fact that they are easily installed during excavation. Fig. 7-19 is a schematic of a type of FRP rod that is in general use. (Note: SD stands for deformed reinforcing bar. D stands for bar diameter.)

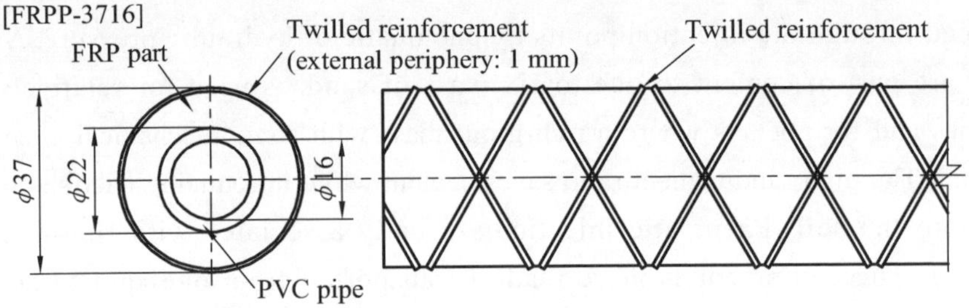

Fig. 7-19 Schematic of an FRP rod

8. Electro-osmosis

An electrolytic action has been used to remove large quantities of moisture from fine-grained soils, including silt clay swamp muck. When clay is electrically charged, ionization affects a chemical change that cements soil particles and causes pore water to flow from a positive to a negative potential. In practice, perforated pipes of 25-30 cm in diameter are driven into the soil to form a negative electrode. Steel rods, beams, or scrap rails are driven to depths of 7.5-15 meter to form the positive electrode or anode, which is charged with a potential of 90-150 V. Water in the soil flows into the cathode and is pumped out through well points by pumps. The process may take several days or weeks to dewater a wet area and may be considered expensive in terms of money per track foot stabilized.

7.3 Subgrade Drainage

7.3.1 Introduction

The importance of efficient drainage with respect for proper drainage in railways is still greater because a slight increase in moisture content would considerably reduce the bearing power of the subgrade. The reduction in bearing power may even result in the subgrade becoming unstable. A railway track is subjected to action of water in the following ways:

(1) Water from rain, dew and snow (if the area is subjected to snow fall).

(2) By capillary action from subsoil water.

(3) Water seeped below the track by seepage from adjoining strata which gets to the sub-grade by capillary action.

(4) Water retained by pores of soil mass due to hydroscopic action.

Fig. 7-20 illustrates how water from different sources finds its way to the sub-grade.

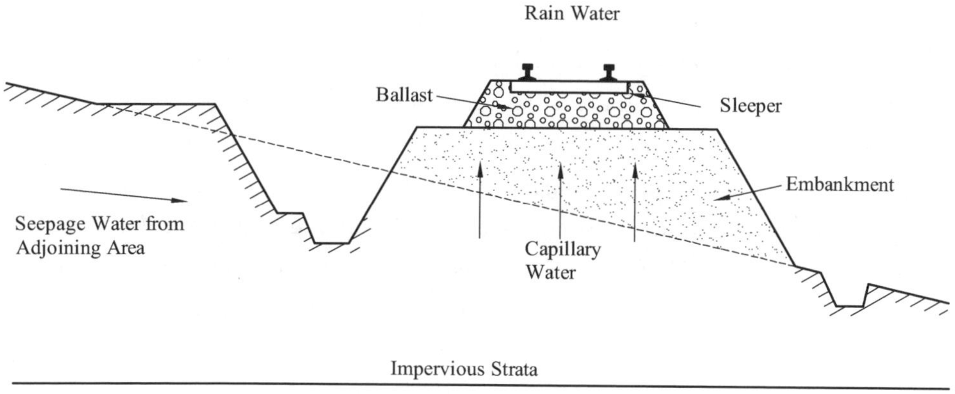

Fig. 7-20 Various ways in which water gets into the track subgrade

The various methods adopted for removal of surface and subsurface water from the subgrade are known as track drainage.

1. Importance of drainage

The effect of moisture on the shearing, and bearing properties have been dealt with as referred to above. In the base of railway track drainage is important on account of the following factors.

(1) In the presence of excess moisture track subjected to heavy and fast loads, tends to deform due to settlement and the stability of the track gets reduced.

(2) Water logged areas formed due to inefficient drainage result in bank slips and land slides. In the case of high moisture content heaving up of soil formation due to swelling and shrinkage due to subsequent drying take place.

(3) The dynamic loads coming on wet soils form slush which .gets into the ballast and clogs it.

(4) The surface and subsurface flow of water causes erosion of the embankment.

(5) If satisfactory drainage is not provided, this may lead derailment.

2. Requirements of drainage system

A good drainage system should be such as to take care of the different ways in which moisture gets into the sub-grade. These requirements can broadly be divided into those of surface water drainage and sub-surface water drainage.

The surface drainage should meet the following requirements:

(1) The surface water should be immediately removed to the side drains by cambering the formation, and provision of side slopes.

(2) The formation should be well above the adjoining ground surface so that surface water from adjoining areas does not flood the formation.

(3) The side drains should have adequate section to cater for the water from the upper reaches as well as the surface water from the track formation.

The sub-surface drainage should meet the following requirements:

(1) The highest underground water level should be brought down sufficiently below the level of the formation by one of the methods described under

(2) Water logged areas require treatment as described under water-logged areas.

(3) As far as possible track alignment should be on pervious naturally drained soil. Coarse texture soils are very well suited for providing quick sub-drainage system.

7.3.2 Drainage system

Track drainage is divided into the following two categories: Surface drainage and sub-surface drainage.

1. Surface drainage

The surface drainage consists of the following.

(1) Side drains. Surface water from the track as well as from the upper reaches is collected on the side drains and discharged into natural streams or water courses.

(2) By provision of cross-drainage works such as bridges and culverts for disposal of the surface water from the side drains and adjoining areas.

(3) In case there is comparatively good cross slope of the natural ground, side drain may be constructed on the higher side of the track. The water from the track on the lower side would get drained off in the natural way.

If no natural stream falls in the alignment for a comparatively large distance, bridges or culverts may be provided for this purpose to drain off the water from higher side.

2. Sub-surface drainage

Changes in the moisture content of the sub-grade soil take place primarily on account of the following:

(1) Seepage water. The drainage should therefore be so designed that the sources responsible for the ingress of water are blocked:

The problem of seepage water finding its way into the sub-grade is more acute in the case of a track in cutting than a formation embankment. The entry of a seepage water to the subgrade or formation is prevented by the following methods:

① By providing catch-water drains at the top of cutting, these catch-water drains should have good longitudinal slope so that water coming from the catchments area above and seeping through is arrested and discharged into the natural outlet. This arrangement reduces the water getting into the track through seepage and also the section of the paved side drain meant for taking surface water is economized. If possible these catch water drains should be paved so that seepage water does not get to the track subgrade by seepage.

② By lowering the water table. Blind drains consisting of rubble and boulders immediately below the paved side drain are provided. These pipes discharge into sumps from where water is pumped out. Alternatively the perforated pipe drain discharges itself to a natural drainage system. Fig. 7-24 shows the section of a track in cutting along with the position of a catchwater drain, side drains and rubble drain below the side drains.

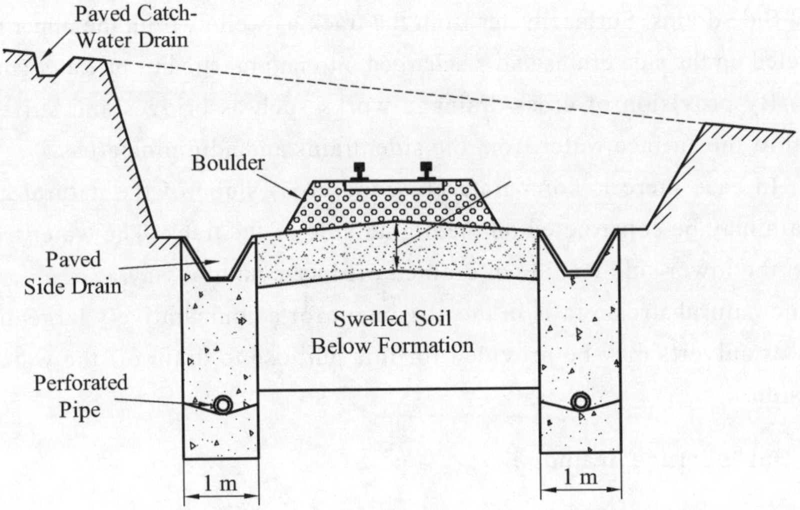

Fig. 7-21 Lowering of water-table

(2) Increase in moisture content due to capillary action. Capillary water is arrested by one of the following methods:

① By providing a pervious layer in the embankment as shown in Fig. 7-22.

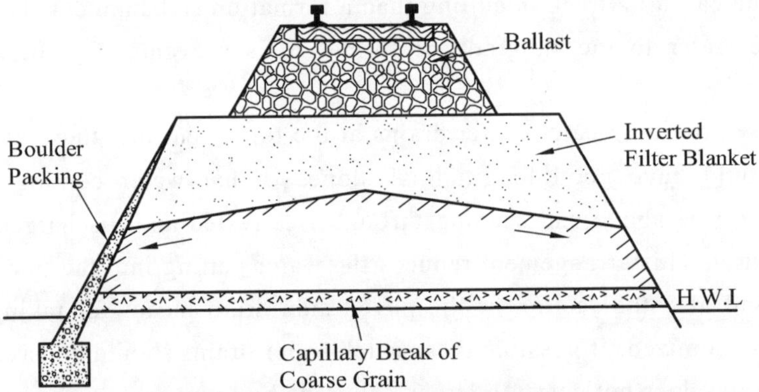

Fig. 7-22 Capillary break

In order that the surface water may not get to the soil below, inverted filter blanket is provided. The water coming from the top is drained off to sides.

The water from below is prevented from coming up by capillary action by providing capillary break of coarse grain sand.

② By the provision of inverted filter of pervious material below the ballast (known as blanket) as shown in Fig. 7-23.

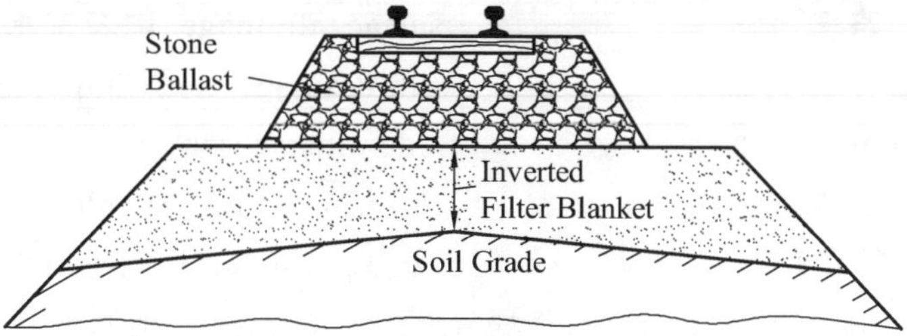

Fig. 7-23 Pervious filter

7.3.3 Drainage problems

Two major problems which result from unsatisfactory drainage of the track are either ballast sinks into the wet earth or the wet earth gets into the ballast. These two problems are described below:

1. Ballast sinking into the wet earth

The moist earth becomes unsafe and is not able to provide a firm bed to the ballast. As a result of this ballast sinks into the subgrade earth formation. The area immediately below the rails gets depressed further and may ultimately lead to the sinking of the track as a whole. The problem can be treated in one of the following ways:

(1) By providing a blanket of sand.

(2) By using sand piles.

(3) By providing capillary break or cut off.

(4) By cement grouting.

2. Wet earth getting into the ballast

As the earth gets softened due to increase in moisture content it gets pumped up under the load of the traffic. The phenomena is known as mud pumping. Wet soil chokes the ballast. The rise of wet earth chokes the drainage system of the track which gets lifted up due to the mud pumping.

The problem can be tackled in one of the following ways:

(1) By lowering the water table

(2) By providing inverted filter blanket

Professional Words and Expressions

Subgrade 路基

ballast pockets 道床底坑

embankment 路堤
cutting 路堑
permanent land 永久占地
temporary land 临时占地
formation 路基本体
slopes of cutting or embankment 路堤或路堑边坡
drainage 排水系统
width of Subgrade 路基宽度
depth of Subgrade 路基深度
slopes of Subgrade 路基边坡
stability of Subgrade 路基稳定性
subsidence 沉降
subgrade Slope Failures 路基边坡失效
weak Ballast Restraint 弱道床阻力
frost Heaving 冻胀
water Pockets 水槽坑
surface drainage 地表排水系统
sub-drainage 地下排水系统
side ditch 边沟
lowering of water-table 降低水位
capillary break 切断毛细渗水
electro-Osmosis 电渗透
mechanical Support 机械防护
sand piles and blast holes 砂桩与炮孔
soil additives 土壤添加剂
cement grouting 水泥灌浆
geotextiles 土工织物
seepage water 渗透水
reinforced subgrade 加固路基
retaining walls 挡土墙
steep cutting slope 陡路堑边坡

CHARPTER 8　TUNNELS AND BRIDGES

【Primary Contents】

(1) Structure and types of tunnel

(2) Construction methods of tunnel

(3) Maintenance of tunnel

(4) Structure and types of bridge

(5) Construction methods of bridge

(6) Maintenance of tunnel bridge

8.1　Tunnels

8.1.1　Overview

A tunnel is an underground or underwater passageway, dug through the surrounding soil/earth/rock and enclosed except for entrance and exit, commonly at each end.

For rail tunnels, the horseshoe profile was generally used, in a higher form for single-track tunnels and a flatter form for two-track tunnels. It can also be designed with vertical inner side surfaces. Today an arched profile with or without invert and vault is more commonly used for conventionally driven tunnels, and a circular profile for tunnels bored by shield machines. In addition to the cross-sectional areas required for the rolling stock and tracks including signal lamps, contact shoes and any other necessary accessories, rail tunnels require a loading gauge that allows for deviations of the wagons through snaking, for example as a result of broken springs. In addition to the loading gauge determined in this way, space also has to be provided for signals, overhead, cables, lighting, pipes and other equipment required for rail operations and escape routes.

8.1.2 Tunnel cross-section

As compared to surface cutting or embankment, the construction of a tunnel specially of a large one, presents a much higher degree of specialization and very high cost of construction. The section adopted therefore should be as small as possible, consistent with the functional requirements. The design will therefore be governed by the following factors: purpose for which required, namely, railroad, highway, rapid-transit, etc.; Clearances prescribed; Method of tunneling; Soil characteristics; Method of lighting and ventilation.

Depending upon the purpose for which the tunnels are to be constructed, a number of design criteria would have to be laid. The shape of the cross-section of tunnels also has to be suitable for the prevailing geological conditions and overburden. The size and direction of external loading mostly depends on the ground pressure. The better the load-bearing capacity of the rock mass being passed through, the less ground pressure has to be assumed in the design of the support, particularly pressure from the side. The higher the lateral pressure is in relationship to the vertical pressure, the more a near-circular cross-section will be suitable. The shape of the cross-section thus depends on the external and internal forces acting on the perimeter of the cavity. In competent rock, which does not tend to be weathered, the excavated profile will stand up without any structural contribution from the support, and a thin layer of shotcrete can resist any effects of weathering. Ways of optimizing the tunnel cross-section to an ideal shape are offered by the laws of structural geo-technical engineering.

Fig. 8-1 to Fig. 8-3 illustrates the common tunnel shapes to include circular, rectangular, arch etc. Although numerous tunnels have rectangular interiors, the tunnel exterior defines the shape of the tunnel. The exterior shape generally correlates with the method of tunnel construction and the encountered ground conditions. Some tunnels may have different shapes along their length because the ground conditions change along its length. For example, a tunnel could start out using shallow cut and cover techniques leading up to the portals, which are usually constructed rectangular in shape. As these tunnels penetrate deeper into the subsurface and cross under obstacles, other tunneling methods may be used such as sequential excavation, drill and blast, or even TBM methods. The exterior shape usually changes with changes in the tunnel construction method or to accommodate greater stresses at depth.[23]

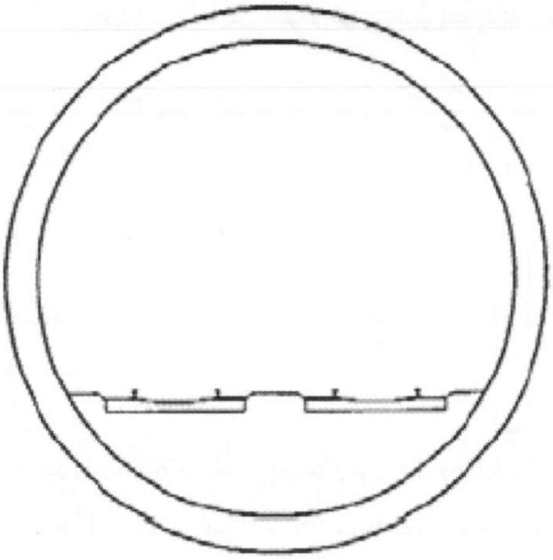

Fig.8-1 Circular tunnel with two traffic lanes and one safety walk

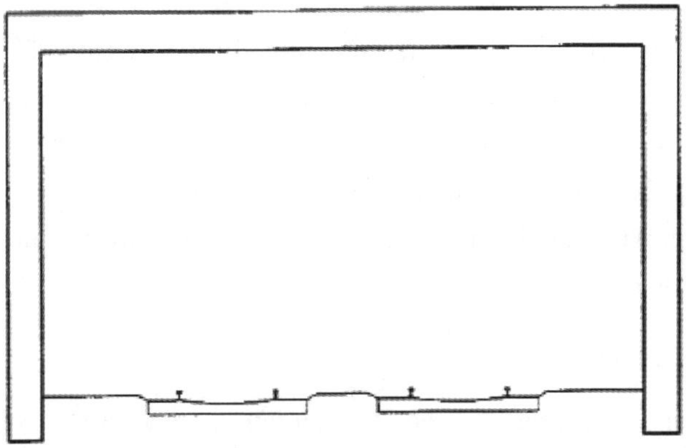

Fig. 8-2 Rectangular shaped tunnels. Left shows twin tunnels each with two lanes and one safety walk.

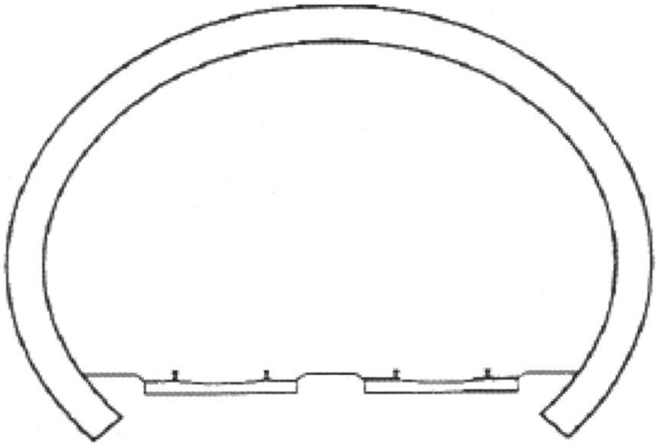

(a) Arch tunnel

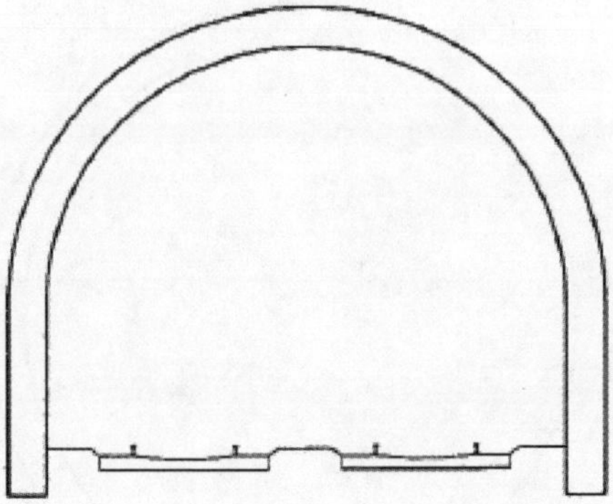

(b) Straight side wall, vaulted roof tunnel

Fig. 8-3 Horseshoe and oval tunnel

8.1.3 Tunnel structure

Tunnel consists of main building and subsidiary building. The main building which is built to maintain the stability of tunnel and ensure the normal use of the tunnel, is composed of lining structure (or called support structure) and portal, and open-cut tunnel is necessary when the tunnel portal is easy to collapse or rock-fall hazard. The subsidiary building refers to ensure the normal use of the required all kinds of tunnels.

1. Lining Structure

After tunnel excavation, in order to maintain the stability of surrounding rock, lining structure should be constructed. The main form of Lining includes Integral Lining, Prefabricated Lining, Shotcrete-bolt supporting, and Composite Lining.

1) Integral Lining(Fig.8-4,Fig.8-5)

Integral Lining refers to the cast-in-place concrete lining. Its features include: suitable for various geological conditions, easy to forming as needed, good integrality, good impermeability, and suitable for various construction conditions.

2) Prefabricated Lining(Fig.8-6, Fig.8-7)

Prefabricated Lining is divided into several blocks of components. These components are prefabricated on site or in a factory, and then transported to the tunnel and will be assembled by mechanical into a ring and a ring. Its characteristic includes: load-bearing immediately when ring closed, mechanized construction, working conditions improved, labor saving. At present, prefabricated lining is widely used in subway which using shield method construction.

Fig. 8-4 Lining trolley

Fig. 8-5 Cast-in-place concrete construction

Fig. 8-6 Shield tunnel segment

Fig. 8-7 Ring of Segment Erection

3) shotcrete-bolt support(Fig.8-8,Fig.8-9) It refers to the shotcrete and bolt, metal mesh and steel frame combined support. Shotcrete-bolt support is suitable for the geological conditions of various rock, but for permanent lining, better used in good, integrity, stability rocks of grade Ⅰ or Ⅱ.

Fig. 8-8 Anchor construction

Fig. 8-9 Sprayed concrete construction

4) Composite lining

Composite lining has outer and inner layers which constructed successively. Initial support (typically shotcrete-bolt support) is the outer flexible support which close contact with the surrounding rock and should be constructed firstly after the tunnel excavation. The tunnel lining with initial support can allow a certain deformation of surrounding rock, but do not result in loose pressure from excessive deformation. Secondary support (usually cast in form-working) is the inner lining which constructed after surrounding rock deformation is stable basically. Waterproof layer between two layers of lining is set as needed or casting waterproof concrete is set as inner lining without doing waterproof layer. Composite lining is a more reasonable structure for a variety of geological conditions surrounding rock, it has broad development prospects.

5) Open-cut tunnel(Fig.8-10,Fig.8-11)

Open-cut tunnel means the lining of tunnels built with open-cut method, commonly used in tunnels of bad geological sections, shallow tunnels, and tunnel inlet and outlet. The structure type of open-cut tunnel depends on the topography, geology, and backfill material, generally consisting of top structure and side wall. If the bottom strata may squeeze into the tunnel, inverted arch must be set. Open-cut tunnel is mainly divided into two categories, namely arch open-cut tunnel and shed tunnel.

Fig. 8-10 Arch open-cut tunnel

Fig. 8-11 shed tunnel

2. Portal

Portal is a retaining structures which is on the tunnel entrance and is built by artificial masonry and architectural decoration. Its main function is to reduce the amount of earth excavation of structure opening, maintain slope stability, drain surface water and decorate structure opening. According to structure type, portal can be divided into: Ring frame portal, End-wall Portal, Wing-wall portal, Column-type portal, Step-type portal and Cutting-style portal.

(1) Ring frame portal. When the end of lining extends outside of tunnel and adds its thickness, a ring frame portal will be formed. It is suit for opening with hard rock, steep terrain and without drainage requirements.

(2) End-wall Portal (Fig. 8-12). End wall portal consists of end wall and drains and is suit for structural opening with wide topography and stable strata, used to support front slope and drain the water on front slope.

Fig. 8-12 End-wall Portal

(3) Wing-wall portal (Fig. 8-13). This type of portal adds wing walls on the side of the end wall, for supporting the end wall and protecting stability of cutting slope. It is suit for the structural opening with poor geological conditions. Top of wing wall and extension surface of front slope must be matched. Ditch would be set on the top of wing wall, which is used to drain water collected by front slope and top of portal into the side ditch of cutting

Fig. 8-13 Wing-wall portal

(4) Column-style portal (Fig. 8-14). Column-style portal is used to increase the stability of the end wall, where local shape is steeper, geological conditions is poor, and wing wall portal is not suitable owing to the limitation of topographical conditions. It is more beautiful and suitable for the suburbs, sights or great tunnel entrance.

Fig. 8-14　Column-style portal

(5) Step-style portal (Fig. 8-15). In hillside areas, in order to reduce the height of the overlaying slope excavation, reducing the amount of earth excavation. The top of the end wall can be built as steps to adapt to the surface slope.

Fig. 8-15　Step-style portal

(6) Cutting-style portal (Fig. 8-16). A series of aerodynamic effects will occur when train travels at high-speed in tunnel, which will affect the comfort and health of passengers on the train and the surrounding environment of the tunnel outlet. But cutting- style portal can reduce the effects effectively. In addition, cutting- style portal is concise, beautiful, environmental protection, conforming to the trend of the ecological and landscape design.

Fig. 8-16 Cutting-style portal

3. Subsidiary Facilities

In order to make use of the tunnel properly and guarantee the safety of train, in addition to the main building of tunnel, subsidiary facilities must be built, including drainage facilities, refuge recess, power and communication facilities and ventilation facilities.

1) drainage facilities

For dealing with the surface water and groundwater properly, a complete and smooth waterproof and drainage system should be arranged inside and outside of the tunnel. The waterproof and drainage system in tunnel should follow the principle: combination of anti-dumping, cut-off and blocking; comprehensive management according to local conditions.

2) refuge recess

When the train passes through a tunnel, in order to ensure the safety of personnel and equipment maintenance, some staggered and uniform caverns are built on both sides of the tunnel wall, to avoid the train, named refuge recess.

According to the size, refuge recess can be divided into large refuge recess (Fig. 8-17) and small refuge recess (Fig. 8-18).

Fig. 8-17 Large refuge recess

Fig. 8-18 Small refuge recess

Large refuge recess: store repair equipment and materials.

Small refuge recess: convenient to avoid trains.

3) Power and communication facilities

In order to prevent wet, rot and man-made destruction, power and communication channel should be set for varieties of cable in tunnel, such as lighting, communication, signal and power cables.

The cable channel is constructed cast-in-site, and on the bottom of the channel covered with sand cushion to all the cables. Cable channel without cover and with cover are shown in Fig. 8-19 and Fig. 8-20 respectively.

Fig. 8-19 Cable channel without cover

Fig. 8-20 Cable channel with cover

4) Ventilation facilities for operation[23]

For trains emitting large amounts of harmful gases and a lot of heat as passing through tunnel , some natural underground harmful gases and moisture penetrating through lining gap from time to time, and maintenance staff always exhaling carbon dioxide continually at work, the air inside the tunnel becomes dirty, hot and humid. For a long time, the concentration of harmful gases increases and will make people breathing difficulties, threaten people's health, reduce the work efficiency, and corrode the line susceptibly. So, the ventilation facilities must be carried out to draw out the harmful gas and heat, and draw in the fresh air. There are two kinds of natural ventilation and mechanical ventilation.

There are five basic types of tunnel ventilation systems:

• Natural ventilation (Fig. 8-21): A naturally ventilated tunnel is simple. The movement of air is controlled only by meteorological conditions and the piston effect from traffic where stale air is pushed out of the tunnel from vehicles traveling through the tunnel in the same direction.

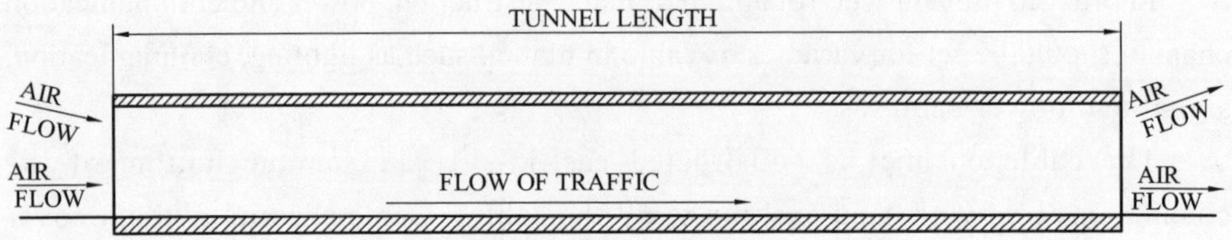

Fig. 8-21 Natural Ventilation

• Longitudinal Ventilation (Fig. 8-22): Longitudinal ventilation is similar to natural ventilation with the addition of mechanical fans to improve the ventilation characteristics. The air is blown through the tunnel bore, which acts as the ductwork for the fans (Fig. 8-23).

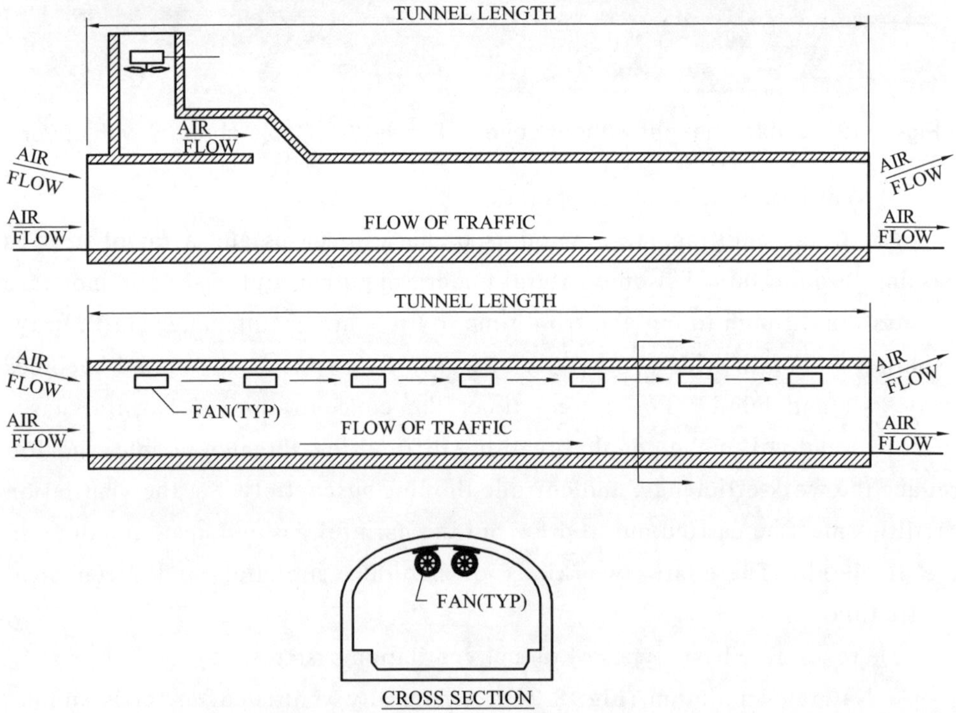

Figure 8-22 Longitudinal ventilation

Fig. 8-23 Mechanical Fan

• Semi-transverse ventilation (Fig. 8-24): Semi-transverse ventilation also makes use of mechanical fans for the movement of air; However, ductwork is added with flues that allow the air to be uniformly distribution throughout the tunnel. This plenum or ductwork is typically located above a suspended ceiling or below a structural slab within a tunnel.

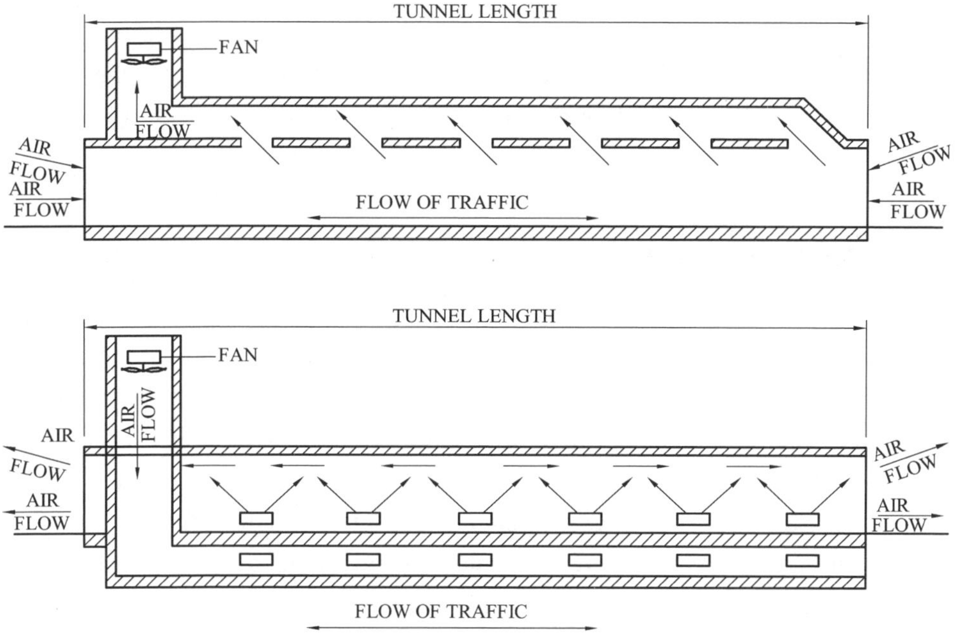

Fig. 8-24 Semi-Transverse Ventilation

• Full-Transverse Ventilation (Fig. 8-25): Full-transverse ventilation systems use two air ducts, one for supply air and one is for exhaust air. With a fully transverse system, the tunnel bore is not used as part of the ductwork. This method is used primarily for longer tunnels with heavy traffic. A pressure difference is created between the supply and exhaust ducts to control the air flow.

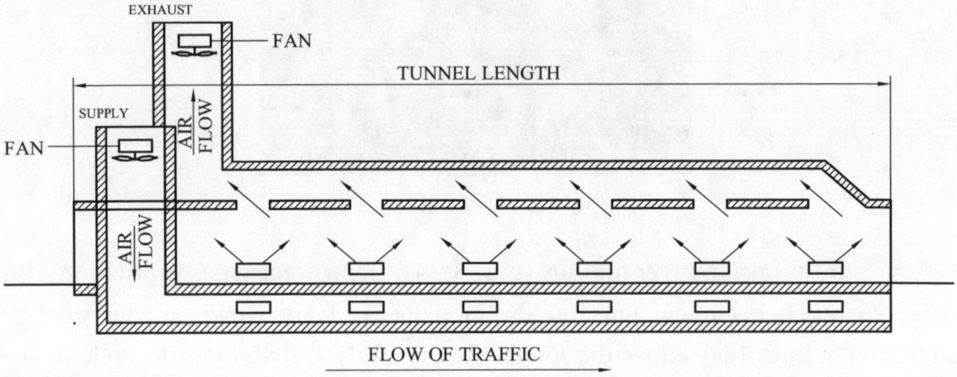

Fig. 8-25 Full-Transverse Ventilation

- Single-point extraction: In conjunction with semi-and full-transverse ventilation systems, single-point extraction can be used to increase the airflow during a fire event. The system works by allowing the opening size of the exhaust flues to increase during the emergency.

8.1.4 Tunnel construction

1. Construction Factors

Tunnels are dug in types of materials varying from soft clay to hard rock. The method of tunnel construction depends on such factors as the ground conditions, the ground water conditions, the length and diameter of the tunnel drive, the depth of the tunnel, the logistics of supporting the tunnel excavation, the final use and shape of the tunnel and appropriate risk management.

There are three basic types of tunnel construction in common use:

(1)Cut-and-cover tunneling method, constructed in a shallow trench and then covered over.

(2) Bored tunnels, constructed in situ, without removing the ground above. They are usually of circular or horseshoe cross-section.

(3) Immersed tube tunnels, sunk into a body of water and sit on, or are buried just under its bed.

Tunnels which are "bored", rather than constructed following excavation down from the surface, need to adopt various building techniques depending on a number of factors. These factors will include the following considerations:

(1) Material through which the tunnel is likely to pass, including the consistency of that material or the degree of variation likely.

(2) Any faults or pockets present in the strata, including those likely to convey local high water pressure.

(3) The level of the water table and any water bearing non-cohesive material likely to be met like "running" sand.

(4) Any disturbance to the original ground that could have occurred previously and then temporarily stabilized. This situation might occur when driving a second tunnel close to a previous tunnel or adjacent to existing foundations, basements or sewers.

(5) Substantial variation in imposed ground pressures, either vertically or horizontally, caused by heavy buildings above or immediately alongside the line of the proposed tunnel.

(6) The length of the proposed tunnel and the required speed of construction. Tunnel construction speeds are generally slow but if considerable lengths have to be constructed it is often worth spending extra money on more sophisticated equipment to increase building speed.

In all civil engineering construction, safety is an essential ingredient. In tunneling this is an absolutely primary consideration and must never be allowed to become secondary to considerations of cost or speed of construction.

Each tunnel construction operation must be carefully considered on its own merits looking at all the factors listed above. A "Method Statement" should then be agreed between the Engineer and the Contractor before operations commence and plant is agreed. The Method Statement should clearly define not only the methods of working but the agreed procedure when work stops between shifts or for longer periods at weekends, etc.

Very accurate surveying of tunnel work, both as the operations proceed and after completion, is essential so that any necessary corrections of line or level can be applied as the work progresses. Railway tunnels usually have very tight clearances to rolling stock and any misalignment in build is difficult if not impossible to compensate in revised track geometry. Even relatively small errors of construction sometimes require a length of tunnel to be rebuilt, which clearly is undesirable and must be guarded against.

2. Construction Methods

1) Cut-and-cover tunneling method

In built up urban areas, tunnels were sometimes necessary because of space limitations and the requirement to place the tracks below ground level. The construction of the first lengths of the metropolitan and district lines in London is "cut-and-cover" method, which is still used today throughout the world for the construction of shallow running tunnels and stations. Cut-and-cover (Fig. 8-26) is a simple method of construction for shallow tunnels where a trench is excavated and roofed over with an overhead support system strong enough to carry the load of what is to be built above the tunnel. Two basic forms of cut-and-cover tunneling are available:

Fig. 8-26 Cut-and-Cover tunnels

Bottom-up method: A trench is excavated, with ground support as necessary, and the tunnel is constructed in it. The tunnel may be of in situ-concrete, precast concrete, precast arches, or corrugated steel arches; in early days brickwork was used. The trench is then carefully back-filled and the surface is reinstated.

Top-down method: Side support walls and capping beams are constructed from ground level by such methods as slurry walling, or contiguous bored piling. Then a shallow excavation allows making the tunnel roof of precast beams or in situ concrete. The surface is then reinstated except for access openings. This allows early reinstatement of roadways, services and other surface features. Excavation then takes place under the permanent tunnel roof, and the base slab is constructed.

A major disadvantage of cut-and-cover is the widespread disruption generated at the surface level during construction.

2) Tunnel Shields (Fig. 8-27) [23]

Fig. 8-27 Tunnel shields

Up to the end of the eighteenth century no tunnels had been successfully constructed under water courses. Marc Brunei, the father of the more famous Isambard Kingdom Brunei, patented a rectangular "tunnel shield" in 1818 which he was later to use on the construction of his Thames Tunnel between Wapping and Rotherhithe in UK. Although the idea was born out of the problem of tunneling through waterlogged ground, the principle of the moving tunnel shield was then established and is now internationally accepted for all safe tunneling work in anything other than hard rock.

Marc Brunei's shield was rectangular in shape with individual cells. It consisted of massive cast-iron frames sitting on shoes at the bottom of the excavation, the working face being supported by heavy oak planks or "poling boards" which were individually held in position by screw jacks bearing on the frames. Each poling board was removed one at a time in each cell, excavated behind by hand to a depth of about 100 mm and then replaced at the new advanced position with the screw jack fully extended. In all there could be up to 36 men working at the face at any one time each in an individual cell. Although safe this method was painfully slow and encouraged contractors to take short cuts to improve progress. The first "tube" underground railway tunnels built in London using "Great-head" shields were commenced in 1886 and now form part of the City branch of the London Underground Northern Line.

Modern tunnel shields used for soft ground tunneling follow the same basic principles as the "Great-head" shield. Some sophistication has been added in the form of hydraulic jacking and "steering" hydraulic arms at the rear to assist in the positioning of tunnel lining segments and power operated tools of various types to excavate the face as well as improved equipment for probing ahead.

3) Tunnel Boring machines (TBM) (Fig. 8-28)

Fig. 8-28 Tunnel boring machines

As mentioned in the previous section, tunneling shields can be used with partial excavation as well as with full face excavation. The latter is known as a tunnel boring machine or TBM exists in many different diameters, ranging from micro-tunnel boring machines with diameters smaller than 1 m to machines for large tunnels, whose diameters are greater than 15 m (the largest TMB is now in excess of 19 m). TBM is available for many different geological conditions. This means that, for example, the type of tunnel face support required and the excavation procedure as well as numerous other technical requirements can be solved in many different ways. Every tunnel is different and hence there are often frequent technical advancements in this field. Although TBM is often designed for specific projects, i.e. with a specific diameter and in order to cope with certain ground conditions, these days refurbished machines are becoming more common and projects are actually designed around the machines available. An example of this is when the diameter of the new project is chosen to suit the old machine, with just the cutter-head being redesigned for the specific ground conditions expected.

There are a variety of TBM designs that can operate in a variety of conditions, from hard rock to soft water-bearing ground. Some types of TBM, the bentonite slurry and earth-pressure balance machines, have pressured compartments at the front end, allowing them to be used in difficult conditions below the water table. This pressurizes the ground ahead of the TBM cutter head to balance the water pressure. The operators work in normal air pressure behind the pressured compartment, but may occasionally have to enter that compartment to renew or repair the cutters. This requires special precautions, such as local ground treatment or halting the TBM at a position free from water. Despite these difficulties, TBM is now preferred over the older method of tunneling in compressed air, with an air lock/decompression chamber some way back from the TBM, which required operators to work in high pressure and go through decompression procedures at the end of their shifts, much like deep-sea divers.

4) Drilling and blasting (Fig. 8-29)

Fig. 8-29 Drilling and blasting

Drill and blast for tunnel construction can be used in geology ranging from hard rock with low strength, e.g. marl, loam, clay, gypsum, chalk, to the hardest rocks, such as granite, gneiss, basalt or quartz. Due to this large range of possible usage, drill and blast can be advantageous for very changeable ground conditions. The drill and blast work and the extent of the tunnel support can be adjusted with every heading advance if required. In addition, tunneling by using drill and blast is often preferable to TBM or road header tunneling if, for example, the tunnel is relatively short so that the high investment costs needed for a tunneling machine are not economic, or when the ground hardness is very high so that a high wear of the cutter tools leads to an uneconomic application of the machine.

Other reason for using drill and blast for tunneling can be when a cross sectional profile is required which does not allow the application of a tunnel machine for technical or economic reasons. As with all tunneling types, tunneling using drill and blast is principally most economic when it is continuous and similar work processes are used. Therefore when planning a tunnel it is beneficial to split the tunnel into sections where the same advancing schema and the same tunnel support intensity can be used. During drill and blast operations the individual job processes are mainly conducted sequentially, which in general results in a slower tunneling speed compared with TBM tunneling. Ground vibrations need to be considered when using drill and blast for the excavation of a tunnel, especially in urban areas, as these can affect surface and subsurface structures (and humans). It is therefore important to make predictions of the likely effect (possibly by conducting blasting trails as part of the site investigation) and to carry out monitoring during the constructions works.

When carrying out drill and blast, the order of the processes generally consists of the following cycle: drilling, charging (including adding the detonator), stemming, blasting, ventilation, mucking (spoiling) and supporting. Tunnel length is a key issue that needs to be addressed because large TBM for a rock tunnel have a high capital cost, but because they are usually quicker than a drill and blast tunnel the price per meter of tunnel is lower. This means that shorter tunnels tend to be less economical to construct with a TBM and are therefore usually constructed by drill and blast. Managing ground conditions can also have a significant effect on the choice with different methods suited to different hazards in the ground.

5) Jacked box tunneling (Fig. 8-30)

Jacked box tunneling involves pushing a precast tunnel section (box) through the ground whilst carrying out excavation at the front face within a shield. Although the technique is not new and has been around for many decades, recent advances in the technique have made it possible to install large section boxes under "live" highways and railways. The cover depth for these tunnels can be very small, down to a couple of metres. The uses for jacked box tunneling have traditionally been for pedestrian subways and portal bridge foundations, with later developments including small boxes being jacked one on top of another and filled with concrete to form bridge abutments.

Fig. 8-30 Jacked box tunnels during the jacking process

It is important, as with all tunneling operations, that a project specific comprehensive site investigation is undertaken to determine the ground conditions, in particular their strength and stability characteristics, essential for the system design. Running parallel must be a survey of overlying infrastructure within the zone of influence of the box installation and the identification of any mitigation measures considered necessary.

6) Pipe jacking method (jack-in method) (Fig. 8-31)

Pipe ramming is a trenchless method for installation of steel pipes and casings. Distances of 30 m or more and over 1,500 mm in diameter are common, although the method can be used for much longer and larger installations. The method is useful for pipe and casing installations under railway lines and roads, where other trenchless methods could cause surface settling or heaving. The majority of installations are horizontal, although the method can be used for vertical installations.

Fig. 8-31 Pipe jacking method

The method uses pneumatic percussive blows to drive the pipe through the ground. The leading edge of the pipe is almost always open, and is typically closed only when smaller pipes are being installed. Its shape allows a small overcut (to reduce friction between the pipe and soil and improve load conditions on the pipe) and to direct the soil into the pipe interior instead of compacting it outside the pipe. These objectives are usually achieved by attaching a soil-cutting shoe or special bands to the pipe.

Further reduction of friction is typically achieved with lubrication, and different types of bentonite and/or polymers can be used (as in horizontal directional boring) for this purpose. Spoil removal from the pipe can be done after the entire pipe is in place (shorter installations). If the pipe containing the spoil becomes too heavy before the installation *s* complete, the ramming can be interrupted and the pipe cleaned (longer installations). Spoil can be removed by auger, compressed air or water jetting.

The principal benefits of jacked box tun nelling are: a non-intrusive construction method; minimal disturbance to surface infrastructure; traffic flows maintained throughout the construction period; traffic flows maintained throughout the construction period; traffic flows maintained with only minor restrictions during box installation; a high quality maintenance free structure.

7) New Austrian Tunneling Method (Fig. 8-32)

Fig. 8-32 New Austrian Tunneling Method

The NATM integrates the principles of the behavior of rock masses under load and monitoring the performance of underground construction during construction. The NATM has often been referred to as a "design as you go" approach, by providing an optimized support based on observed ground conditions. More correctly it can be described as a "design as you monitor" approach, based on observed convergence and divergence in the lining and mapping of prevailing rock conditions. It is not a set of specific excavation and support techniques.

NATM has seven elements:

(1) Exploitation of the strength of native rock mass-relies on the inherent strength of the surrounding rock mass being conserved as the main component of tunnel support. Primary support is directed to enable the rock to support itself.

(2) Shotcrete protection-loosening and excessive rock deformation must be minimised. This is achieved by applying a thin layer of shotcrete immediately after face advance.

(3) Measurement and monitoring-potential deformations of the excavation must be carefully monitored. NATM requires installation of sophisticated measurement instrumentation. It is embedded in lining, ground, and boreholes. In the event of observed movements, additional supports are installed only when needed, with a resultant overall economy to the total cost of the project.

(4) Flexible support-the primary lining is thin and reflects recent strata conditions. Active rather than passive support is used and the tunnel is strengthened by a flexible combination of rock bolts, wire mesh and steel ribs, not by a thicker concrete lining.

(5) Closing of the invert-especially crucial in soft ground, the quick closing of the invert (the bottom portion of the tunnel) which creates a load-bearing ring is important, and has the advantage of engaging the inherent strength of the rock mass surrounding the tunnel.

(6) Contractual arrangements-since the NATM is based on monitoring measurements, changes in support and construction method are possible, but only if the contractual system enables them.

(7) Rock mass classification, ranging from very hard to very soft, determines the minimum support measures required and avoids economic waste that comes from needlessly strong support measures. Support system designs exist for each of the main rock classes. These serve as the guidelines for tunnel reinforcement.

3. Vertical and Sloping Shafts

All but the very shortest railway tunnels require some vertical shafts, both for the purpose of construction, and for final ventilation or draught relief. These shafts are build "top down" with each ring being completed and grouted before the next lower is started beneath it. Segments are individually maneuvered into position by hand, the space required having been carefully excavated rather like in underpinning. As rings are completed the "dumpling" inside the shaft can be excavated by machine loading into buckets and craned away or simply "grabbed" out by crane. Much care must be taken when water or running sand is encountered when special precautions may be necessary.

Sloping shafts are necessary to accommodate escalators, usually at about thirty degrees to the horizontal. These are constructed in a similar manner and can be very difficult to build, especially nearer the surface when going through made ground and surface water pockets. Escalator shafts often require de-watering, pressure grouting, chemical grouting, ground freezing or other ground treatment and need careful investigation well before starting operations.

8.1.5 Tunnel maintenance

An effective maintenance program helps reduce costs, decrease the number of tunnel closures, increase public safety, and ensure adequate levels of service. To maximize efficient use of resources and minimize costs, maintenance programs should be optimized. When large-scale repairs and upgrades are implemented, these projects are typically referred to as tunnel rehabilitation. Maintenance activities range from simple tasks to complex endeavors as indicated in the hierarchy below:

- Removing debris, snow, and ice.
- Washing tunnel structures, flushing drains, tightening bolts, and changing light bulbs.
- Servicing equipment, painting fixtures, and restoring pavement.
- Tests, verifications, measurements, and calibrations.
- Planned interventions.
- Unplanned interventions. Ideally, the maintenance strategies of a tunnel facility should strike a balance between preventative maintenance and on-demand maintenance. Safety, service requirements, and costs must be considered. When approximately 70% to 80% of all maintenance activities are performed under a preventative maintenance approach, it is considered to be good practice.
- Rehabilitation.

1) Removing debris, snow and ice

Debris, snow, and ice present a number of safety concerns. Debris should be removed from the tunnel on a regular basis since it could obstruct vision, damage vehicles, foul equipment, or present a fire or safety hazard. In cold regions, ices above the railway should be removed since they could damage vehicles. Deicing agents should be used to clear ice from tunnel. Ice should also be removed from areas that are not designed to carry potentially ice loads. Fig. 8-33 shows the process of washing the tunnel.

2) Groundwater Seepage through Liners

Groundwater seepage can be controlled temporarily by interim solutions using catchment troughs and interior composite liners; however, these temporary solutions do not protect the final liner from long-term corrosion and degradation. Before implementing these methods, an engineer should evaluate the potential for:

Fig. 8-34 Washing the tunnel

• Fine soil particle migration, void creation, and redistribution of the stresses around the tunnel liner.

• Fine soil migration, re-deposition, and drain clogging.

• Protection of structural materials from corrosion and further degradation.

• Settlement of adjacent structures because of soil or rock mass dewatering.

• Vehicle strikes due to insufficient clearance of new installed materials.

• Obscuring important safety defects during future inspections of the final liner.

Fig. 8-35 Leakage at a construction joint through the cementitious coating

3) Repairs for structural concrete (Fig.8-34)

When the concrete has areas impacted by spalling, mortar patches can be applied by hand to patch smaller areas while larger areas are more effectively treated using shotcrete based application methods and economies of scale. When cracks in the concrete need to be repaired the cracks can bc injected with grout.

4) Maintenance of Functional Systems

Functional systems include the mechanical, electrical, lighting, fire and life safety, security, sign, and protective systems installed in the tunnel. The equipment rooms for these functional systems, such as the ventilation buildings, pump rooms, and emergency generator rooms, should be kept clean. Remove any debris, grease and oil. Loose debris can damage equipment. All gauges, sight glasses, indicator lights, and safety equipment must be cleaned and checked. Some components might require painting. Movable components should be exercised periodically. Ideally, maintenance programs can be enhanced by collecting data and managing the maintenance activities.

8.2 Bridges

8.2.1 Bridge components (Fig. 8-35)

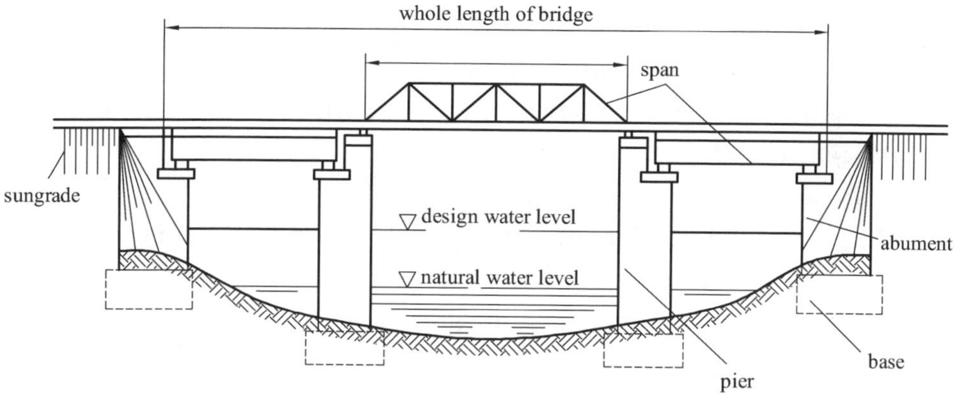

Fig. 8-36 The components of bridge

Definition: A bridge is a structure providing passage over an obstacle without closing the way beneath. The required passage may be for a road, a railway, pedestrians, a canal or a pipeline. The obstacle to be crossed may be a river, a road, railway or a valley.

The main parts of a bridge are: the deck, the superstructure (girder, truss, or arch), the substructure (abutments and piers) and foundation. All parts must work together to create a strong, long-lasting bridge.

1) Deck

The deck is the roadway or railway surface. In roadway applications it is usually a poured reinforced concrete slab, but can also be steel grid or wood plank. The deck includes any road lanes, medians, sidewalks, parapets or railings, and miscellaneous items like drainage and lighting.

2) Superstructure

The superstructure is what supports the loads and is the most visible part of the bridge. The supporting structure consists of the steel or concrete span structure supporting the deck. This includes the girders themselves, diaphragms or cross-braces, and (if applicable) the truss or arch system. In a girder bridge this would include only the girders and the bracing system. The girders are the primary load support, while the bracing system both allows the girders to act together as a unit, and prevents the beams from toppling.

The job of the bearing pads is to allow the superstructure to move somewhat independently of the foundation. All materials naturally expand and contract with temperature-if a bridge were completely rigid, this would cause unnecessary stress on the structure and could lead to failure or damage. By fixing the superstructure at one end, while allowing the other end of a span to move freely in the longitudinal direction, thermal stresses are alleviated and the lifespan of the bridge increased.

3) Substructure

The portion of the bridge structure below the level of the bearing and above the foundation is generally referred to as substructure. The substructure transfers the loads from the superstructure to the ground, including abutment, piers and other components.

An abutment is the support for the end of a bridge span or lateral support for the soil or rock on which the roadway rests immediately adjacent to the bridge, functioning as a pier and a retaining wall. The abutment can of masonry, plain concrete or reinforced concrete. An abutment generally consists of the following three distinct structural elements: the breast wall which directly supports the static and live loads of the superstructure, and retains the filling of the embankment in its rear. the wing walls, which act as extensions of the breast wall in retaining the fill though not taking any loads from superstructure; and the back wall, which is a small retaining wall just behind the bridge seat, preventing the flow of material from the fill on to the bridge seat

A pier is the main body of the substructure. It is a vertical intermediate supporting structure, such as a pillar, transferring the load from the superstructure, through the cap, down to the footer. Types of piers include: solid, cellular, trestle, hammer-headed. The general shape and features of a pier depend to a larger extent on the type, size and dimensions of the superstructure and on the environment.

The cap is the part that supports the bearing pads. Depending on the type of support structure, there may or may not be a cap. Wall piers and stub abutments do not require a cap, while a multi-column, hammerhead, or pile-bent pier will have a cap.

4) Foundation

The role of the bridge foundation is to bear all the load from the superstructure and transfer them and the substructure load to the natural ground.

There are two basic types of substructure foundations, shallow and deep. Shallow foundations typically utilize spread footings to transfer structure loads to the soil at a relatively shallow level below the ground surface. Deep foundations utilize some type of driven pile, drilled shaft or caisson to transfer the structure load to some lower stratum of soil or rock. The choice of whether to use a shallow or deep foundation depends on soil conditions and the potential for scour at the site.

Foundations are used when it is necessary to carry the structure load through a zone of weak or compressible material to firmer foundation material at a deeper level. Piles are also used to found a structure below the depth of potential scour. End bearing piles develop their load capacity through their tip by bearing on hard material. Friction piles develop their load capacity by skin friction between the pile and soil over their length.

The space, called bridge clearance, consists of the bottom of bridge superstructure, the top of design water level and the side of two adjacent piers. Bridge clearance should meet the requirements of flood discharge, drainage and navigation of the ship. The distance between two piers is called bridge span. The whole length of bridge is the distance between the ends of the wing-wall or side-wall of two bridge abutments, or the whole length of the vehicle lane if the bridge has no abutments.

8.2.2 Bridge type

Bridges may be classified in many ways. According to the form or type of superstructure, bridges may be classified as slab, beam, truss, arch or suspension bridge. According to the material of construction of superstructure they may be classified as timber, masonry, iron, steel, reinforced concrete, prestressed concrete, composite bridge.

The choice of an appropriate type of bridge and planning of its basic features usually constitute a crucial decision to be taken by the bridge engineer. The designer must consider all the preliminary data made available to him from the detailed investigation before arriving at a solution. The entire completed structure should be the most suitable to carry the desired traffic, adequately strong to support the incident loads, economical and aesthetically pleasing.

1. Fixed or movable types

Fixed (Fig. 8-36)—Majority of bridges are fixed, with no moveable parts to provide higher clearance for river/sea transport that is flowing below them. They are designed to stay where they are made to the point they are deemed unusable or demolished.

Fig. 8-37　Fixed bridges

Temporary bridges—Bridges made from modular basic components that can be moved by medium or light machinery. They are usually used in military engineering or in circumstances when fixed bridges are repaired.

Moveable bridges(Fig. 8-37)—They have moveable decks, most often powered by electricity.

Fig. 8-38 Moveable bridges

Most bridges are fixed bridges, meaning they have no moving parts and stay in one place until they fail or are demolished. Temporary bridges, such as Bailey bridges, are designed to be assembled, and taken apart, transported to a different site, and re-used. They are important in military engineering, and are also used to carry traffic while an old bridge is being rebuilt. Movable bridges are designed to move out of the way of boats or other kinds of traffic, which would otherwise be too tall to fit. These are generally electrically powered.

2. Bridge by use

A bridge can be categorized by what it is designed to carry, such as trains, pedestrian or road traffic, a pipeline or waterway for water transport or barge traffic. An aqueduct is a bridge that carries water, resembling a viaduct, which is a bridge that connects points of equal height. A road-rail bridge carries both road and rail traffic.

Some bridges accommodate other purposes, such as the tower of Nový Most Bridge in Bratislava, which features a restaurant, or a bridge-restaurant which is a bridge built to serve as a restaurant. Other suspension bridge towers carry transmission antennas.

Car Traffic—The most common type of bridge, with two or more lanes designed to carry car and truck traffic of various intensities.

Pedestrian bridges—Usually made in urban environments, or in terrain where car transport is inaccessible (rough mountainous terrain, forests, etc.).

Double-decked bridges—Built to provide best possible flow of traffic across bodies of water or rough terrain. Most often they have large amount of car lanes, and sometimes have dedicated area for train tracks.

Train bridges—Bridges made specifically to carry one or multiple lane of train tracks.

Pipelines—Bridges made to carry pipelines across water or inaccessible terrains. Pipelines can carry water, air, gas and communication cables.

Viaducts—Ancient structures created to carry water from water rich areas to dry cities.

Commercial bridges—Modern bridges that host commercial buildings such as restaurants and shops.

3. Bridge by material

1) Wooden bridge

Selection of materials is very important in bridge construction, as in any structural project. Early wood or vine bridges would eventually rot. We still see many wooden road bridges and walk bridges. Today's wooden bridges life span is expanded by treating the wood with chemicals. These bridges will still eventually rot and are limited by their lack of strength. Wooden decking were easily destroyed by animal hooves at one time, and today traffic and snow plow blades can quickly wear the deck. Besides not being weather proof, wooden bridges can burn. Many communities or areas have experienced more than an inconvenience when local bridges have burned due to lightening, accidents or even vandalism.

2) Stone bridge

Stone bridges have strong and long lasting bridges. They could span longer distances than wooden beam bridges as well, but could not span extremely long distances as would be required in time. The development of railroads caused a revival of semicircular-arch construction, and cut stone was used in certain localities where it was economical. The demand for longer spans than what arch bridges could safely serve led to the development of suspension bridges.3) Steel bridge.

Not only did the style of bridge change in time, so did the material of choice. In the beginning of the 1800's Iron was replacing wood, and by the late 1800's, steel starting to replace iron. iron is much stronger than wood and, as a result, can span greater distances. It is plentiful, in fact it makes up 5% of the earth's crust. It is malleable, or can be shaped and bent quit easily. It is also weather proof (when painted) and heat resistant.

Steel is simply an iron and carbon alloy (which means a mixture of both iron and carbon that has been put through a special process). Other alloys (additives) can also be added to the recipe to make it really hard, strong, wear resistant and so on. As a result steel has become a much more reliable material and versatile than iron.

Each new material or design technique builds off the lessons of the past. Modern bridges often use steel in the form of cables or girders, and/or concrete as construction materials. Steel is durable and is relatively light considering the strength and size of the components. The aestitics are also very appealing when built in steel. In other words, people find that the structure can be made to look very beautiful, or cool. Another very big plus is that steel components can be made elsewhere and assembled on the site. This speeds up the construction of the bridge considerably.

4) Concrete bridge

Concrete is a relatively inexpensive, versatile, tough, but it is a heavy material. It is widely used in modern bridge building, as well as the building of other modern structures. It is made by mixing the proper proportions of sand, stone, cement, and water. When the water dries up, the concrete becomes hard and dry. Concrete can be poured into forms on site to become permanent fixtures. Concrete can also be poured into a molds such as the puzzle shaped wall pieces being unloaded above, or as beams or other prefabricated (made ahead of time to be assembled later or elsewhere) components to be transported and assembled on site. Concrete is a material that has good compression properties, but does not hold up so well under tension. However, reinforced concrete. is made when steel mesh or rods are embedded into the concrete for increased strength in tension. It was soon after the turn of the 20th century when the development of reinforced concrete brought about great progress in concrete-arch bridge construction. Even stronger, pre-tensioned concrete has embedded steel bars or cables which are stretched into tension before the concrete hardens. In post-tensioned concrete, the embedded steel bars or cables are stretched into tension after the concrete hardens.

4. Bridge by Aesthetics

Most bridges are utilitarian in appearance, but in some cases, the appearance of the bridge can have great importance. Often, this is the case with a large bridge that serves as an entrance to a city, or crosses over a main harbor entrance. These are sometimes known as signature bridges. Designers of bridges in parks and along parkways often place more importance to aesthetics, as well. Examples include the stone-faced bridges along the Taconic State Parkway in New York.

To create a beautiful image, some bridges are built much taller than necessary. This type, often found in east-Asian style gardens, is called a Moon bridge, evoking a rising full moon. Other garden bridges may cross only a dry bed of stream washed pebbles, intended only to convey an impression of a stream. Often in palaces a bridge will be built over an artificial waterway as symbolic of a passage to an important place or state of mind.

5. Bridge by Structure

Bridges may be classified by how the forces of tension, compression, bending, torsion and shear are distributed through their structure. Most bridges will employ all of the principal forces to some degree, but only a few will predominate. The separation of forces may be quite clear. In a suspension or cable-stayed span, the elements in tension are distinct in shape and placement. In other cases the forces may be distributed among a large number of members, as in a truss, or not clearly discernible to a casual observer as in a box beam.

1) Beam bridges (Fig. 8-38)

Beam bridges are horizontal beams supported at each end by substructure units and can be either simply supported when the beams only connect across a single span, or continuous when the beams are connected across two or more spans.

are the simplest of forms – one or several horizontal beams that can either simply span the area between abutments or relieve some of the pressure on structural piers. The core force that impacts beam bridges is the transformation of vertical force into shear and flexural load that is transferred to the support structures (abutments or mid-bridge piers).

The earliest beam bridges were simple logs that sat across streams and similar simple structures. In modern times, beam bridges can range from small, wooden beams to large, steel boxes. The vertical force on the bridge becomes a shear and flexural load on the beam which is transferred down its length to the substructures on either side. They are typically made of steel, concrete or wood. Beam bridge spans rarely exceed 76 m long, as the flexural stresses increase proportional to the square of the length (and deflection increases proportional to the 4th power of the length). Beam bridges are the most common bridge type in use today. Pre-stressed concrete is an ideal material for beam bridge construction; the concrete withstands the forces of compression well and the steel rods imbedded within resist the forces of tension. Pre-stressed concrete also tends to be one of the least expensive materials in construction.

Fig. 8-39 Beam bridges

2) Truss bridges (Fig. 8-39)

A truss bridge is a bridge whose load-bearing superstructure is composed of a truss. It is a very popular bridge design that uses a diagonal mesh of most often triangle-shaped posts above the bridge to distribute forces across almost entire bridge structure. Individual elements of this structure (usually straight beams) can endure dynamic forces of tension and compression, but by distributing those loads across entire structure, entire bridge can handle much stronger forces and heavier loads than other types of bridges. The triangular pieces of truss bridges are manufactured from straight and steel bars, according to the truss bridge designs. A truss bridge is economical to construct owing to its efficient use of materials.

Fig. 8-40 Truss bridges

3) Arch bridges (Fig. 8-40)

These bridges uses arch as a main structural component (arch is always located below the bridge). With the help of mid-span piers,they are made with one or more arches, depending of what kind of load and stress forces they must endure. Arch bridges have abutments at each end. The weight of the bridge is thrust into the abutments at either side. Stone, brick and other such materials that are strong in compression and somewhat so in shear. The earliest known arch bridges were built by the Greeks, and include the Arkadiko Bridge.The world's current largest arch bridge is the Chaotianmen Bridge over the Yangtze River with a length of 1,741 m and a span of 552 m. The bridge was open April 29, 2009 in Chongqing, China.

Fig. 8-41 Arch bridges

4) Cantilever bridges (Fig. 8-41)

Cantilever bridges are somewhat similar in appearance to arch bridges, but they support their load, not through a vertical bracing but trough diagonal bracing with horizontal beams that are being supported only on one end. Most cantilever bridges use a pair of continuous spans that extend from opposite sides of the supporting piers to meet at the center of the obstacle the bridge crosses. Cantilever bridges are constructed using much the same materials and techniques as beam bridges. The difference comes in the action of the forces through the bridge. Some of the most famous cantilever bridges in the world are Quebec Bridge in Canada, Forth Bridge in Scotland and Tokyo Gate bridge in Japan.

Fig. 8-42 Cantilever bridges

5) Tied arch bridges (also called bowstring-arch or bowstring-girder bridge, Fig. 8-42)

Similar to arch bridges, but they transfer weight of the bridge and traffic load to the top chord that is connected to the bottom cords in bridge foundation. They are often called bowstring arches or bowstring bridges. Tied arch bridges have an arch-shaped superstructure, but differ from conventional arch bridges. Instead of transferring the weight of the bridge and traffic loads into thrust forces into the abutments, the ends of the arches are restrained by tension in the bottom chord of the structure,and they transfer weight of the bridge and traffic load to the top chord that is connected to the bottom cords in bridge foundation. They are also called bowstring arches.

Fig. 8-43 Tied arch bridges

6) Rigid-frame bridge (Fig. 8-43)

Rigid-Frame Bridge is a bridge in which the superstructure and substructure are rigidly connected to act as a continuous unit. Typically, the structure is cast monolithically, making the structure continuous from deck to foundation. The connections between members are rigid connections which transfer bending moment, axial forces, and shear forces. A bridge design consisting of a rigid frame can provide significant structural benefits, but can also be difficult to design and/or construct.

Fig. 8-44 Rigid-frame bridge

7) Suspension bridges (Fig. 8-44)

Suspension bridges are suspended from cables. Bridges that use ropes or cables from the vertical suspender to hold the weight of bridge deck and traffic. The earliest suspension bridges were made of ropes or vines covered with pieces of bamboo. In modern bridges, the cables hang from towers that are attached to caissons or cofferdams. The caissons or cofferdams are implanted deep into the floor of a lake or river. Sub-types include the simple suspension bridge, the stressed ribbon bridge, the under-spanned suspension bridge, the suspended-deck suspension bridge, and the self-anchored suspension bridge. The cables are usually made of steel cables coated with Zinc, along with most of the bridge, but some bridges are still made with steel reinforced concrete. The suspension bridge can cover a vast span but has a serious drawback: It is very flexible and traffic loading may produce a large deflection, particularly when it acts near the quarter point of the span, for this reason a stiffening beam or box girder is almost always provided to supplement the cables. Even so, this type is rarely used for railway bridge as, trains are heavier, and their loading more concentrated than road traffic. Suspension bridges are, however, the solution for the longest spans, since wire for the cables can be produced cheaply with much greater strength than the steel suitable for beam construction. A compromise which is now popular for intermediate span is the cable –stayed bridge which has stays joining the towers and deck.

Fig. 8-45 Suspension bridge

8) Cable-stayed bridges (Fig. 8-45)

Cable-stayed bridges, like suspension bridges, are held up by cables. However, in a cable-stayed bridge, less cable is required and the towers holding the cables are proportionately higher. Cable-stayed bridge that uses deck cables that are directly connected to one or more vertical towers. Cables are usually connected to towers in two ways – harp design (each cable is attached to the different point of the towers, creating harp like design of "strings" and fan design (all cables connect to one point at the top of the towers). The first known cable-stayed bridge was designed in 1784 by C. T. (or C. J.) Löscher.

Fig. 8-46 Cable-stayed bridges

8.2.3 Bridge construction

Bridge construction has been improved tremendously with the advancement in science and technology. Better and lighter materials are now available that can endure greater loads. The construction is now much faster due to the introduction of a variety of heavy construction equipment.

1. Bridge construction planning

Bridge construction tends to involve huge projects that encompass the utilization of skills related to several engineering disciplines including geology, civil, electrical, mechanical, and computer sciences. Therefore, integrating the efforts of all involved must be meticulous. The initial plans are prepared regarding the project, including the characteristics of the desired bridge, the site details, and the requirement of resources. The bridge design will be determined by the type of bridge being constructed. The main types of the bridges are beam, arch, truss, cantilever, and suspension. The beam bridge is one of the popular types. Bridges can also be categorized by the planned use, like road and rail bridge, pedestrian pavement, material to be used like steel or concrete, and fixed or moveable. Moveable bridges are constructed when the ship height may be more than the bridge floor. In such situations, the road has the capability to be lifted or pivoted, to permit marine traffic movement under it.

2. Bridge foundation

Construction of the foundations is the first step toward building a bridge. This process involves detailed geotechnical investigations of the bridge site. The type of bridge foundation has to be selected, such as the well foundation, pile foundation, and the opened foundation. Each foundation is suitable for specific soil strata, and the desired bridge characteristics.

The soil-bridge foundation characteristics will determine the load bearing capacity, and other important parameters. The superstructure is basically designed in accordance with the technical requirements, aesthetic reasons, and the construction methodology. Excavation required for the foundations may need to be executed to sizeable depths, involving hard ground, before the solid rocks are reached. Engineering feats will be involved to avoid water, and prevent collapse of the diggings. Tunnels specifically may be subjected to sudden failures.

3. Bridge construction equipment

Heavy equipment will be used extensively during the bridge construction including bulldozers, excavators, asphalt mixers, formworks, and fabrication equipment. The construction and other equipment needs to be identified thoroughly, according to their capability and other desired functions. The foundation and the superstructure design will need to be considered. This expensive equipment should Wheel Excavator, equipment not remain idle, and must be used cautiously to obtain optimum advantage.

4. Bridge loads

Several loads act on a bridge, and the bridge is designed accordingly. Dynamic loads are particularly of prime significance. A bridge is designed to endure the normal vehicle loads, and other forces created due to winds and earthquakes. Several bridges have bridge failure, loads collapsed due to high-speed winds. Even if the wind speeds are reasonably low, the dynamic forces can become excessive for the bridge to resist. Initially, the bridge may vibrate violently, causing the bridge structure to fail at a few weak elements, or even damage the major components. Investigations conducted after bridge failures have revealed that the real forces on bridges that collapsed were significantly less compared to the loads for which the bridge was designed. However, the oscillations created due to the winds were enough to cause the failure. Therefore, special reinforcement may be necessary for prevention against high-speed winds and earthquakes. Thus, lighter materials are used that are arranged in suitable geometric structures, and it is ensured that the configuration is aerodynamically stable.

5. Testing of bridges

Since bridge construction is an expensive project, it is essential that all necessary tests may be conducted prior to the actual construction. These tests and investigations can reveal the bridge behavior under different dynamic loads. Computer aided design bridge testing and testing are powerful tools that must be used to assist in the bridge design. Bridge design has benefited considerably due to the growth of computer programs. Such computer programs reveal immense information concerning the effect of different forces being applied on a bridge. Wind tunnels are being used extensively for the analysis of aircraft designs. Now these techniques are also being applied for bridge design examination. A wind tunnel is basically a space that is enclosed. Air at a fast speed is moved through the bridge model. Likely design and structural defects can be discovered by photography and study of the air movement pattern over the model

8.2.4 Bridge maintenance

Bridge maintenance consists of a combination of structural health monitoring and testing. This is regulated in country-specific engineer standards and includes e.g. an ongoing monitoring every three to six months, a simple test or inspection every two to three years and a major inspection every six to ten years. The lifetime of welded steel bridges can be significantly extended by after treatment of the weld transitions. This results in a potential high benefit, using existing bridges far beyond the planned lifetime. The cost of maintenance is higher than spending on new bridges, such as in Europe.

High-speed railway bridge with steel hollow box sections, performed for lifetime extension by welding after treatment.

1. Bridge failure

The failure of bridges is of special concern for structural engineers in trying to learn lessons vital to bridge design, construction and maintenance. The failure of bridges first assumed national interest during the Victorian era when many new designs were being built, often using new materials.

In the United States, the National Bridge Inventory tracks the structural evaluations of all bridges, including designations such as "structurally deficient" and "functionally obsolete".

2. Bridge monitoring

There are several methods used to monitor the stress on large structures like bridges. The most common method is the use of an accelerometer, which is integrated into the bridge while it is being built. This technology is used for long-term surveillance of the bridge.

Another option for structural-integrity monitoring is "non-contact monitoring", which uses the Doppler effect (Doppler shift). A laser beam from a Laser Doppler Vibrometer is directed at the point of interest, and the vibration amplitude and frequency are extracted from the Doppler shift of the laser beam frequency due to the motion of the surface. The advantage of this method is that the setup time for the equipment is faster and, unlike an accelerometer, this makes measurements possible on multiple structures in as short a time as possible. Additionally, this method can measure specific points on a bridge that might be difficult to access.

8.3 Choice of Tunnels vs. Bridges

Bridges and tunnels are two basic ways to cross rivers and straits, each has its own advantages and disadvantages. The comparison of them are as below:

(1) First of all, the underwater tunnel is obviously superior to the bridge as for the influence of the shipping channel. Because the underwater tunnel does not invade the net of the waterway, does not affect the shipping of rivers, straits, bays and ports, and does not interfere with the command and connection of any aircraft and aircraft.

(2) Secondly, the underwater tunnel is the operating channel of the whole day, and is not affected by the climate changes such as wind, heavy rain, heavy snow, heavy fog, and severe freezing. The bad climate conditions have obvious influence on the operation of the bridge.

(3) Thirdly, the underwater tunnel reduces the land occupation, demolition and interference, greatly reduces the comprehensive cost of the project, and is sure to start on schedule. Bridges usually require a larger footprint on each shore than tunnels.

(4) In addition, the structure of the underwater tunnel has a good durability. The underwater tunnel has a great load capacity.

(5) However, for water crossings, a tunnel is generally more costly to construct than a bridge. There are particular hazards with tunnels, especially

from vehicle fires when combustion gases can asphyxiate users.

(6) Compared with the tunnel, bridge engineering has such advantages as low requirements for geological survey, good driving conditions and convenient operation and maintenance.

Water-crossing tunnels built instead of bridges include the Holland Tunnel and Lincoln Tunnel between New Jersey and Manhattan in New York City, the Queens-Midtown Tunnel between Manhattan and the borough of Queens on Long Island, and the Elizabeth River tunnels between Norfolk and Portsmouth, Virginia, the 1934 River Mersey road Queensway Tunnel, the Western Scheldt Tunnel, Zeeland, Netherlands, and the North Shore Connector tunnel in Pittsburgh, Pennsylvania. Some water crossings are a mixture of bridges and tunnels, such as the Denmark to Sweden link and the Chesapeake Bay Bridge-Tunnel in Virginia.

Professional Words and Expressions

tunnel 隧道
tunnel cross-section 隧道横断面
lining structure 衬砌结构
integral lining 整体式衬砌
prefabricated lining 装配式衬砌
shotcrete-bolt supporting 喷锚支护
composite lining 复合式衬砌
open-cut tunnel 明挖隧道
ring frame portal 环框门
end-wall portal 端墙式洞门
sing-wall portal 翼墙式洞门
column-style portal 立柱式洞门
step-style portal 步进式洞门
cutting-style portal 切割式门
subsidiary facilities 辅助设施
drainage facilities 排水设施
refuge recess 避车洞
power and communication facilities

New Austrian Tunneling method 新奥法
vertical and sloping shafts 竖井斜井
inverted arch 仰拱
bridge 桥梁
deck 桥面
superstructure 桥梁上部结构
bearing pads 桥梁支座
bridge cap 桥梁墩帽
substructure 桥梁下部结构
abutment 桥台
pier 桥墩
foundation 桥梁基础
bridge span 桥梁跨度
bridge clearance 桥下净空
double-decked bridges 双桥面桥梁
pedestrian bridges 人行桥
viaducts 高架桥

动力通信设施

ventilation facilities 通风设施

cut-and-cover tunneling method 明挖法

bored tunnels 钻孔隧道

immersed tube method 沉埋法

tunnel shields 盾构机

Tunnel Boring machines (TBM) 隧道掘进机

drilling and blasting 钻孔爆破

jacked box tunneling

pipe jacking method(jack-in method) 顶进法

beam bridge 梁桥

truss bridge 桁架桥

arch bridge 拱桥

cantilever bridge 悬臂桥

rigid frame bridge 刚架桥

tied arch bridge 弓弦式拱桥

suspension bridge 悬索桥

cable-stayed bridge 斜拉桥

bridge failure 桥梁失效

bridge monitoring 桥梁监测

aqueduct 渡槽

TEST SHEET

1. True-False (Mark a "T" for true and an "F" for false.)

(1) Broadening the gage of track on sharp curves prevents derailment.

(2) A profile shows the horizontal alinement as well as the vertical curves of a railroad.

(3) In comparing 60-75 kg/m rail, you would find that the 75 kg/m rail is the stiffer of the two.

(4) Concrete sleepers are preferred to wooden ones because of their resistance to impact loads.

(5) A locomotive with a long, rigid wheelbase may have difficulty going around sharp curves.

2. Cluster True-False

(Each question of this kind consists of a series of statements related to the stem that precedes them. Indicate which are true and which false with respect to the stem)

(1) Wooden sleepers have a number of advantages, some of which are their:

A. Resistance to rot in damp climates.

B. Resistance to impact loads.

C. Resistance to abrasive wear.

D. General availability.

E. Suitability for holding rails by spikes.

(2) A good subgrade is essential to a railroad because it:

A. Receives train weight from ballast above and transmits it to ground below.

B. Compensates for irregularities of terrain.

C. Supports ballast above adjacent ground to provide run-off for water.

D. Provides the stability that a track needs.

E. Should be spongy to reduce shock to rails and provide a comfortable ride.

(3) A crossing is installed in a turnout so that a train's wheels and wheel flanges can cross the rails.

It is true of a crossing that:

A. While the wing rail of a spring crossing is being held open by spring tension, the train can follow the alternate path through the crossing.

B. The bolted-rigid type may be made from standard rail.

C. When a train passes over its actual point, the wheel is unsupported.

D. Its theoretical and actual points are between its heel and throat.

E. A train never reaches it when a trailing-point move is made.

(4) A spiraled curve is built between a tangent and a circular curve. Of spiraled curves, it is

true that they:

A. Are called easements because of their function.

B. Provide correct superelevation needed without suddenly altering the track's banking.

C. Differ from circular curves in that their curvature is constant throughout their length.

D. Become sharper where they join tangents.

E. Can be designed by most section foremen.

(5) When you speak of a railroad's horizontal layout, you are referring to its:

A. Curves and tangents.

B . Ups and downs.

C. Centerline.

D. Ground plan.

E. Grades.

3. Matching

(Match the terms in column II with the definitions in column I. Terms in column II may be used once, more than once, or not at all)

Column I	Column II
(1)Distance between the two rails of track.	A.Superelevation
(2)Relationship between the height of the two rails.	B.Cross level
(3)Prevents rail from moving longitudinally	C.Gauge

(4) Resists lateral thrust on rail (5) Prevents vehicle from overturning.	D.Rail creep E. Rail brace F.Rail Anchor G.Super-elevation H.Gauge-widening

4. Multiple Choice

(Each question in this group contains one and only one correct answer. Circle thealternative which represents your choice.)

(1) Rail anchors are used to restrain the movement of track where there is: ______.

A. Excessive lateral thrust.

B. Continually spreading track on a curve.

C. Excessive vertical thrust.

D. Longitudinal movement.

(2) When a rail joint is installed in cold weather, the gap left between rail sections, in comparison with that left in warm weather, is: ______.

A. Smaller.

B. The same.

C. Greater.

D. Governed by the humidity.

(3) The gauge of the track on a particularly sharp curve in your section was increased slightly to prevent binding. The passage of trains, however, is spreading the gage even farther. To correct the situation, you should install: ______.

A. Gage rods.

B. Track gages.

C. Rail braces.

D. Rail anchors.

(4) The sketch shows a typical rail section. Which of the following correctly identifies its three main parts ?

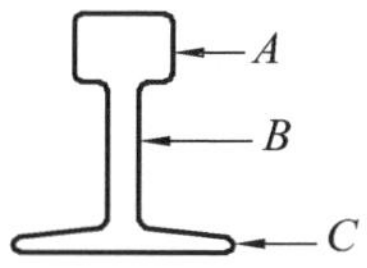

A. head; B, waist; C, foot.

B. foot; B, head; C, waist.

C. head; B, foot, C, waist.

D. base; B, waist; C, foot.

(5) The rails connected by switch rods so that they may be moved simultaneously are called____________________ rails.

A Closure

B. Switch-throwing

C. Stock

D. Switch

5. Answer questions briefly

(1)Please describe the functions and types of rail.

(2)Please describe influence factors on gauge widening and give the calculation principle.

(3)Please describe the functions of easement curve of rail line.

(4)Please describe the functions and types of turnouts.

(5) Please give the advice to improve the train speed trough turnouts.

(6) Please give the advice to protect roadbed(subgrade) from water damage.

6. Calculation

(1) Radius of one curve line in a railway is 350 m. According to statistical data trains going through the round curve are listed as follows:

a. there are 10 high-speed passenger trains and speed ;

b. there are 4 normal speed passenger trains and speed ;

c. there are 40 freight trains and speed .

Please calculate the Super-elevation of outer rail in the curve line.

(2) In a city, the top temperature is 40 °C and the least temperature is − 5 °C. A section of continuous welded rail track (whose length is 2,500 m)is fastened down at the temperature which is 4 °C higher than middle rail temperature and its sectional area is 65.8 cm^2. Please calculate the maximum temperature pressure and the maximum temperature tension.(α=0.011,8 mm/m °C).

REFERENCE

[1] Clifford F Bonnett. Practical railway engineering(2nd Edition). London: Imperail College Press, 2005

[2] The railway theory and practice of the construction and maintenance of the railroad track.Alejandro Carrascosa Hernandez.USA: 2014. http://www.ICGtesting.com

[3] 杨寿康. 新编铁路科技英语[M]. 北京：中国铁道出版社，2000.

[4] Tore Dahlberg. Railway track dynamic-a survey[R]. Solid Mechanic/IKP, linkoping Universit. linkoping Sweden:2003

[5] http://www.comhacer.info/wp-content/uploads

[6] The army institute for professional development army correspondence course program. SUBCOURSE EDITION TR0670-RAILWAY TRACK MAINTENANCE 1 (EDITION 8)[M]. Virginia

[7] The army institute for professional development army correspondence course program. SUBCOURSE EDITION TR0670-RAILWAY TRACK MAINTENANCE 2 (EDITION 8)[M]. Virginia

[8] 马国忠，唐智慧. 线路基础[M]. 成都：西南交通大学出版社，2010.

[9] Office of rail regulation.Level Crossings: A guide for managers, designers and operators[M]. Railway Safety Publication 7. December2011

[10] GoranC´irovic´a,1,DraganPamucˇarb. Decision support model for prioritizing railway levelcrossings for safety improvements:Application of the adaptive neuro-fuzzy system[J]. Expert Systems with Applications. 40(2013) 2208–2223

[11] Martin Lindahl. Track geometry for high-speed railways: A literature survey and simulation of dynamic vehicle response[D]. Stockholm: Railway Technology Department of Vehicle Engineering of Royal Institute of Technology，2001.

[12] ABDUR ROHIM BOY BERAWI. IMPROVING RAILWAY TRACK MAINTENANCE USING POWER SPECTRAL DENSITY (PSD) [D]. PORTO: FACULDADE DE ENGENHARIA UNIVERSIDADE DO PORTO, 2013.

[13] Coenraad Esveld. Moden railway track [M]. 2nd ed. Netherlands: MRT-Productions, 2001. http://www.ICGtesting.com.

[14] Ping wang. Design of hign-speed railway turnouts-theory and application[M]. 成都：西南交通大学出版社，2015.

[15] F. Lanza di Scalea, I. Bartoli, R. Phillips, C. Nucera, and S. Coccia. Automated Measurement of Stress in Continuous Welded Rail[R]. US Department of transportation Federal Railroad Administration, 2010.12

[16] MICHAEL J. KOOB. THE DEVELOPMENT OF A VIBRATION TECHNIQUE FOR ESTIMATION OF NEUTRAL TEMPERATURE IN CONTINUOUSLY WELDED RAILROAD RAIL[D]. Illinois: Science in Civil Engineering in the Graduate College of the University of Illinois at Urbana-Champaign, 2005.

[17] M.A. Van. Buckling analysis of continuous welded rail track[J]. HERON, 1996, 41(3): 175-186. http://www.doc88.com/p-7038945216545.html

[18] Nam-Hyoung Lim, Sang-Yun Han, Taek-Hee Han, and Young-Jong Kang. Parametric Study on Stability of Continuous Welded Rail Track-Ballast Resistance and Track Irregularity [J]. International journal of steel structures. 2008(9): 171-181. https://www.researchgate.net/publication/260267455

[19] Dong-Ho Choi, Ho-Sung Na. Parametric Study of Thermal Stability on Continuous Welded rail[J]. International Journal of Railway, 2010, 3(4): 126-133.

[20] Georgios Michas. Slab Track Systems for High-Speed Railways[D]. Stockholm, Sweden: Architecture and the Built Environment Royal Institute of Technology, 2012.

[21] Kish, Andrew,Mui, Wesley. Track Buckling Research. U.S. DEPARTMENT OF TRANSPORTATION[M]. John A. Volpe National Transportation Systems Center (U.S.):2013

[22] Railway Technical Research Institute. Design Standards for Railway Structures and Commentary (Concrete_Structures) 2007-03(OCR)[M].

Osaka：Maruzen Co., Ltd，2007.

[23] William Bergeson, PE and Steve Ernst, PE (FHWA). Tunnel Operations, Maintenance, Inspection, and Evaluation Manual[R]. Washington DC: Federal Highway Administration Office of Bridges and Structures，2015

[24] Ports, Circuits, and Tunnels Operations Guide. SmartEdge OS.Release 5.0.3.Part. http://www.redback.com[22]

[25] L McKibbins, R Elmer, K Roberts. Tunnels:inspection, assessment and maintenance[M]. London：2009. http://www.ciria.org/

[26] Vernon R. Schaefer, David J. White, Halil Ceylan, Larry J. Stevens. Design Guide for Improved Quality of Roadway Subgrades and Subbases[R]. Washington DC：Iowa Highway Research Board (IHRB Project TR-525)，2008. https://www.ctre.iastate.edu

[27] FAN PENG. SCHEDULING OF TRACK INSPECTION AND MAINTENANCE ACTIVITIES IN RAILROAD NETWORKS. Illinois：University of Illinois at Urbana-Champaign, 2011.

[28] Gerard Parke,Nigel Hewson. ICE manual of bridge engineering(2nd Edition). London: Thomas Telford Ltd, 2008.

[29] Louise Butcher. Railways: level crossings[R]. http:// researchbriefings.parliament.uk

[30] B. L.Gupta. Nai Sarak, Delhi. Road, railway, bridge & tunnel engineering[M]. United states：standard book house, 1982.

[31] 中华人民共和国标准 TB 10082—2017，J448—2017，铁路轨道设计规范.

[32] 中华人民共和国标准 TB 10001—2016，J447—2016，铁路路基设计规范